Reflections

*Edited and
with an Introduction
by Peter Demetz*

Walter Benjamin

REFLECTIONS

Essays,
Aphorisms,
Autobiographical
Writings

Translated by Edmund Jephcott

A Helen and Kurt Wolff Book
Harcourt Brace Jovanovich
New York and London

These essays have all been published in Germany. "A Berlin Chronicle" was published as *Berliner Chronik,* copyright © 1970 by Suhrkamp Verlag; "One-Way Street" as *Einbahnstrasse,* copyright 1955 by Suhrkamp Verlag; "Moscow," "Marseilles," "Hashish in Marseilles," and "Naples" as *"Moskau," "Marseille," "Haschisch in Marseille,"* and *"Neapel"* in *Gesammelte Schriften,* Band IV-1, copyright © 1972 by Suhrkamp Verlag; "Paris, Capital of the Nineteenth Century," "Karl Kraus," and "The Destructive Character" as *"Paris, die Hauptstadt des XIX. Jahrhunderts," "Karl Kraus,"* and *"Der destruktive Charakter"* in *Illuminationen,* copyright 1955 by Suhrkamp Verlag; "Surrealism," "On Language as Such and on the Language of Man," and "On the Mimetic Faculty" as *"Der Sürrealismus," "Über die Sprache überhaupt und über die Sprache des Menschen,"* and *"Über das mimetische Vermögen"* in *Angelus Novus,* copyright © 1966 by Suhrkamp Verlag; "Brecht's *Threepenny Novel*" as *"Brechts Dreigroschenroman"* in *Gesammelte Schriften,* Band III, copyright © 1972 by Suhrkamp Verlag; "Conversations with Brecht" and "The Author as Producer" as *"Gespräche mit Brecht"* and *"Der Autor als Produzent"* in *Versuche über Brecht,* copyright © 1966 by Suhrkamp Verlag; "Critique of Violence," "Fate and Character," and "Theologico-Political Fragment" as *"Zur Kritik der Gewalt," "Schicksal und Charakter,"* and *"Theologisch-politisches Fragment"* in *Schriften,* Band I, copyright 1955 by Suhrkamp Verlag.

Printed in the United States of America

Library of Congress Cataloging in Publication Data

Benjamin, Walter, 1892–1940.
Reflections: essays, aphorisms, autobiographical writings.
"A Helen and Kurt Wolff book."
Bibliography: p.
Includes index.
I. Demetz, Peter, 1922–   II. Title.
PT2603.E455A26 1978   834'.9'12   77-92529
ISBN 0-15-176189-2

First edition
B C D E

Contents

Introduction

In the mid-fifties, Theodor W. Adorno presented the first collection of Walter Benjamin's essays to German audiences, and in the late sixties, Hannah Arendt prepared a similar volume for American readers. It was, both in Frankfurt (1955) and in New York (1968), a matter of rescuing Walter Benjamin from near-oblivion and of transforming what had been, in the late twenties and early thirties, a rumor among the *cognoscenti* into an incisive challenge to our ossifying habits of thought. Today, the situation has radically changed, and Walter Benjamin has become a new classic, at least among the members of the philosophical left on the European continent, who study his essays as avidly as those of Antonio Gramsci, Georg Lukács, or Ernst Bloch. We now have a nearly complete edition of his collected works in which even some of his improvised reviews are preserved (as they should be) with a philological care never bestowed on Sainte-Beuve or N. G. Chernyshevski; and many groups of partisan interpreters ally their political cause, by quoting chapter and verse, with the ideas of a writer obsessed with protecting the privacy of his experience. Reading and interpreting an author have never been activities that evolve outside a complex net of committed interests and social pressures, and I cannot pretend to approach Walter Benjamin from a more impersonal view than others have done. My difficulty is that I find myself unable to share his assumptions in the traditions of Romantic metaphysics or Hegelian dialectics, but I hope to balance these serious deficiencies by a compassionate effort to understand the tragic quality of his life and the internal contradictions of his thought, which was intent, at least at times, upon a vision of history violently disrupted by the coming of the Messiah and/or the revolution of the proletariat.

Over a long period, Gershom (Gerhard) Scholem and Theodor W. Adorno collaborated loyally in editing Benjamin's revealing letters and in suggesting diverse ways in which we should understand his ideas and commitments. Gershom Scholem, who was instrumental in introducing Benjamin to the Jewish spiritual tradition, continues to suggest in his memoirs that his restless friend was a religious if not a mystical thinker who may have been tempted, against the grain of his sensibilities, to superimpose the terms of Marxist discourse upon his metaphysical vision of God, language, and a society ontologically in need of salvation.

Theodor W. Adorno, Benjamin's irascible friend and his first editor of substantial merit, was inclined to make some allowances for an early metaphysical infatuation that was followed, to be sure, by a more important though uneasy alliance with a critical philosophy basically incarnated in the work of the Frankfurt Institut für Sozialforschung, which was continued, after Hitler had come to power, in Geneva and New York. In his own sophisticated way, Fredric Jameson, in one of the first important essays on Benjamin published in this country, fully supports Adorno's claims and adds a dash of inevitable melancholy characteristic of American academic Marxists in their frustrating search for an old-fashioned proletariat. Yet the neat division between a metaphysical and a materialist reading of Benjamin, advanced by Scholem and the critical Marxists respectively, has been modified more recently by the German critic Helmut Heissenbüttel and some younger interpreters emerging from the radical German student movement of the late sixties, who rightly stress the substantial differences between Adorno's and Benjamin's way of using Marxist ideas. These critics say, with a good deal of justification, that we cannot entirely understand Benjamin's particular brand of Marxism without looking more closely at his creative friendship with the playwright Bertolt Brecht, a relationship very little appreciated by either Scholem or Adorno. Scholem's religious views thus compete with a rich array of highly differentiated Marxist readings of Benjamin, and yet I prefer a third way, suggested by Martin Jay's sober history of the Frankfurt Institut, Hannah Arendt's biographical essays concerning the paradoxes of Benjamin's personality, and René Wellek's judicious panorama of his critical views. I am less concerned with constructing a systematic pigeonhole than with sketching a biographical account of Benjamin's experiences against crucial years of Central European history and with trying to ease, if it can be done at all, the exhilarating difficulties of reading some of his best writings, which are totally alien to the pragmatic and analytic orientations long prevalent in American thought.

In many Jewish families of late nineteenth-century Europe, gifted sons turned against the commercial interests of their fathers, who were largely assimilated (after moving from the provinces to the more liberal cities) to bourgeois success, and, in building their counterworlds in spiritual protest, they incisively shaped the future of science, philosophy, and literature. Articulating an insight of far-reaching implications, Karl Kraus, the belligerent Viennese satirist, suggested in his *Magical Operetta* (much enjoyed by Benjamin) that little Jewish family dramas were being played all over, the stern fathers concerned with *tachles*—profitable business ploys—and the spiritual sons with *shmonzes*—the less profitable matters of the pure mind. Whether we think of Sigmund Freud, Edmund Husserl, or Franz Kafka, we need few modifications to apply this description to what happened in these families, and in the story of Benjamin's development, the fundamental pattern reasserts itself with particular clarity. Walter Benjamin's parents belonged to the Berlin Jewish upper-middle class, and his childhood was protected by an elegant household of refined *diners* and prescribed shopping excursions, the inevitable governesses, and the best schools. His father was a knowledgeable auctioneer, art dealer, and investor who believed that he was distantly related to the poet Heinrich Heine. His mother came from a clan of lawyers and merchants successfully established in the Jewish communities of Prussia's eastern provinces. There was a sister, Dora, and a brother, George, who, as a physician, loyally served the working people in the northern industrial districts of Berlin, joined the German Communist Party, and later died in a concentration camp (his wife, Hilde Benjamin, was to serve the German Democratic Republic as a fierce state prosecutor and appeared, in fictional shape, in Le Carré's *Spy Who Came in from the Cold*). Walter received his first education in the Kaiser Friedrich School, a rather liberal institution (whatever he was to say about it later), and spent some time in an élite prep school in Thuringia, well known for the pedagogical experiments it directed against petrified educational tradition. One of his teachers there was Gustav Wyneken, the later founder of the "Free School Community" (Freie Schulgemeinde) under whose guidance the young student enthusiastically immersed himself in the ideas—or, rather, feelings—of the idealistic German Youth Movement, the counterculture of Wilhelmine Germany; "my thinking," young Benjamin wrote, "has its origins in my first teacher, Wyneken, and returns to him again and again."

In Berlin Benjamin actively participated in organizing the collective life of the "Free Students," who were aligned with the romantic ideology and the conservative orientations of the Youth Movement, rather than with the young Zionists or Socialists, who were competing for the allegiance of middle-class students in revolt against their fathers and the advances of industrial civilization. In 1912 he went to the University of Freiburg for a while because of the neo-Kantians there, and a year later traveled to Paris (the future capital of his sensibilities), but returned to Berlin again. There he published neo-Romantic poetry and essays concerning the need for change in the educational system, and was duly elected president of the Berlin "Free Students," who defended Wyneken's ideas about friendship, Eros, and the purity of the mind. On the first day of the war, Benjamin and his friends immediately volunteered for service in the Prussian army (the argument of his later left-wing defenders, that the young people simply wanted to stay together, obscures the patriotic enthusiasm of the Youth Movement volunteers who died *en masse* on the Western Front and were later hailed by the Nazis as true war heroes). Fortunately, however, his induction was postponed, and when his number came up later, he prepared for the physical examination by drinking innumerable cups of coffee and was, as he appeared before the recruiting board pale and with trembling hands, promptly rejected on medical grounds.

In 1915, Benjamin wrote an abrupt letter to Gustav Wyneken, breaking with him and the Youth Movement, but it would be difficult to say that he actively committed himself to political opposition to the monarchy and the war. If Franz Kafka, on August 2, 1914, laconically noted in his diary that war had broken out and that he went swimming in the afternoon, Benjamin kept a similarly studious distance from political and military events for a long time, read Kant and the German Romantics, collected rare editions, and branched out, rather early in his studies, into the philosophy of language and contemporary linguistics. During the first year of the war, he wrote about Hölderlin as any young German intellectual close to the Youth Movement would have done at that time. In October 1915, he went to Munich, less attracted by the university than by the presence of Dora Pollak, née Kellner (whom he was to marry after she obtained her divorce). At the same time he met Gershom Scholem, an active Zionist and scholar who, for the next twenty years or so, untiringly involved Benjamin in the study of Jewish religious traditions and, though disappointed again and again, kept encouraging him to think of moving to Palestine in order to write and teach in the homeland of the Jews. In the spring of 1917, Walter and Dora married and, with the permission of the German authorities, moved to Bern, Switzerland, where Benjamin continued his studies of philosophy, literature, and aesthetics; he was by

deepest inclination a true *Privatgelehrter*, most happy when
he could hide behind his papers and rare editions, but (possibly because his parents wished him to do so) he submitted a
professionally done dissertation entitled "The Concept of Art
Criticism in German Romanticism" and received his doctoral
degree *summa cum laude* (1919). While the battles of the civil
war were raging in many cities and regions of Germany, Benjamin in his Swiss retreat devoted critical attention to his
studies of Baudelaire and Adalbert Stifter, an Austrian conservative writer, and in his letters indulged in a Swiftian game
of establishing a new university that would gather in one distinguished place the silliest and most pedestrian minds of the
German university world.

The progressing inflation in Germany forced Benjamin,
Dora, and their three-year-old son, Stefan, to return home, and
in the subsequent years in Berlin (when the young family
lived in his parents' villa in the fashionable Grunewald district) Benjamin turned critic, translator of Baudelaire and
Proust, and, for pressing financial reasons, reviewer for the
Frankfurter Zeitung and the *Literarische Welt,* reporting with
equal interest on Charlie Chaplin, old toys (which he continued to love), odd assortments of Russian novels, and new
publications about German literary history. These were, in
terms of productivity and challenging friendships, intense
and strong years, coinciding with the most creative epoch of
the Weimar Republic: Benjamin developed an intense interest in anarchist theory (Sorel); his interpretation of Goethe's
novel *Elective Affinities,* moving to a mythopoeic approach,
was much admired by Hugo von Hofmannsthal; and he wrote
his difficult study of the origins of the German *Trauerspiel,*
which constitutes a pioneering philosophical analysis of allegory, symbol, and the "play of lament" in German tradition
and in European tradition as a whole. (This study accompanied his half-hearted application for a nonsalaried lecture-
ship at the University of Frankfurt, but Benjamin preferred
to withdraw the application, rather than let it be rejected by

an uncomprehending faculty involved in Byzantine intrigues.) In 1923, Benjamin met the young philosopher Theodor W. Adorno for the first time and, on a vacation trip to Capri in the summer of 1924, the Latvian actress Asja Lacis, an active Bolshevik (and later, through Stalinist justice, for nearly ten years a prisoner in the Gulag Archipelago) who, as he confessed, immediately inspired him to a feeling of the vital relevance of radical Communism; these feelings, however, did not prevent his subscribing, at about the same time, to the ultraconservative *Action Française,* or from saying that its viewpoints were the best antidote to German political stupidity. In the winter of 1926–27, Asja Lacis had Benjamin invited to Moscow, but although he accepted a commission to write the entry on Goethe (never published) for the *Bol'shaia Entsiklopediia,* he did not join the Communist Party, cryptically alluding to his "old anarchism" when the question came up in his correspondence. Somewhat later, he readily accepted a fellowship provided by the good offices of Gershom Scholem and the Jewish citizens of Palestine to concentrate on studying Hebrew in preparation for a teaching job in Jerusalem. It is difficult to say why Benjamin (who was divorced in 1930) once again rejected Scholem's urgent invitation to leave Germany; on January 20, 1930, he wrote a long and melancholy letter to his friend explaining in French why he had been dilatory in his Hebrew studies (which were not to be continued) and declaring that he had made up his mind to become Germany's most outstanding literary critic. Three years later, Hitler was in power, the brown shirts roamed through the streets of Berlin, and Benjamin was an exile, without a roof over his head, or, rather, without his collection of rare editions to protect him against a world of merciless enemies.

For the last seven years of his life, Walter Benjamin was condemned to a way of life closely resembling that of the émigré extras in Rick's Café in *Casablanca,* but there was nothing fictional about his efforts to be paid a decent fee for an occasional review, to avoid the attention of the French police (who were eager to collaborate with the German authorities when it came to Jewish and leftist refugees), or to find somebody willing to help with a visa that would open the doors to England or the United States. He continued publishing little reviews in Germany under his own name until April 1933, and under the playful pseudonyms of Detlev Holz and K. A. Stampflinger until the summer of 1935, but by that time Nazi control of the press, including the once liberal newspapers, was totally consolidated, and he was lucky if he could publish here and there in Switzerland, in Czechoslovakia, or in the *Gazette des amis des livres* (Paris). German radicals have lately accused Adorno and the Institut für Sozialforschung of dealing with Benjamin in less than humane ways, but the record shows that in spite of the frank views that he exchanged with Adorno in letters, Benjamin was made a member of the Institut (1935), received a regular stipend that came with the membership, and published his seminal study of Baudelaire in a periodical sponsored by the former Frankfurt group; and it was Max Horkheimer, of the Institut, who secured for Benjamin (who thought of himself as the "last of the Europeans" and a rather hesitant candidate for emigration to America) an affidavit and entry visa for the United States. Yet in these most difficult years of his life Benjamin felt closer than ever to Bertolt Brecht, with whom he stayed again and again in Brecht's Danish *dacha,* discussing Kafka, the uneasy situation of the radical left in the age of the Stalinist purges, and the importance of technological changes in the revolutionary arts. It was Benjamin who (perhaps in the wrong place and at the wrong time) became the first philosophical defender of Brecht's revolutionary experiments in the arts. In late September 1940, Benjamin (who had picked up his U.S. visa in Marseilles) crossed the French-Spanish border with a small band of fellow exiles, but was told on the Spanish side by the local functionary (who wanted to blackmail the refugees) that Spain was closed to them and that they would be returned in the morning to the French authorities, who were just waiting to hand them over to the Gestapo. Benjamin—totally exhausted and possibly sick—took an overdose of morphine, refused medical help, and died in the morning, while his fellow refugees were promptly permitted to proceed through Spanish territory to Lisbon. He is buried in Port Bou, but nobody knows where, and when visitors come (Scholem tells us), the guardians of the cemetery lead them to a place that they say is his grave, respectfully accepting a tip. We have neither monument nor flower, but we have his texts, in which his elusive, vulnerable, and terribly tense mind continues to survive.

In *Illuminations* (1968) Hannah Arendt gathered some of Benjamin's most important literary essays, and in the present companion volume she wanted (if I judge her intentions correctly) to show the many rich strains of his writings and the variegated forms in which he articulated his experience of thoughts, places, books, and people. Here she arranged his philosophical essays, aphorisms, and autobiographical writings in a sequence in which the chronologies of his life and of his developing ideas often cooperate, but I would recommend that the reader (particularly one approaching Benjamin for the first time) study and enjoy these texts in a more meandering way. We would keep together particular clusters of texts, as Hannah Arendt would have wanted us to do, and yet move on to a different finale—not to the pure metaphysics of his luminous early thought, as suggested by Dr. Arendt's arrangement, but to later essays in which the metaphysical and the Marxist elements confirm and contradict one another. I would suggest that the reader first approach those of Benjamin's writings that can loosely be termed autobiographical, including the ironic self-exploration in "The Destructive Character" (pages 301–03), and then proceed to a group of early writings in which a systematic and metaphysical orientation predominates. In consonance with his intellectual development, we would, in the next step, deal with a third cluster of essays in

which Benjamin moved to the speculative left or tried to formulate what he thought he had learned from Bertolt Brecht;
and once we had learned something about his Marxist commitments, we might feel better prepared to deal with those
particularly difficult texts in which, to the despair of partisan
interpreters, spiritual and materialist ideas appear in cryptic
configurations. In these (as, for example, the Paris précis) the
failure of the systematic thinker constitutes the true triumph
of the master of hermeneutics who, in "reading" the things
of the world as if they were sacred texts, suddenly decodes the
overwhelming forces of human history.

Benjamin's "Berlin Chronicle," a relatively late text sketched
during his first stay (1932) in Ibiza, Spain, and never published
while he lived, looks back in many important passages upon
his early childhood experiences and upon the emotional vicis-
situdes of the thinker as a young man of the idealist *jeunesse
dorée*. He himself suggests how we should read the text; the
"Chronicle," precisely because it explicates the nature of
memory by testing its powers, is a far more restless and profound text than his "Berlin Childhood Around the Turn of
the Century," in which individual memories are neatly ordered in a static if not mannered way. In the "Berlin Chronicle," his intimate childhood and the city of his youth emerge
luminously: the shaft of light under his bedroom door revealing the consoling presence of his parents nearby, the first experience of a threatening thunderstorm over the city, the
smell of perspiration in the classroom, the confusions of pu-
berty, the pale whore in the blue sailor-suit dominating (as
in an Antonioni movie) his recurrent dreams, the famous
Romanische Café as well as the more modest Princess Café,
where he wrote his first essays on a marble table-top. The details are vivid and precise, but Benjamin is not satisfied with
the informative splinter: he wants to explore the process of
remembering itself—unfolding, dredging up—and to analyze
the particular movement of his thoughts that gives shape to
the materials and isolates the illuminating significance of

what is close to the center of his sensibilities. We are, as readers, involved in a Proustian exercise in creating a past by using the finest snares of consciousness; to remember, Benjamin writes, is to "open the fan of memory," but he who starts to open the fan "never comes to the end of its segments; no image satisfies him, for he has seen that it can be unfolded and only in its folds does the truth reside: that image, that taste, that touch for whose sake all this has been unfurled and dissected; and now remembrance advances from small to smallest details, from the smallest to the infinitesimal, while that which it encounters in these microcosms grows ever mightier." Memory is the "capability of endlessly interpolating." In an extended image (implying an allusion to Schliemann and his discovery of Troy), Benjamin praises the writer as an archeologist who is never satisfied with the first stroke of the spade and returns again and again to the same place to dig deeper and deeper.

Benjamin himself is aware that his memories are characterized by a remarkable absence of people, and he tells us of a sudden epiphany that revealed to him in what way modern cities take their revenge upon the many claims human beings make upon one another. Memory ruled by the city does not show encounters and visits, but, rather, the scenes in which we encounter ourselves or others, and such an insight betrays an entire syndrome of Benjamin's ideas about life in the modern world: his concern with the "thingness" of the cities, the only places of historical experience in industrial civilizations; his obsession (shared by the French Surrealists) with walking the streets and boulevards; his fundamental urge to rearrange everything lived by fixing it on maps, in graphic schemes, spatial order. In his imagination, as in that of Rainer Maria Rilke, space rules over time; his "topographical consciousness" shapes experience in architectonic patterns, in neighborhoods, and in particular in urban districts the borders of which have to be crossed in trembling and sweet fear. The "Berlin Chronicle" is a misnomer, because it actually offers a map of coexistent apartments, meeting places, elegant salons, shabby hotel rooms, skating rinks, and tennis courts; social distinctions are expressed in terms of different urban landscapes in which the rich and the poor are enclosed without knowing one another; and certain streets, dividing the red-light districts around the railway station from the quarters of the *haute bourgeoisie,* are ontological thresholds on which the young man likes to dwell, tasting the terrible and magic moments of confronting a totally "other" life or the "edge of the void," the whores being "the household goddesses of [a] cult of nothingness." Benjamin always looked for threshold experiences, and not only in a private way. As a young man he may have loitered near the railway stations to face another way of living that radically negated all his personal values of absolute purity, and as a philosopher he continued moving toward thresholds of speculative potentialities, tasting, confronting, exploring, without really caring to cross over into a total commitment to the "other" once and for all. His early fascination with the other world of the red lights may be emblematic of the most secret bents of his mind.

"One-Way Street" was originally planned to be a highly personal record of observations, aphorisms, dreams, and prose epigrams assembled from 1924 to 1928 for a few intimate friends; the title suggests, in its urban metaphor, the fortunate turn of a street that opens onto a striking view of an entire new panorama, and indicates to readers that they should confront each of the little pieces as an abruptly illuminating moment of modern experience—intimate, literary, and political. The "Imperial Panorama," Benjamin's diagnosis of German inflation, was possibly the first piece, to which others were added. It is a first-rate document, in which his private shock (often articulated in terms of his incipient Marxism) and the social dissolution of the age closely correspond. He wrote these observations from the double perspective of the reluctant bourgeois son who had been living on the financial resources of his father (the capitalist), and the revolutionary

Marxist who was beginning to grasp, from his conversations with Asja Lacis and his readings of Georg Lukács, in what way middle-class stability, now seemingly destroyed forever, had caused the unstable fate of the less privileged. He rightly observes how inflationary pressures make money the destructive center of all interests, and yet he sounds very much like the disappointed middle-class idealist in the German Romantic tradition when he deplores the loss of communal warmth in human relationships, the disappearing feeling for a free and well-rounded personality, and the new dearth of productive conversation, due to the sudden predominance of the question of the cash nexus. But it is difficult to separate Benjamin the social commentator from the moralist in the French tradition; his brief and lucid observations on the fragility of feelings between men and women forcefully remind me of Stendhal's *De l'amour,* and he is particularly impressive when he fiercely comments on the analogies between books and prostitutes (variations of a leitmotif), discusses the insecurities of the modern writer, or playfully works out rules for writing bad books. Looking far into the future, he demands new forms of publications that would be more easily accessible, in an industrial mass society, to people averse to the "universal gesture of the book," and he speculates, as a pioneer in the semiotic tradition, about the literary and technological changes effected by new modes of print, advertising, and the developing cinema. As if in passing, and yet with astonishing foresight, he approaches problems that today dominate our changing awareness of literature and the media in the age of concrete poetry, Marshall McLuhan, and Jacques Derrida.

Peter Szondi suggested that in his "images of the cities" Benjamin offers an "exegesis of creation," but I would distinguish between his exercises and his pieces of perfection. Whether or not the portrait of "Naples" (1924) was sketched by Benjamin alone, as Adorno believed, or with his friend Asja, it strikes me as a preliminary essay in future possibilities, rich in precise observations (as if preserved by Lina Wertmüller's camera), and yet unusually relaxed in idiom, a funny and lovable travel reportage. The pages on "Marseilles" (1929) are of an entirely different order and of highly personal importance. They were especially dear to him, Benjamin confessed in 1928 to the Austrian writer Hugo von Hofmannsthal, because he had to "fight" Marseilles more than any other city. Marseilles was the toughest of adversaries, and to "squeeze a single sentence out of Marseilles was more difficult than to write an entire book about Rome." Hiding his own obsessions behind a quotation from André Breton (who speaks about the city streets as the only place of authentic experience), Benjamin consistently relies on his topographical approach again, breaks up the city into its constituent components, and, mobilizing striking and precise metaphors, shows himself an absolute master of reading the hidden meaning of the sparse detail. Certain of his total isolation in the toughest of all cities, Benjamin decided, as soon as he arrived in his small hotel room and read a little in Hermann Hesse's *Steppenwolf*, to continue the hashish experiments he had been undertaking for a number of years under the medical supervision of Dr. Ernst Joël, one of his oldest friends from the time of the Youth Movement. Benjamin wanted to sharpen his sensibilities to pierce the essence of the city, but "Hashish in Marseilles" (introduced by a long quotation from Dr. Joël's medical report) revises and transforms an actual record of his experiment (dated September 29, 1928) into a distinct work of art in which fluid and inchoate experience has changed into an ordered narrative of precision and radiance. Inarticulate consumers of hashish who merely want their narcissistic kicks surely cannot claim to follow Benjamin's example.

In the essays written during and immediately after the years of World War I, Benjamin wants to confront central questions about the order of the universe. He speaks of these writings as contributions to a new "metaphysical" philosophy and does not conceal his systematic interest in providing in-

clusive answers; the form of the essay may indicate some of
his hesitations, yet it is always our knowledge of the entire
kosmos—of God, man, and things—that is at stake. In a fragment about the essential tasks of (his) philosophy, Benjamin
shows himself deeply impressed by Kant's epistemological
fervor, but sharply contrasts a genuine philosophy, "conscious
of time and eternity," with the Enlightenment, which unfortunately admitted to scrutiny only knowledge of the lowest
kind (elsewhere he speaks of the "hollow" and the "flat" concerns of the Enlightenment). What he seeks is a theory dealing
with higher knowledge that is not limited by mathematical
and mechanical norms of certainty, but sustained by a new
turn to language, which alone communicates what we philosophically know.

Benjamin's essay "On the Mimetic Faculty," with its sudden
shifts of attention and compressed arguments of astonishing
range and illuminating suggestions, energetically seeks to close
the gap between the universe of things and the world of
signs, a gap widened by modern linguistics. It is man's mimetic
faculty in the widest sense that brings together what seems
split and divided; the wholeness of the universe is sustained,
Benjamin suggests, by "natural correspondences" that in turn
stimulate and challenge man to respond by creating analogies,
similarities, something that is akin. Man's mimetic responses
have their own history; and although Benjamin is inclined
to believe in a distinct weakening of some forms of the mimetic
force, he introduces the concept of a "nonsensuous similarity"
that operates beyond the evidence of the senses. Astrology,
dancing, and the onomatopoeic element in speech reveal the
oldest forms of man's capabilities, but "nonsensuous similarity" (or in more recent parlance, a paradoxical nonsensuous
iconicity of the sign, I would suspect) continues to reside in
speech as well as in writing and guarantees wholeness and
unity; "it is nonsensuous similarity that establishes the ties
not only between the spoken and the signified but also between the written and the signified, and equally between the

spoken and the written." Implicit in these arguments are two of Benjamin's most essential ideas—his belief that language is far from being a conventional system of signs (an idea further developed in his essay on language) and his hermeneutic urge to read and understand "texts" that are not texts at all. The ancients may have been "reading" the torn guts of animals, starry skies, dances, runes, and hieroglyphs, and Benjamin, in an age without magic, continues to "read" things, cities, and social institutions as if they were sacred texts.

His essay "On Language as Such and on the Language of Man" (written in 1916) clearly offers a central attempt to re-establish a metaphysical view of the word, in which the over-whelming power of language spoken and heard puts forth a truth that was hidden before; and whatever Marxists may say about his allegiances, here the enemy of the Enlightenment has his place between gnostic traditions and Martin Heidegger. Quoting, against Kant, the German Romantics Hamann and Friedrich M. Müller, Benjamin separates his own ideas from a "bourgeois" (i.e., commonplace) and a "mystical" philosophy of language; the bourgeois theory unfortunately holds that language consists of mere conventional signs that are not necessarily related to Being, and the mystical view falsely identifies words with the essence of things. In his own view, the being of a richly layered world, as divine creation, remains separate from language, yet cannot but commune "in" rather than "through" it. Language, far from being a mere instrument, lives as a glorious medium of being; all creation participates in an infinite process of communication (communion), and even the inarticulate plant speaks in the idiom of its fragrance. "There is no event or thing in either animate or inanimate nature that does not in some way par-take of language, for it is in the nature of all to communicate their mental meanings. . . . We cannot imagine a total absence of language in anything."

Following the gnostic tradition, Benjamin looks for his cue in biblical texts, and after a halfhearted attempt at reconciling the two creation narratives of the Old Testament, he develops his ideas from a close reading of Genesis 1, for he feels that the recurrent rhythm of "Let there be," "He made," and "He named" clearly indicates a striking relationship of creation to language. The hierarchies of the world and the order of language, or, rather, "words," intimately correspond: although the word of God is of absolute and active power, in man's realm the word is more limited, and it is "soundless" in the "silent magic of things." Man's dignity consists in mirroring God's absolute and creative word in "names" on the threshold between finite and infinite language; the names he gives to and receives from others may be but a reflection (*Abbild*) of the divine Word, but name giving sustains man's closeness to God's creative energies and defines his particular mode of being; "of all beings man is the only one who himself names his own kind, as he is the only one whom God did not name." To name is man's particular fate; he alone among the created beings (as Rilke and Hölderlin would confirm) responds to the silent language of things by "translating" their speechless communication. Thus "translation," in a complex meaning, acquires a central ontological importance because the communication of the lower strata of creation has to be translated (that is, elevated and made pellucid) to the higher orders. The speechless word of the things or the silent speech on the lowest level is translated by man into the "naming word" (*nennendes Wort*), the language of the anthropological stratum, and finally offered to God, who, in His word of creation (*schaffendes Wort*) guarantees the legitimacy of the translation, because it is He who has created the silent word of things as well as that of translating man. "Translating" means solving a task that God has given to man alone; and such a task would be impossible to fulfill "were not the name-language of man and the nameless one of things related in God, released from the same creative word, which in things became the communication of matter in magic community, and in man the language of knowledge and name in blissful mind." We are in a universe structured by the presence or absence of "linguistic" articulation, and all the levels of creation (articulate and inarticulate) are alien and yet intimately related to one another by the potentialities of the "name" (not less powerful than in Gertrude Stein's godless theory of poetry).

Benjamin's "Theologico-Political Fragment" (written 1920–21), a striking statement of the Messianism prevalent in his thought for a long time, connects his early meditations about language, knowledge, and the world with his "Critique of Violence" (1921), in which his experience of changing German society in the age of the Spartakus uprisings and his readings of Sorel's anarchist theories combine with his unshaken belief in a postlapsarian world crying for sudden eschatological change. In his "Fragment," he wants to cope, at least by suggestion, with the seeming incompatibility of the profane (or historical) and the Messianic (or divine) order; and he bravely demands that a new philosophy of history (his own) try to relate the distinct forces in some way to one another. These forces do not move in a consonant rhythm, and yet, "if one arrow points to the goal toward which the profane dynamic acts, and another marks the direction of Messianic intensity, then certainly the quest of free humanity for happiness runs counter to the Messianic direction; but just as a force can, through acting, increase another that is acting in the opposite direction, so the order of the profane assists, through being profane, the coming of the Messianic Kingdom." Benjamin suggests that in the profane urge for being happy the most tender coming of the divine order announces itself, and we are left with hope in fragile and painful abeyance.

Benjamin's fragment "Fate and Character," like many of his earlier essays, compresses far-reaching suggestions into a few pages, and it would be foolish to separate the strains of anthropology, autobiographical implication, and genre criticism too neatly. It is an impressive and tortuous example of how Benjamin brings together and divides again in a new and radical way what more traditional minds have related in superficial fashion. His concern with guilt, the law, and the gods, and his separation of the moral and the divine order, indicate that (though questions of characterology and the poetic predominate) we are still moving in a universe of metaphysical consistence. In the early passages, the fragment suggests why Benjamin, in search of a sign system of human experience, is far less ashamed of his intense interest in graphology (of which he was a gifted practitioner), chiromancy, and physiognomy than his critics. Later he argues that our concepts of fate and character have been mistaken, because we put these concepts in the wrong contexts—ethics and religion. But fate relates to guilt and misfortune (rather than to happiness, which would be a way of escaping fate) and belongs therefore to the world of the law, which is but a relic of the demonic stage in human development; and it is in tragedy that the genius of man first arises above the "mist of guilt"— not, as Hegel and his many disciples would suggest, restoring the disturbed order of the universe, but manifesting human resistance "by shaking up [the] tormented world." Similarly, the concept of character should be removed from the realm of ethics and related to "nature in man"; and if tragedy seeks to go beyond the "guilt context of the living," comedy shows character (for instance, in Molière's plays) "like a sun, in the brilliance of its single trait, which allows no other to remain visible in its proximity." We do not judge in moral terms but feel "high amusement," and far from presenting to us a monstrous puppet that is totally unfree, comedy—with its commitment to an emancipated physiognomy—introduces a new age of the genius of humanity.

The "Critique of Violence" hides its paradoxes and disturbing self-subversion in a deceptively tight structure of arguments in which, as if he were a lawyer or a legal philosopher, Benjamin proposes to develop, with an almost merciless power of deduction, a close sequence of professional distinctions; and yet, on the later pages of the essay, the entire

system of initial reasoning, if not an entire world of preliminary values, is pushed aside, and the expert lawyer changes
into an enthusiastic chiliast who rhapsodically praises the violence of divine intervention, which will put a sudden end to
our lives of insufficiency and dearth (the essay subverts its
own fundaments in order to enact something of the ontological "break" in which the old world is abruptly transformed
into a new). As in his other essays of the time (1916–21), Benjamin first wants to separate his own philosophical perspective
from that of other traditional approaches, and in a technical
argument of high sophistication he reviews the manner in
which the "natural law" and the "positive law" have been
dealing with the problems of violence. He shows that the one
conceives of violence as a product of unchangeable nature,
whereas the other deals with violence as a result of historical
becoming (*Gewordenheit*). Both, however, are constantly concerned with the close interrelationships of means and ends
within the legal system, and both fail to ask the question
(central to his own interest) of how certain means of violence
might be paradoxically justified totally outside the law. Benjamin surveys the legal implications of strikes, wars, and capital punishment and concludes that all violence in the human
realm functions so that it is either constituting or sustaining
the law (*rechtssetzend/rechtserhaltend*); and in a passage certain to challenge the liberal reader, he suggests that legal
institutions forgetful of the latent presence of violence inevitably decay, that parliaments (ignoring the dignity of violence)
err in trying to reach compromises, and that anarchists and
Bolsheviks are right in fiercely attacking parliamentary systems. Fortunately, there is still a private sphere in which a
"cultured heart," politesse, and trust in our fellow beings may
come to subjective but nonviolent accords.

But here we are suddenly elevated from the profane to the
mythical and divine orders, and violence, of a more radical
kind, turns into an eschatological necessity. Not only is it
difficult, Benjamin asserts, to think about solving any prob-

lems in the human world in a nonviolent way, but it is completely inconceivable that man's salvation from all historical modes of existence should ever occur without violence. We are compelled to postulate another kind of violence, one that operates outside the realm of legal principles, violence not as a means of legality but as a manifestation of Olympian power: "Niobe's arrogance calls down fate upon itself not because her arrogance offends against the law but because it challenges fate—to a fight in which fate must triumph, and can bring to light a law only in its triumph." Yet in his thirst for purity, plenitude, and otherness, Benjamin again relegates the violence of myth or the "manifestation of the Gods" to a dubious state of wordliness, because even mythical violence cannot finally escape an involvement with, or, rather, a definition of, profane legalities. True otherness is only in God, who asserts himself in a third and absolute type of violence completely alien to the order of profanity and myth; "if mythical violence is lawmaking, divine violence is law-destroying; if the former sets boundaries, the latter boundlessly destroys them; if mythical violence brings at once guilt and retribution, divine power only expiates; if the former threatens, the latter strikes; if the former is bloody, the latter is lethal without spilling blood." The anarchist mystic Benjamin sees the coming of the Messiah as abrupt, sudden, destructive, ending all human history and its barrenness by freeing pure, glorious, divine violence from contagion with myth or the regions below. Once again we have moved through all the strata of creation, but Benjamin does not tell us how we are to *live* after God's violent lightning has struck, when a timeless and crystalline space of terrible perfection, as in paradise, surrounds us again.

We cannot speak about anybody's Marxism in a general and abstract way any more, and to approach productively those of Benjamin's essays in which Marxist ideas predominate is to define the particular implications of these ideas and to describe their specific function in an individual moment of

Central European politics and intellectual history. Whatever
can be said about Benjamin as melancholy Marxist, I would
stress above all that he, in his rather unobtrusive way, sided
with those artists and critics on the radical left who were
arguing against the growing traditionalism of the Soviet establishment and, often in close combat with the defenders of an
ossifying party line, continued to believe that Marxists should
not participate in construing a totally closed world, but should
spontaneously respond to new technological changes in contemporary civilization. There are few indications that Benjamin, who was a secretive and studious man, often attended
political mass meetings or marched under red banners through
the streets of Berlin. His Marxism was a library affair (more
Lenin and Trotsky than Marx, and more early Lukács than
Engels), and the challenging way in which he speaks of Surrealism, Sergei Tretiakov, and Bertolt Brecht suggests that
he was, in the concrete context of the late twenties and thirties, attracted by the impressive power of the Communist
Party and inclined toward increasing opposition to the Stalin-
ists, the dogma of Socialist Realism (after 1934), and the
revolutionary decree from above.

His report from Moscow, published immediately after his
return from the Soviet Union in 1927, shows the self-styled
convert in the initial moments of his first encounter with a
revolutionary world that claims his instinctive sympathies and
yet does not assuage the strong doubts of the middle-class in-
trovert. He bravely declares at the outset that the only guarantee of true insight is that he took sides before going to Russia,
and yet, while doing his best to understand and to sympathize,
he continues to walk through the streets of Moscow in the
manner of a Baudelairean *flâneur,* simultaneously very close
to and very distant from what he hears and sees. Of the twenty
sections of the report, more than half offer impressions of
streets, squares, parks, and public buildings; and although he
can show enthusiasm about the public quality of revolutionary

life, he is also able without effort to keep his mind cool and unendangered by the compassionate transports of too much empathy. In contrast to the Prussian cleanliness and the order of Berlin, Moscow nearly overwhelms Benjamin with an aesthetic surfeit of colors, disorganization, and teeming humanity. Against the snow and the gray winter sky, reds and greens glow with Mediterranean intensity, and the streets are filled with children, beggars (sketched with Dickensian flair), and ordinary citizens, hastening to offices, markets, and meetings. Modern technology and old-fashioned ways of life hurtle against one another; occasionally subverting his own ideological resolutions, Benjamin speaks of the "Asiatic" time sense of the Russians, of the rough quality of daily life, which suggests a gold miners' camp in the Klondike, or describes the female ticket collectors in the rickety streetcars as "Samoyed women." Something obsolete and yet essential survives in the inexorable transformations of the city; and in a moving moment Benjamin reveals his exquisite tactile pleasures when, riding in a sleigh, he tenderly and quickly brushes against people, horses, and stones and feels a touch of life on his skin.

I suspect that Benjamin was puzzled by the social realities of the Moscow winter of 1926–27. Armed with bookish and radical notions about the Revolution, he finds himself confronted with the attempt of the Soviet bureaucracy to increase the efficiency of commerce and the public services by creating a new middle class (of a hypothetical kind) and to push economic productivity by granting new privileges to technical experts; in literature, the staunchest revolutionaries agree to an armistice with productive and traditionalist "fellow travelers," discussions about problems of writing are dominated by a crude interest in ideological content, the graphic experiments of the futurists and constructivists have disappeared from public view, and in a few theaters are staged performances that would horrify the progressive Berlin audiences. As one committed to believe, Benjamin is rather naïve about the government and active opposition, but he is not willing to disregard what he sees with his own eyes when he describes daily life as a great laboratory (which does not change the inventive language of simple people) or when he, with good reason, praises public efforts to educate the waifs of the civil war and the inarticulate peasants by means of museums, movies, and a didactic theater (Asja Lacis's particular field of work). Benjamin anticipates Milovan Djilas's later analyses when he remarks that the Soviet system represents a "state of castes" in which the life of each individual citizen is fully determined by his relationship to the ruling Party; a "reliable viewpoint" constitutes the only guarantee that goods may be enjoyed. I find it difficult to decide in which way to read the concluding passages of section 14, where Benjamin speaks of the inevitable disappearance of the free *homme de lettres,* who is bound to the fate of the withering middle classes. He seems to record Soviet developments with the undisturbed voice of the historian, and yet it is impossible to believe that he does not speak about his own concerns when he describes how the revolutionary artist has turned into a functionary, working for the departments of censorship, justice, or finance, and finds himself a member of the new ruling class. If his friend Asja had read these pages more carefully, she would have discovered the answer to her perpetual question why Walter did not join the Communist Party, as had his brother the physician.

I would include Benjamin's essay "Surrealism," originally published as three installments in *Die Literarische Welt* in the late winter of 1929, among his most cryptic and important texts. Written from the distance of the German observer at a time of growing conflicts within the French Surrealist group, the essay offers a panoramic view of what the Surrealist poets had done since 1919 and, perhaps more essentially, reveals personal ideas that were to obsess Benjamin for the rest of his life. A consciousness in crisis seizes on the crisis of a poetic movement to define itself; and it is important to see how Benjamin characterizes the pressing problems of a "humanist concept of freedom" for one disenchanted with "eternal discussions" and longing 'for vital decisions to go beyond the alternatives of the "anarchist *fronde*" (close to his sensibilities) and "revolutionary discipline" (demanded by the organized Communists). He describes how the Surrealists have exploded traditional poetry from within by pushing the idea of "poetic life" to the utter limits of the possible; inevitably they have reached a tortuous moment of transition in which the heroic period of Surrealism, or the intimate years of the "inspiring wave of dreams," have to give way to a public struggle for power, political commitment, and involvement with revolutionary action. Yet the key concept of the "profane illumination," which emerges here to characterize Surrealist vision, suggests Benjamin's own way of unveiling, in his materialist hermeneutics, how history resides in some of the things of the world and institutions of society; and by attributing to the Surrealists the virtue of "seeing" and "freeing" revolutionary energies in things nearly obsolete, Benjamin describes what he is actually going to do in his later essays on Paris and French society. The Surrealists (who may not always have been equal to their task) have discovered revolutionary forces in particular objects and everyday use (e.g., the first iron constructions, early photographs, dresses almost out of fashion); André Breton and his beloved Nadja change into revolutionary resolution, if not action, what others have felt in uncertain and frustrated moods when taking a trip in a sad railway carriage or looking, from a new apartment, out through the window and the rain. But Benjamin does not want to tolerate any irrational romantic, or intoxicating element in that secularized epiphany or the overwhelming moment of "profane illumination"; in spite of his hashish experiments (or, rather, because of them), he asserts that it is not productive to accentuate the mystical element in the mystery of discovering hidden forces and meanings, "for histrionic or fanatical stress on the mysterious side of the mysterious takes us no further; we penetrate the mystery only to the degree that we recognize it in the everyday world, by virtue of a dialectical optic that perceives the everyday as impenetrable, the impenetrable as everyday." There are few lines in which Benjamin reveals the intent of his late writings more clearly and openly.

Hannah Arendt speaks about the importance of the Svendborg conversations between the critic Benjamin and the playwright Brecht, but I have to confess that I feel both exhilarated and depressed by these dialogues in exile, which show much intellectual brilliance and a good deal of constitutional inability to see, in the age of Dachau and the Gulag Archipelago, the political realities hidden behind a fine veil of self-created illusions about the alternatives to fascism (less Hegel and more common sense would have been useful). The trouble is that Benjamin, who recorded these conversations without any intent to publish his notes, does not care to indicate his own views and arguments in more than fleeting detail, and what we have is an interesting document of Brecht's intelligent and foolish utterances about a wide range of questions, including Kafka and the political and literary situation in the Stalinist Soviet Union. On approaching Kafka, the friends clearly disagree; Benjamin likes to explore the far corners of a metaphysical universe, but Brecht thinks above all of grist for his theatrical mill. With almost boyish charm, Brecht admits (against his theories) that an artist should have the privilege of playing games; he has witty things to say about Kafka's Prague milieu, and he does not avoid ideological simplification when he declares Kafka to be a prophet of terrible bureaucracies (a view generally expressed at the East European Kafka Conference near Prague in 1963) or asks what usable elements (*Brauchbares*) Kafka has to offer to his left-wing readers. Later conversations briefly touch on internal problems of Communist cultural policies; and whereas Benjamin refuses to speak up, Brecht rants against Georg Lukács and other adversaries and suggests that the Soviet Union shows signs of being run by a "personal regiment" that has created a "dictatorship over the proletariat" or a "worker's monarchy" as monstrous as a fish with horns. Not so long before, the playwright Brecht had publicly admonished his audiences to "embrace the butcher" in the interest of world revolution, but here in private conclave he recites the names of friends arrested during the purges and puts the blame for these heinous deeds on a "criminal clique." He reminds me of the German *petits bourgeois* who at approximately the same time busily told one another that a small group of SA men were responsible for all Nazi atrocities, but that the system was entirely innocent of any transgressions against humanity.

In his lecture "The Author as Producer," given at the Paris Institute for the Study of Fascism (1934), Benjamin concentrates on important questions often discussed with Brecht; and I wonder how the functionaries responded to his nostalgic memories of the Soviet "Left Front," or *Levyi Front,* group (he did delete a long Trotsky quotation from his manuscript). The lecture begins in good Brechtian fashion by separating the "bourgeois entertainer" (Brecht would have said the "culinary" writer) from the progressive artist who has thrown his lot in with the revolutionary proletariat, but Benjamin does not want to accept the traditional idea that the correct tendency alone assures the quality of the text. Trying to redefine the old problem of content/form in a dialectical way, he rightly argues that it is insufficient to analyze "a book, work, or novel" independently of social relationships, and, dexterously shifting to his central question, he suggests that the question about the work and the social structure should be revised; instead of asking how a work of art relates "to" modes of production, we should ask how it operates "within" them (he is thinking of modes of property as well as of technology). Like the *Levyi Front* writers and Brecht since the late twenties, Benjamin demands that left-wing writing use the technological advances in the media, and he praises Sergei Tretiakov as a true "operative" (not merely "informational") author who energetically seized on new technologies and forms of expression, joined the peasant communes in the Russian countryside, organized *st'engazety* (newspapers on the walls), and brought radio and movies to the villages. Benjamin's image of the Soviet press may be rather romantic, but what he really wants is a radical democratization of cultural life, based on the potentialities of the mass media; he hopes (as does Herbert Marcuse later) that these new forms would not be easily absorbed by the capitalist apparatus of production/distribution, but would instead revolutionize the apparatus itself (a rather optimistic idea, if we remind ourselves of the experiments of the Italian futurists, allied with the Fascists, or of Leni Riefenstahl's experimental movies in praise of the butchers on the right). Benjamin finds little consolation in the German writing of his time; expressionists and activists, from Heinrich Mann to Alfred Döblin, have wanted "spiritual transformation" rather than "technical innovation," and even the *Neue Sachlichkeit* (New Objectivity) of the mid-twenties, with all its striking interest in photography and reportage techniques, has delivered its goods to the capitalist culture machinery, rather than change it. Yet we should not ignore the beginnings of a countermovement: "the revolutionary strength of Dada" tested the authenticity of art, John Heartfield used photo montage to teach the working people, and Bertolt Brecht, above all in plays like *The Measures Taken* (*Die Massnahme*), created the new paradigms of a theater obstinately refusing to be absorbed by capitalist society. Brecht (whose *Threepenny Novel* Benjamin vastly overrates) emerges as the master of what artists and the arts should do; his epic theater constitutes a model of production able to teach other producers what to produce and, by requiring a different kind of theatrical apparatus, transforms the old cultural institutions in a revolutionary way. There is much tragic irony in Benjamin's last stand as a theoretician of "operative" literature. He demands a new, open, and experimental Marxist art in the manner of Tretiakov and Brecht exactly at the moment when, in the Soviet Union, Karl Radek is attacking James

Joyce, and eager Party functionaries are declaring that nineteenth-century traditions are the best way to the future.

Sectarian interpreters of Benjamin are fond of referring exclusively to one group of essays and ignoring others, but such divisive tactics are of little help to his readers, because they impose a reductive pattern of either/or on an intricate surfeit of paradoxes, abrupt changes of orientation, internal contradictions, and thoughtful self-subversions. It is not difficult to include the author of the Brechtian essay "The Author as Producer" (1934) among the revolutionary Marxists of his time or to characterize the writer of the essay on language (1916) as a belated Romantic, but it is far more challenging to read these two essays as demarcating an extensive field of intellectual possibilities within which Benjamin moves with piercing insights, a distinct aversion to inherited orthodoxies, and surprising reversals of direction. Only if we are willing to accept the entire Benjamin, and not just an essay here or a tag there quoted in support of somebody's narrow dogma, are we really qualified, at least in a preliminary way, to deal with those of his puzzling texts in which whole syndromes of divergent ideas work with and against one another. The essay "Karl Kraus" and the précis "Paris, Capital of the Nineteenth Century" surely are representative and challenging examples of meditations in which speculative and Marxist views of the world forcefully collide.

Karl Kraus (1874–1936) has for a long time been a towering cult figure for a particular generation of Austrian and German writers, but outside of his time and place, it is almost impossible to communicate something of his ambivalent charisma. He was to many the Isaiah of decaying old Europe or at least the Jewish Swift of Vienna, and in order to suggest his many and uncanny gifts I would have to say that he combined the interests and energies of H. L. Mencken, Sören Kierkegaard, and a demonic Woody Allen, all in one. As editor of the influential periodical *Die Fackel* (*The Torch*, 1899–1936), which

for decades he himself wrote from cover to cover, as author of
the superdrama *The Last Days of Mankind* (1922), crying from
the depth of despair against the powerful of the world, and as
fierce critic and polemicist in the age of Fritz Mauthner and
Ludwig Wittgenstein, he was obsessed with judging the virtues
and perversions of his contemporaries, famous and infamous,
by looking closely at how they spoke and wrote. He would discover a cheap adjective and, with thunder and undisputed authority in his voice, reveal the unspeakable degradation of
ethical norms hidden behind a microscopic detail of style.

Benjamin's perplexing and rich essay on Karl Kraus (of
which I can hope to explicate only a major strain) argues from
a late gnostic as well as from a Marxist perspective, in which
the postlapsarian and the capitalist worlds seem to be synony-
mous. Kraus (who confessed that he himself did not really
understand what Benjamin said about him) emerges as a ma-
jestic judge who, touched by the last rays of the day of creation,
stubbornly upholds theological norms in a fallen (i.e., bourgeois) world of inauthenticity, base journalism, and meretricious
newspapers—above all, the Viennese *Neue Freie Presse*. On
trial are language and the press, or, rather, the outrageous
cheapening of authentic language into mere prattle (*Ge-
schwätz*), in which base relevance wants to triumph over the purity of all created things. Kraus actually stands for Adam, who
"names" in the original sense of the word, and takes his revenge on writers like Heine or Nietzsche who, in the absence
of binding norms, confuse the naming power of language with
mere "essayism" and the *feuilleton*. But by quoting again and
again (a device that Benjamin himself liked), Kraus restores
the original purity of the word by lifting it out of its undignified context and by pushing it back toward its origins. Quotations, emancipating words from the demeaning bondage of
context, actually purify what is being said and paradoxically
reflect something of the original language of the angels, "in
which all words, startled from the idyllic context of meaning,
have become mottoes on the book of Creation."

Benjamin is not blind to the intricate mode of Kraus's polemical discourse, in which a radical technique of unmasking the enemy combines with an intense art of self-expression continually sustained by demonic vanity. The critic Kraus behaves like an actor who anxiously waits for applause, and his famous public readings from Shakespeare and the popular Viennese playwright Johann Nestroy have been but crucial tests of his power of mimicking other voices and *personae*. Kraus employs these powers when attacking his enemies, literally creeping "into those he impersonates, in order to annihilate them." Benjamin does not hesitate to say that "Kraus will pay any price to get himself talked about," but he also knows that his elemental vanity generates a self-torture that forces him to sacrifice to his initiated reader, in each modest comma and obscure fact, "a piece of his mutilated flesh." In Kraus's writings, idiosyncrasy has been elevated to the most supreme instrument of criticism, and his obsessive self-concern is put to the most noble use.

But the Marxist Benjamin does not hesitate to judge the judge of language, who unfortunately binds his revolutionary practice, the liberation of words from the vicious contexts, to a reactionary theory suggesting (as did young Benjamin) the possibility of restoring the original glory of language without totally revolutionizing nature; "that to him the fit state of man appears not as the destiny and fulfillment of nature liberated through revolutionary change, but as an element of nature *per se*, of an archaic nature without history, in its pristine, primeval state, throws uncertain, disquieting reflections even on his idea of freedom and of humanity." Karl Kraus, as the Austrian conservative Adalbert Stifter did before him, sides with "the party of nature" and inevitably turns a blind eye to the social realm. His indubitable virtues are, originally, those of the last bourgeois, who wants to be judged on being an unpolitical citizen, and only in close combat with the enemies of the naming word have his "operating powers" (Benjamin uses the military term *"Einsatzkräfte"*) acquired a belligerent ap-

pearance. Unfortunately, people do not see the historical necessity of these developments any more, and it is highly important to show why "this guardian of Goethe's linguistic
values" became "a comedian and why this honorable man
went berserk." I think it is not impossible to read Benjamin's
Kraus essay as an ambivalent critique of his own metaphysical
concept of language. Exorcizing Karl Kraus in himself, Benjamin comes to see his own romantic ideas of language as
regressive, and yet he says, as if with unrepentant pride, that
his ideas are strangely and successfully operative in his protracted fight against the perversions of the Adamic word in
bourgeois society. It is his gnosticism, Benjamin almost im-
plies, that makes him a better Marxist.

Translating Proust and studying the French Surrealists in
the middle and later twenties, the *flâneur* Benjamin began to
collect materials for a substantial book about Paris that was to
be central to his efforts and achievements. It was to investigate historical forms of culture in the wildest sense, proceed-
ing from historical and literary texts (Baudelaire) and, as he
had done before in his images of cities, from "going through"
a metropolitan topography as if it were a revealing record of
historical forces. "Paris, Capital of the Nineteenth Century"
constitutes part of a précis submitted to the Institut für Sozialforschung; and while it would be useful to read it in close con-
junction with some of his remarks on Baudelaire, it shows even
in splendid isolation an important late moment of his thought,
in which his Marxist analysis of institutional structures relies
productively on his earlier habits of "reading" things as if they
were texts. The individual sections of the text, concluded by a
programmatic coda, follow a recurrent pattern of seizing upon
an architectural development (shopping arcades or boulevards), an industrial event (exhibitions), or a fashion in the
arts (the panorama) of mid-nineteenth-century Paris. After
isolating the individual "fact," Benjamin searches for its sociological and technological causes and/or correspondences,
suggests links to economic trends and political tendencies of

the time, and literally forces the "fact" to yield, to reveal, to deliver to his and to our minds what it hides and preserves of the wishful thinking of the ruling classes—"the development of the forces of production reduced the wish symbols of the previous century to rubble even before the monuments representing them had crumbled." Yet for all his concern with historical time, the text (as has often been observed) has a strikingly static quality, which reflects Benjamin's compulsion to deal with spaces, vistas, buildings, and monuments, rather than with sequences of events. His regular use of mottoes and quotations (creating graphic "blocks") and of a striking syntax, in which paratactic statements far outnumber hypotactic constructions, generates a discourse in which history has come to a halt in "things" of monumental stillness and deceptive immobility.

Benjamin's problem, which he shares with other Marxists, is to link the individual fact or institution with the overall development of economic history (the prime mover). Behind, or, rather, "in," the elegant shopping arcades, Benjamin sees as first cause the boom of the French textile industry and the economic necessity of storing a variety of expensive goods. But there is also a secondary cause—the technological advances of cast-iron construction accelerated by the growth of the railways and, in turn, the use of cast iron in building railway stations and exhibition halls, wherever transients gather. Benjamin speaks about correspondences where many other Marxists would refer to economic basis and cultural superstructure; and he often suggests these correspondences by parallel sentence structures, neatly arranging the semantic elements in the required relationships ("as . . . as"; "as little . . . as").

But Benjamin's quick and productive perceptions did not go unchallenged, even among his close friends. In a letter (November 10, 1938) much discussed by Marxist metacritics, Theodor W. Adorno energetically accused his friend of linking pragmatic content "directly" with a few elements of social history, and, using Hegelian terms, he disparaged Benjamin's inclination to give "a materialist turn" to a few selected features from the realm of the intellectual superstructure. Benjamin's dialectic, he added, lacked proper mediation, and his thought inevitably oscillated between "magic and positivism." I am not in sympathy with Adorno's prescription of what proper Marxism should be, but I think he was right in pointing out to Benjamin the "theological motif" of calling things "by their names" and the "deeply romantic element" hidden in his vision; in looking at Paris, Benjamin certainly had not yet ceased to pursue the old Adamic ways of naming the individual things of the universe and releasing, in a blessed word, the energy of meaning that God, or, rather, human history, had gathered in the particularity of these things. It is still an attitude of paradisiac hermeneutics, even if Benjamin, as a kind of Marxist Hölderlin (in prose), in the age of postlapsarian capitalism cannot but rely on a more secular code.

As I continue reading Benjamin thirty and more years after his death, I cannot close my eyes to the obsolescence of many of his beliefs (including his demand that the artist join the revolutionary proletariat), and yet I find myself constantly impressed by the erudite range of his conflicting interests and by his stubborn loyalties, which do not easily fit into the schematic image of a Central European left-wing intellectual *entre deux guerres.* He is well known to us as a sophisticated and cosmopolitan translator and critic of Baudelaire and Proust, but he also loved "naïve" art (as we would say today) and the didactic narratives of Johann Peter Hebel, an Alemannic writer concerned with the moral education of simple village people. Benjamin was the first philosophical defender of Brecht's revolutionary plays, but he also felt attracted by Franz Kafka for a long time and critically studied the Austrian Catholic Adalbert Stifter. His continued readings of the Bolshevik classics did not diminish his interest in Max Kommerell, whose literary essays showed high regard for Stefan George and Hölderlin, essential to the more refined members of the German Youth Movement. Benjamin wrote pioneering studies of Goethe and the baroque drama and was (together with Siegfried Kracauer) among the first intellectuals of the Weimar Republic to think seriously about the new technological possibilities of photography and film. He studied the traditions of Jewish mysticism and the German Romantics, and yet never gave up reading contemporary thrillers and detective stories, including those by Emile Gaboriau and, later, Simenon. One would wish that his interpreters, busy with developing complex terminologies thrice removed from our cultural experience, would be half as open as he was to the literature and the arts of our time.

But there are other contradictions, astonishing and difficult to discuss. Benjamin's friends all agree that he was a man of quiet, fastidious, and extremely polite manners, and yet there was in his character and in his thought a half-hidden thirst for violence (more poetic than political), ill according with his life in the library and his later will to believe in revolutionary discipline. His studies of Sorel and his defense of anarchist spontaneity (as suggested in his essay on violence) against any Marxist "programming" of action reveal something in him that precedes all political theory and perhaps has its origins in a mystic vision of a Messiah who comes with the sword to change the world into white-and-golden perfection. His recurrent images of barricades, exploding dynamite, and the furies of civil war (as, for instance, in the essay on Surrealism) have an almost sexual if not ontological quality, and should not be obfuscated by pious admirers who would like to disregard the deep fissures in his thought and personality. A future discussion of his philosophies and politics may well come to the conclusion that his constitutional inability to come to terms with the problem of anarchy (spontaneity, intoxication, salvation) and order (programming, reason, and discipline) is more characteristic of his central conflicts than is his movement back and forth between romantic metaphysics and Marxism, closely bound to each other by Hegel's philosophy.

The Austrian Marxist Ernst Fischer once suggested that Benjamin contributed much to an interpretation of capitalism but little to changing the world, and added that his philosophy, sustained by utter loneliness, rather than by the concerns of the masses, particularly attracts those intellectuals who restlessly search for a better world and yet shy away from the grubbier commitments of a practical kind. Benjamin was tempted at times to say that in the age of Hitler, his brand of Communism was the "lesser evil" (May 6, 1934) and to picture himself as a shipwrecked mariner who had little choice. Whatever his motivation, he substantially participated in developing a sophisticated Marxist theory of history, society, and culture, and by at least sketching a systematic apologia for Mallarmé, Dada, and the Surrealists on Marxist grounds, he substantially aided the artists and critics of the independent left who were (and are) engaged in ever-renewed conflicts with orthodox party functionaries hiding their power games behind clichés about progressive realism (if the Eurocommunists develop a theory of culture, Benjamin will be one of their saints). Yet these are issues surviving from the early thirties, and it would be wrong, I think, to define Benjamin's importance to us solely in terms of a political anachronism, however resilient. He has more to offer to his readers now, and we should not disregard those of his essential concerns that go far beyond the agenda of his own day. In articulating his vision of language, Benjamin soon developed a strong interest in a theory of the sign and renewed semiotic tradition (which in Germany went back to the mid-eighteenth century). His romantic opposition to the idea that the meaning of the sign was mere convention pushed him on to courageous speculations about the sign and the mimetic urge of mankind, and his later interest in the technology of the new media forcefully widened his thinking about signs to include problems of book production, graphic experiments, and advertising. He has few equals in restoring semiotics to our attention.

I wonder whether it would be possible to listen to Benjamin in a musical rather than a literary way, and to concentrate, as if his individual writings were fragments of an inclusive score, on the thematic orchestration of his ideas and arguments. His ultimate secret, I believe, is that he works with a few intimate leitmotifs that fascinate him throughout his life, regardless of the particular stage of his ideological transformations. The name and the sign, divine violence and mundane discipline, the threshold and the city, the *flâneur* and the archeologist of culture—these are a few of his elemental *topoi* and recurrent figures, absent occasionally, submerged perhaps for a while, yet never totally absent from his ken. Perhaps the best way to approach Benjamin's writings would be to imitate his willingness to keep the sensibilities open to the sober and profane illuminations that come to people who quietly and attentively walk through the astonishing streets of a foreign city. It is not a matter of reducing distances but of keeping them, and in confronting Benjamin, we should not try to diminish or explain away what is strange, difficult, and a productive provocation. It is precisely his fine and fierce otherness that is going to change our thought.

ONE

A Berlin Chronicle

For my dear Stefan

Now let me call back those who introduced me to the city. For although the child, in his solitary games, grows up at closest quarters to the city, he needs and seeks guides to its wider expanses, and the first of these—for a son of wealthy middle-class parents like me—are sure to have been nursemaids. With them I went to the Zoo—although I recall it only from much later, with blaring military bands and "Scandal Avenue" (as the adherents of *art nouveau* dubbed this promenade)—or, if not to the Zoo, to the Tiergarten. I believe the first "street" that I discovered in this way that no longer had anything habitable or hospitable about it, emanating forlornness between the shopfronts and even danger at the crossings, was Schillstrasse; I like to imagine that it has altered less than others in the West End and could even now accommodate a scene rising irresistibly from the mist: the saving of the life of "little brother." The way to the Tiergarten led over the Herkules Bridge, the gently sloping embankment of which must have been the first hillside the child encountered—accentuated by the fine stone flanks of the lion rising above. At the end of Bendlerstrasse, however, began the labyrinth, not without its Ariadne: the maze surrounding Frederick William III and Queen Louise, who, rising sheer from the flower beds on their illustrated, Empire-style plinths, seemed as if petrified by the signs that a little rivulet inscribed in the sand. Rather than the figures, my eyes sought the plinths, since the events taking place on them, if less clear in their ramifications, were closer in space. But that a particular significance attaches to this Hohenzollern laby-

3

rinth I find confirmed even now by the utterly unconcerned, banal appearance of the forecourt on Tiergartenstrasse, where nothing suggests that you stand but a few yards from the strangest place in the city. At that time, it is true, it must have corresponded more than closely to what was waiting behind it, for here, or not far away, were the haunts of that Ariadne in whose proximity I learned for the first time (and was never entirely to forget) something that was to make instantly comprehensible a word that at scarcely three I cannot have known: love. Here the nursemaid supervenes, a cold shadow driving away what I loved. It is likely that no one ever masters anything in which he has not known impotence; and if you agree, you will also see that this impotence comes not at the beginning of or before the struggle with the subject, but in the heart of it. Which brings me to the middle period of my life in Berlin, extending from the whole of my later childhood to my entrance to the university: a period of impotence before the city. This had two sources. First was a very poor sense of direction; but if it was thirty years before the distinction between left and right had become visceral to me, and before I had acquired the art of reading a street map, I was far from appreciating the extent of my ineptitude; and if anything was capable of increasing my disinclination to perceive this fact, it was the insistence with which my mother thrust it under my nose. On her I lay the blame for my inability even today to make a cup of coffee; to her propensity for turning the most insignificant items of conduct into tests of my aptitude for practical life I owe the dreamy recalcitrance with which I accompanied her as we walked through the streets, rarely frequented by me, of the city center. But to this resistance in turn is due who knows how much that underlies my present intercourse with the city's streets. Above all, a gaze that appears to see not a third of what it takes in. I remember, too, how nothing was more intolerable to my mother than the pedantic care with which, on these walks, I always kept half a step behind her. My habit of seeming slower, more maladroit, more stupid than I am, had its origin in such walks, and has the great attendant danger of making me think myself quicker, more dexterous, and shrewder than I am.

I have long, indeed for years, played with the idea of setting out the sphere of life—bios—graphically on a map. First I envisaged an ordinary map, but now I would incline to a general staff's map of a city center, if such a thing existed. Doubtless it does not, because of ignorance of the theater of future wars. I have evolved a system of signs, and on the gray background of such maps they would make a colorful show if I clearly marked in the houses of my friends and girl friends, the assembly halls of various collectives, from the "debating chambers" of the Youth Movement to the gathering places of the Communist youth, the hotel and brothel rooms that I knew for one night, the decisive benches in the Tiergarten, the ways to different schools and the graves that I saw filled, the sites of prestigious cafés whose long-forgotten names daily crossed our lips, the tennis courts where empty apartment blocks stand today, and the halls emblazoned with gold and stucco that the terrors of dancing classes made almost the equal of gymnasiums. And even without this map, I still have the encouragement provided by an illustrious precursor, the Frenchman Léon Daudet, exemplary at least in the title of his work, which exactly encompasses the best that I might achieve here: *Paris vécu*. "Lived Berlin" does not sound so good but is as real. And it is not just this title that concerns me here; Paris itself is the fourth in the series of voluntary or involuntary guides that began with my nursemaids. If I had to put in one word what I owe to Paris for these reflections, it would be "caution"; I should scarcely be able to abandon myself to the shifting currents of these memories of my earliest city life, had not Paris set before me, strictly circumscribed, the two forms in which alone this can legitimately—that is, with a guarantee of permanence—be done; and had I not forsworn the attempt to equal the first as firmly as I hope one day to realize the second. The first form was created in the work of Marcel Proust, and the renunciation of any dalliance with related possibilities could scarcely be more bindingly embodied than in the translation of it that I have produced. Related possibilities—do they really exist? They would certainly permit no dalliance. What Proust began so playfully became awesomely serious. He who has once begun to open the fan of memory never comes to the end of its segments; no image satisfies him, for he has seen that it can be unfolded, and only in its folds does the truth reside; that image, that taste, that touch for whose sake all this has been unfurled and dissected; and now remembrance advances from small to smallest details, from the smallest to the infinitesimal, while that which it encounters in these microcosms grows ever mightier. Such is the deadly game that Proust began so dilettantishly, in which he will hardly find more successors than he needed companions.

How totally unlike this (the music at the Zoo) was some other park music that had begun to reach my ears at an earlier time. It came from Rousseau Island and drove the skaters looping and whirling on New Lake. I was among them long before I had any conception of the source of the island's name, not to mention the difficulty of his style. Through its position this ice rink was comparable to no other, and still more by virtue of its life through the seasons: for what did summer make of the rest? Tennis courts. But here, under the overhanging branches of the trees along the bank, stretched a lake connected to labyrinthine waterways, and now one skated under the little arched bridges where in summer one had leaned on balustrades, or on chains held by lions' mouths, watching the boats gliding in the dark water. There were serpentine paths near the lake and, above all, the tender retreats of lonely old men, benches for "adults only" at the edge of the sand pit with its ditches, where toddlers dig or stand sunk in thought until bumped by a playmate or roused by the voice of a nursemaid from the bench of command; there she sits, stern and studious, reading her novel and keeping the child in check while hardly raising an eyelid until, her labor done, she changes places with the nurse at the other end of the bench, who is holding the baby between her knees and knitting. Old, solitary men found their way here, paying due honor, amid these scatterbrained womenfolk, among the shrieking children, to the serious side of life: the newspaper. Even if the girl I loved, after tarrying long on the paths of this garden, had left at last, there was nowhere I liked staying to think of her better than on a backless bench in one of those playgrounds, and I never swept the sand from where I was going to sit down. All these pictures I have preserved. But none would bring back New Lake and a few hours of my childhood so vividly as to hear once more the bars of music to which my feet, heavy with their skates after a lone excursion across the bustling ice, touched the familiar planks and stumbled past the chocolate-dispensing slot machines, and past the more splendid one with a hen laying candy-filled eggs, through the doorway behind which glowed the anthracite stove, to the bench where you now savored for a while the weight of the iron rails on your feet, which did not yet reach the ground, before resolving to unbuckle them. If you then slowly rested one calf on the other knee and unscrewed the skate, it was as if in its place you had suddenly grown wings, and you went out with steps that nodded to the frozen ground.

And then my fifth guide: Franz Hessel. I do not mean his book *On Foot in Berlin,* which was written later, but the *Celebration* that our walks together in Paris received in our native city, as if we were returning to harbor, the jetty still rising and falling as on waves under the feet of strolling seamen. The centerpiece of this *Celebration,* however, was the "Green Meadow"—a bed that still stands high above the couches spreading all around, on which we composed a small, complaisant, orientally pallid epilogue to those great, sleeping feasts with which, a few years earlier in Paris, the Surrealists had unwittingly inaugurated their reactionary career, thus fulfilling the text that the Lord giveth unto his own in sleep. On this meadow we spread out such women as still amused us at home, but they were few. From beneath lowered lids our gaze often met, better than on drafty stairways, the palms, caryatids, windows, and niches from which the "Tiergarten mythology" was evolving as the first chapter of a science of this city. It prospered, for we had been astute enough to gather to us girls from the most latinate quarter and in general to observe the Parisian custom of residing in the *quartier*. True, the *quartier* in Berlin is unfortunately an affair of the well-to-do, and neither Wedding nor Reinickendorf nor Tegel bears comparison on this account with Ménilmontant, Auteuil, or Neuilly.

All the more gratifying, therefore, were marauding Sunday-afternoon excursions on which we discovered an arcade in the Moabit quarter, the Stettin tunnel, or liberty in front of the Wallner Theater. A girl photographer was with us. And it seems to me, as I think of Berlin, that only the side of the city that we explored at that time is truly receptive to photography. For the closer we come to its present-day, fluid, functional existence, the narrower draws the circle of what can be photographed; it has been rightly observed that photography records practically nothing of the essence of, for example, a modern factory. Such pictures can perhaps be compared to railway stations, which, in this age when railways are beginning to be out of date, are no longer, generally speaking, the true "gateways" through which the city unrolls its outskirts as it does along the approach roads for motorists. A station gives the order, as it were, for a surprise attack, but it is an outdated maneuver that confronts us with the archaic, and the same is true of photography, even the snapshot. Only film commands optical approaches to the essence of the city, such as conducting the motorist into the new center.

The fourth guide.* Not to find one's way in a city may well be uninteresting and banal. It requires ignorance—nothing more. But to lose oneself in a city—as one loses oneself in a forest—that calls for quite a different schooling. Then, sign-

* Benjamin is referring to Paris.—ED.

boards and street names, passers-by, roofs, kiosks, or bars must speak to the wanderer like a cracking twig under his feet in the forest, like the startling call of a bittern in the distance, like the sudden stillness of a clearing with a lily standing erect at its center. Paris taught me this art of straying; it fulfilled a dream that had shown its first traces in the labyrinths on the blotting pages of my school exercise books. Nor is it to be denied that I penetrated to its innermost place, the Minotaur's chamber, with the only difference being that *this* mythological monster had three heads: those of the occupants of the small brothel on rue de la Harpe, in which, summoning my last reserves of strength (and not entirely without an Ariadne's thread), I set my foot. But if Paris thus answered my most uneasy expectations, from another side it surpassed my graphic fantasies. The city, as it disclosed itself to me in the footsteps of a hermetic tradition that I can trace back at least as far as Rilke and whose guardian at that time was Franz Hessel, was a maze not only of paths but also of tunnels. I cannot think of the underworld of the Métro and the North-South line opening their hundreds of shafts all over the city, without recalling my endless *flâneries*.

The most remarkable of all the street images from my early childhood, however—more so even than the arrival of the bears, which I witnessed at the side of a nursemaid, or it may have been my French governess—more remarkable than the racecourse that passed Schillstrasse or ended there, is—it must have been about 1900—a completely deserted stretch of road upon which ponderous torrents of water continuously thundered down. I had been caught up in a local flood disaster, but in other ways, too, the idea of extraordinary events is inseparable from that day; possibly we had been sent home from school. In any case, this situation left behind an alarm signal; my strength must have been failing, and in the midst of the asphalt streets of the city I felt exposed to the powers of nature; in a primeval forest I should not have been more abandoned than here on Kurfürstenstrasse, between the columns of water. How I reached the bronze lions' mouths on our front door with their rings that were now life belts, I cannot remember.

Rides to the station in the rattling taxi, skirting the Landwehr Canal while, among the dirty cushions, the weekly evening gathering in the drawing room or the living room of my parents' apartment, which had just neared its end, for a week at least, was revived with stricken violence. And so it was not what impended that weighed so terrifyingly upon me, or even the parting from what had been, but that which still continued, persisted, asserting itself even in this first stage of the journey. The destination of such rides would usually have been the Anhalt Station—where you took the train to Suderode or Hahnenklee, to Bad Salzschlirf or—in the later years—to Freudenstadt. But now and again it was Arendsee, too, or Heiligendamm, and then you went by the Stettin Station. I believe it is since that time that the dunes of the Baltic landscape have appeared to me like a *fata morgana* here on Chausseestrasse, supported only by the yellow, sandy colors of the station building and the boundless horizon opening in my imagination behind its walls.

But this vista would indeed be delusive if it did not make visible the medium in which alone such images take form, assuming a transparency in which, however mistily, the contours of what is to come are delineated like mountain peaks. The present in which the writer lives is this medium. And in it he now cuts another section through the sequence of his experiences. He detects in them a new and disturbing articulation. First, his early childhood, enclosing him in the district where he lived—the old or the new West End, where the class that had pronounced him one of its number resided in a posture compounded of self-satisfaction and resentment that turned it into something like a ghetto held on lease. In any case, he was confined to this affluent quarter without knowing of any other. The poor? For rich children of his generation they lived at the back of beyond. And if at this early age he could picture the poor, it was, without his knowing either name or origin, in the image of the tramp who is actually a rich man, though without money, since he stands—far removed from the process of production and the exploitation not yet abstracted from it—in the same contemplative relation to his destitution as the rich man to his wealth. The child's first excursion into the exotic world of abject poverty characteristically took written form (only by chance, perhaps, one of his first excursions to do so), being the depiction of a sandwich man and his humiliation at the hands of the public, who did not trouble even to take the leaflets he held out to them, so that the wretched man—thus the story ended—secretly jettisoned his entire consignment. Certainly a wholly unfruitful solution to the problem, already announcing the flight into sabotage and anarchism that later makes it so difficult for the intellectual to see things clearly. Perhaps the same sabotage of real social existence is to be found even later in my manner, already described, of walking in the city, in the stubborn refusal under any circumstances to form a united front, be it even with my own mother. There is no doubt, at any rate, that a feeling of crossing the threshold of one's class for the first time had a part in the almost unequaled fascination of publicly accosting a whore in the street. At the beginning, however, this was a crossing of frontiers not only social but topographical, in the sense that whole networks of streets were opened up under the auspices of prostitution. But is it really a crossing, is it not, rather, an obstinate and voluptuous hovering on the brink, a hesitation that has its most cogent motive in the circumstance that beyond this frontier lies nothingness? But the places are countless in the great cities where one stands on the edge of the void, and the whores in the doorways of tenement blocks and on the less sonorous asphalt of railway platforms are like the household goddesses of this cult of nothingness.

So on these erring paths the stations became my especial habitat, each with its outskirts like a city: the Silesian, Stettin, Görlitz stations, and Friedrichstrasse.

Just as there are, for children, fairy tales in which a witch or even a fairy holds a whole forest in thrall, as a child I knew a street that was ruled and occupied entirely by a woman, even though she was always enthroned in her bay window, one minute's walk from the house in which I was born: Aunt Lehmann. The stairs rose steeply to her room from just behind the hall door; it was dark on them, until the door opened and the brittle voice bid us a thin "good-morning" and directed us to place before us on the table the glass rhombus containing the mine, in which little men pushed wheelbarrows, labored with pickaxes, and shone lanterns into the shafts in which buckets were winched perpetually up and down. On account of this aunt and her mine, Steglitzer Strasse could henceforth, for me, never be named after Steglitz. A goldfinch [*Stieglitz*] in its cage bore greater resemblance to this street harboring the aunt at her window than the Berlin suburb that meant nothing to me. Where it joins Genthiner Strasse, it is one of the streets least touched by the changes of the last thirty years. In the back rooms and attics, as guardians of the past, numerous prostitutes have established themselves here, who, during the inflation period, brought the district the reputation of being a theater of the most squalid diversions. Needless to say, no one could ever determine on which stories the impoverished opened their drawing rooms, and their daughters their skirts, to rich Americans.

Climbing the stairs in this fashion,* with nothing before me but boots and calves, and the scraping of hundreds of feet in my ears, I was often seized—I seem to remember—by revulsion at being hemmed in by this multitude, and again, as on

* The beginning of this passage is missing in the manuscript; Benjamin is talking about his school experiences.—ED.

those walks in the city with my mother, solitude appeared to me as the only fit state of man. Very understandably, for such a mob of school children is among the most formless and ignoble of all masses, and betrays its bourgeois origin in representing, like every assembly of that class, the most rudimentary organizational form that its individual members can give their reciprocal relationships. The corridors, and the classrooms that finally came into view, are among the horrors that have embedded themselves most ineradicably in me, that is to say, in my dreams; and these have taken revenge on the monotony, the cold torpor that overcame me at each crossing of the classroom thresholds, by turning themselves into the arena of the most extravagant events. The backdrop was often the fear of having to take the *Abitur* again (under more unfavorable conditions), a position in which I had been placed by my own recklessness and folly. Undoubtedly, these rooms lend themselves to dreamlike representation; there is something nightmarish even in the sober recollection of the damp odor of sweat secreted by the stone steps that I had to hasten up five times or more each day. The school, outwardly in good repair, was in its architecture and situation among the most desolate. It matched its emblem, a plaster statue of the Emperor Frederick, which had been deposited in a remote corner of the playground (admittedly one favored by hordes engaged in martial games), puny and pitiful against a fire wall. According to a school legend it was, if I am not mistaken, a donation. This monument, unlike the classrooms, was never washed, and had acquired in the course of years an admirable coat of dirt and soot. It still stands today in its appointed place. But soot descends upon it daily from the passing municipal railway. It is far from impossible that my uncommon aversion to this railway dates from this time, since all the people sitting at their windows seemed enviable to me. They could afford to ignore the school clock that held sway above our heads, and quite unawares they cut through the invisible bars of our timetable cage. They could only be seen, incidentally, during the breaks, for the lower panes of the classroom windows were of frosted glass. "Vagabond clouds, sailors of the skies" had for us the absolute precision that the verse holds for prisoners. Moreover, little about the actual classrooms has remained in my memory except these exact emblems of imprisonment: the frosted windows and the infamous carved wooden battlements over the doors. It would not surprise me to hear that the cupboards, too, were crowned with such adornments, not to mention the pictures of the Kaiser on the walls. Heraldic and chivalrous obtuseness shone forth wherever possible. In the great hall, however, it was most ceremoniously united with *art nouveau*. A crude, extravagant ornament stretched with stiff gray-green limbs across the paneling of the walls. References to objects were no more to be found in it than references to history; nowhere did it offer the eye the slightest refuge, while the ear was helplessly abandoned to the clatter of idiotic harangues. All the same, one of these occasions is perhaps noteworthy for the effect it had on me for years afterward. It was the leave-taking ceremony for those who had graduated. Here, as in several other places, I find in my memory rigidly fixed words, expressions, verses that, like a malleable mass that has later cooled and hardened, preserve in me the imprint of the collision between a larger collective and myself. Just as a certain kind of significant dream survives awakening in the form of words when all the rest of the dream content has vanished, here isolated words have remained in place as marks of catastrophic encounters. Among them is one in which for me the whole atmosphere of the school is condensed; I heard it when, having hitherto received only private tutoring, I was sent for my first morning, on a trial basis, to what was later to become the Kaiser Friedrich School, but at that time was still situated on Passauerstrasse. This word that still adheres in my mind to a phlegmatic, fat, unbecoming figure of a boy is the following: ringleader. Nothing else is left of this earliest school experience. It was re-enacted in similar form, however, some six years later, when I spent my first day in alien and threatening circumstances in Haubinda and was asked by a tall, hostile-seeming lout who played a prominent part in the class whether my "old man" had already left. This common piece of schoolboy parlance was entirely unfamiliar to me. An abyss opened before me, which I sought to bridge with a laconic protest. Here in the great hall it was the verses with which the school choir began the farewell song to the leavers —"Brother now may we / your companions be / in the world so wide"—followed by something containing the words "loyally by your side"; at any rate these were the verses that enabled me year by year to take the measure of my own weakness. For no matter how palpably the abominable goings-on at school were daily before my eyes, the melody of this song seemed to surround the departure from this hell with infinite melancholy. But by the time it was addressed to me and my class it must have made little impression, for I remember nothing of it. More remarkable are some other verses that I heard once in the gymnasium dressing room after the lesson, and never forgot. Why? Perhaps because "Schulze"—as the imprudent boy who knew the lines was called—was rather pretty, perhaps because I thought them true, but most probably because the situation in which they were spoken, one of frenetic, military hyperactivity, was so utterly appropriate. "Loitering at the rear / you never need fear / neurasthenía."

If I write better German than most writers of my generation, it is thanks largely to twenty years' observance of one little rule: never use the word "I" except in letters. The exceptions to this precept that I have permitted myself could be counted. Now this has had a curious consequence that is intimately connected to these notes. For when one day it was suggested that I should write, from day to day in a loosely subjective form, a series of glosses on everything that seemed noteworthy in Berlin—and when I agreed—it became suddenly clear that this subject, accustomed for years to waiting in the wings, would not so easily be summoned to the lime-

light. But far from protesting, it relied on ruse, so successfully
that I believed a retrospective glance at what Berlin had become for me in the course of years would be an appropriate
"preface" to such glosses. If the preface has now far exceeded
the space originally allotted to the glosses, this is not only the
mysterious work of remembrance—which is really the capacity
for endless interpolations into what has been—but also, at the
same time, the precaution of the subject represented by the
"I," which is entitled not to be sold cheap. Now there is one
district of Berlin with which this subject is more closely
connected than any other that it has consciously experienced.
To be sure, there are parts of the city in which it was destined
to have equally deep and harrowing experiences, but in none
of them was the place itself so much a part of the event. The
district I am talking of is the Tiergarten quarter. There, in
a back wing of one of the houses standing nearest the municipal railway viaduct, was the "Meeting House." It was a small
apartment that I had rented jointly with the student Ernst
Joël. How we had agreed on this I no longer remember; it can
hardly have been simple, for the student "Group for Social
Work" led by Joël was, during the term in which I was president of the Berlin Free Students' Union, a chief target of my
attacks, and it was precisely as leader of this group that Joël
had signed the lease, while my contribution secured the rights
of the "debating chamber" to the Meeting House. The distribution of the rooms between the two groups—whether of a
spatial or a temporal character—was very sharply defined, and
in any case, for me at that time only the debating group
mattered.

My cosignatory, Ernst Joël, and I were on less than cordial
terms, and I had no inkling of the magical aspect of the city
that this same Joël, fifteen years later, was to reveal to me.
So his image appears in me at this stage only as an answer
to the question whether forty is not too young an age at which
to evoke the most important memories of one's life. For this
image is already now that of a dead man, and who knows

how he might have been able to help me cross this threshold, with memories of even the most external and superficial things? To the other threshold he had no access, and of all those who once had it I alone remain. I should never have thought that I should seek him by this topographical route. But if I call to mind the first trial run I made in this direction, more than ten years ago now, the earlier and more modest essay has the better of the comparison. It was in Heidelberg, during what was undoubtedly self-forgetful work, that I tried to summon up, in a meditation on the nature of the lyric, the figure of my friend Fritz Heinle, around whom all the happenings in the Meeting House arrange themselves and with whom they vanish. Fritz Heinle was a poet, and the only one of them all whom I met not "in real life" but in his work. He died at nineteen, and could be known in no other way. All the same, this first attempt to evoke the sphere of his life through that of poetry was unsuccessful, and the immediacy of the experience that gave rise to my lecture asserted itself irresistibly in the incomprehension and snobbery of the audience, who came to hear it at the house of Marianne Weber. No matter how much memory has subsequently paled, or how indistinctly I can now give an account of the rooms in the Meeting House, it nevertheless seems to me today more legitimate to attempt to delineate the outward space the dead man inhabited, indeed the room where he was "announced," than the inner space in which he created. But perhaps that is only because, in this last and most crucial year of his life, he traversed the space in which I was born. Heinle's Berlin was the Berlin of the Meeting House. He lived at this period in closest proximity to it, in a fourth-floor room on Klopstockstrasse. I once visited him there. It was after a long separation resulting from a serious dissension between us. But even today I remember the smile that lifted the whole weight of these weeks of separation, that turned a probably insignificant phrase into a magic formula that healed the wound. Later, after the morning when an express letter awoke me with the

words "You will find us lying in the Meeting House"—when
Heinle and his girl friend were dead—this district remained
for a period the central meeting place of the living. Today,
however, when I recall its old-fashioned apartment houses, its
many trees dust-covered in summer, the cumbersome iron-
and-stone constructions of the municipal railway cutting
through it, the sparse streetcars spaced at great intervals, the
sluggish water of the Landwehr Canal that marked the district off from the proletarian quarters of Moabit, the splendid
but wholly unfrequented cluster of trees in the Schlosspark
Bellevue, and the unspeakably cruel hunting groups flanking
its approach at the star-shaped intersection of roads—today
this point in space where we chanced then to open our Meeting House is for me the strictest pictorial expression of the
point in history occupied by this last true élite of bourgeois
Berlin. It was as close to the abyss of the Great War as the
Meeting House was to the steep slope down to the Landwehr
Canal, it was as sharply divided from proletarian youth as the
houses of this *rentiers'* quarter were from those of Moabit, and
the houses were the last of their line just as the occupants of
those apartments were the last who could appease the clamor-
ous shades of the dispossessed with philanthropic ceremonies.
In spite—or perhaps because—of this, there is no doubt that
the city of Berlin was never again to impinge so forcefully on
my existence as it did in that epoch when we believed we
could leave it untouched, only improving its schools, only
breaking the inhumanity of their inmates' parents, only making a place in it for the words of Hölderlin or George. It was
a final, heroic attempt to change the attitudes of people
without changing their circumstances. We did not know that
it was bound to fail, but there was hardly one of us whose
resolve such knowledge could have altered. And today, as
clearly as at that time, even if on the basis of entirely different
reasoning, I understand that the "language of youth" had to
stand at the center of our associations. Nor do I know today
of any truer expression of our impotence than the struggle

that seemed the pinnacle of our strength and our exuberance, even if the shadow of downfall, cast by the incomprehension of the audience, was seldom more palpable than on that evening. I think here of an altercation between Heinle and myself on an evening at the *Aktion*.* Originally only a speech by me entitled "Youth" had been on the agenda. I took it for granted that its text should be known to our closest circle before it was delivered. Scarcely had this happened, however, when Heinle raised objections. Whether he wanted to speak himself, or to impose alterations on me that I refused—the upshot was an ugly quarrel into which, as always happens on such occasions, the whole existence of each participant was drawn—Heinle's side being taken by the youngest of the three sisters† around whom the most important events used to gravitate, as if the fact that a Jewish widow was living with her three daughters represented, for a group seriously intent upon the abolition of the family, an appropriate base from which to launch an attack. In short, the girl reinforced her friend's demands. But I was not prepared to yield, either. So it happened that on that evening at the *Aktion*, before an astonished but less-than-captivated audience, two speeches with the same title and almost exactly identical texts were delivered, and in truth the latitude within which the "Youth Movement" had to maneuver was no larger than the area bounded by the nuances of those speeches. Thinking about the two speeches today, I should like to compare them to the clashing islands in the legend of the Argonauts, the Symplegades, between which no ship can pass in safety and where, at that time, a sea of love and hatred tossed. Assemblies of bourgeois intellectuals were then far commoner than nowadays, since they had not yet recognized their limits. We may say, however, that we felt those limits, even if much time

---

* *Die Aktion,* a political journal of revolutionary tendency, founded in 1911 by Franz Pfemfert, dedicated to the revolution in literature and the visual arts.—ED.

† Traute, Carla, and Rika Seligson.—ED.

was to pass before the realization matured that no one can improve his school or his parental home without first smashing the state that needs bad ones. We felt these limits when we held our discussions, at which the younger among us spoke of the brutalities they had to endure at home, in drawing rooms kindly made available by parents who at bottom thought no differently from those we wished to oppose. We felt them when we older members held our literary evenings in rooms at beerhouses that were never for a moment safe from the serving waiters; we felt them when we were obliged to receive our lady friends in furnished rooms with doors we were not at liberty to lock; we felt them in our dealings with owners of public rooms and with porters, with relations and guardians. And when, finally, after August 8, 1914, the days came when those among us who were closest to the dead couple did not want to part from them until they were buried, we felt the limits in the shame of being able to find refuge only in a seedy railway hotel on Stuttgart Square. Even the graveyard demonstrated the boudaries set by the city to all that filled our hearts: it was impossible to procure for the pair who had died together graves in one and the same cemetery. But those were days that ripened a realization that was to come later, and that planted in me the conviction that the city of Berlin would also not be spared the scars of the struggle for a better order. If I chance today to pass through the streets of the quarter, I set foot in them with the same uneasiness that one feels when entering an attic unvisited for years. Valuable things may be lying around, but nobody remembers where. And in truth this dead quarter with its tall apartment houses is today the junk room of the West End bourgeoisie.

That was the time when the Berlin cafés played a part in our lives. I still remember the first that I took in consciously. This was much earlier, immediately after my graduation. The Viktoria Café, where our first communal jaunt ended at three in the morning, no longer exists. Its place—on the corner of

Friedrichstrasse and Unter den Linden—has been taken by one of the noisiest luxury cafés of new Berlin, against which the earlier one, however luxurious it may have been in its day, stands out with all the magic of the age of chandeliers, mirrored walls, and plush comfort. This old Viktoria Café was on that occasion our last port of call, and we doubtless reached it a depleted group. It must have been more than half empty —at any rate I can discern, through the veils that mask the image today, no one apart from a few whores, who seemed to have the spacious café to themselves. We did not stay long, and I do not know whether I paid the Viktoria Café, which must have disappeared soon after, a second visit. The time had not yet arrived when the frequenting of cafés was a daily need, and it can hardly have been Berlin that fostered this vice in me, however well the vice later adapted itself to the establishments of that city, which leads far too strenuous and conscious a life of pleasure to know real coffeehouses. Our first café, accordingly, was more a strategic quarter than a place of siesta. And I have thus unmistakably revealed its name: as is well known, the headquarters of bohemians until the first war years was the old West End Café. It was in this café that we sat together in those very first August days, choosing among the barracks that were being stormed by the onrush of volunteers. We decided on the cavalry on Belle-Alliance Strasse, where I duly appeared on one of the following days, no spark of martial fervor in my breast; yet however reserved I may have been in my thoughts, which were concerned only with securing a place among friends in the inevitable conscription, one of the bodies jammed in front of the barracks gates was mine. Admittedly only for two days: on August 8 came the event that was to banish for long after both the city and the war from my mind. I often saw Heinle in the West End Café. We usually met there late, about twelve. I cannot say that we had close relations to the literary Bohemia whose days, or nights, were spent there; we were a self-contained group, the world of our "movement" was dif-

ferent from that of the emancipated people around us, and
contacts with them were only fleeting. A mediator between
the two sides for a period was Franz Pfemfert, editor of *Die
Aktion*; our relations with him were purely Machiavellian.
Else Lasker-Schüler once drew me to her table; Wieland
Herzfelde, then a young student, was to be seen there, and
Simon Guttmann, to whom I shall return; but the list here
reaches the boundaries of our narrower world. I believe we
were alien to the café; the feverish concentration induced by
concern with so many rival actions, the organization of the
Free Students' Union and the development of the debating
chambers, the elaboration of our speeches in large assemblies
of pupils, help for comrades in need, care for those imperiled
by entanglements either of friendship or of love—all this set
us apart from the sated, self-assured bohemians about us.
Heinle was more closely acquainted with one or another of
them, such as the painter Meidner, who drew him; but this
connection remained unfruitful for us. Then, one day in
Switzerland, I read that the West End Café had been closed.
I had never been much at home in it. At that time I did not
yet possess that passion for waiting without which one cannot thoroughly appreciate the charm of a café. And if I see
myself waiting one night amid tobacco smoke on the sofa
that encircled one of the central columns, it was no doubt in
feverish expectation of the outcome of some negotiation at
the debating chamber, or of one of the mediators who were
brought into play when tensions had once again reached an
unbearable pitch. I came to be on much more intimate terms
with the neighboring café, which had its beginning during
the period I now refer to. This was the Princess Café. In an
attempt to create a "Physiology of Coffeehouses," one's first
and most superficial classification would be into professional
and recreational establishments. If, however, one leaves aside
the most brazen entertainment places run along industrial
lines, it becomes very noticeable that in the development of
most hostelries the two functions coincide. A particularly tell-

ing example is the history of the Romanische Café from exactly the moment when the proprietor of the West End Café evicted his clientele. Very soon the Romanische Café accommodated the bohemians, who, in the years immediately after the war, were able to feel themselves masters of the house. The legendary, now-departed waiter Richard, distributor of newspapers—a hunchback who on account of his bad reputation enjoyed high esteem in these circles—was the symbol of their dominance. When the German economy began to recover, the bohemian contingent visibly lost the threatening nimbus that had surrounded them in the era of the Expressionist revolutionary manifestoes. The bourgeois revised his relationship to the inmates of the Café Megalomania (as the Romanische Café soon came to be called) and found that everything was back to normal. At this moment the physiognomy of the Romanische Café began to change. The "artists" withdrew into the background, to become more and more a part of the furniture, while the bourgeois, represented by stock-exchange speculators, managers, film and theater agents, literary-minded clerks, began to occupy the place—as a place of relaxation. For one of the most elementary and indispensable diversions of the citizen of a great metropolis, wedged, day in, day out, in the structure of his office and family amid an infinitely variegated social environment, is to plunge into another world, the more exotic the better. Hence the bars haunted by artists and criminals. The distinction between the two, from this point of view, is slight. The history of the Berlin coffeehouses is largely that of different strata of the public, those who first conquered the floor being obliged to make way for others gradually pressing forward, and thus to ascend the stage.

Such a stage, for Heinle and me, was the Princess Café, which we were in the habit of patronizing as occupants of private boxes. The latter should be taken almost literally, for this café, designed by Lucian Bernhard, an interior decorator and poster artist much in demand at that time, offered its

visitors an abundance of snug recesses, standing historically
midway between the *chambres séparées* and the coffee parlors.
The profession primarily served by this establishment is therefore clear. And when we visited it, indeed made it for a time
our regular meeting place, it was certainly on account of the
cocottes. Heinle wrote "Princess Café" at that time. "Doors
draw coolness over through the song." We had no intention of
making acquaintances in this café. On the contrary—what
attracted us here was being enclosed in an environment that
isolated us. Every distinction between us and the literary
coteries of the city was welcome to us. This one, to be sure,
more so than all others. And that certainly had to do with the
cocottes. But this leads into a subterranean stratum of the
Youth Movement, reached by way of an artist's studio in
Halensee, to which we shall return. It is quite possible that
S. Guttmann, its occupant, met us here, too, from time to time.
I have no recollection of it, just as in general, here more than
elsewhere, the human figures recede before the place itself,
and none of them is as vividly present to me as a forlorn, approximately circular chamber in the upper story, hung with
violet drapery and illuminated with a violet glow, in which
many seats were always empty, while on others couples took
up as little space as possible. I called this amphitheater the
"anatomy school." Later, when this epoch was long since
closed, I sat long evenings there, close to a jazz band, discreetly
consulting sheets and slips of paper, writing my *Origin of
German Tragic Drama.* When one day a new "renovation"
set in, turning the Princess Café into Café Stenwyk, I gave up.
Today it has sunk to the level of a beerhouse.

Never again has music possessed so dehumanized and shameless a quality as that of the two brass bands that tempered
the flood of people surging torpidly along "Scandal Avenue"
between the café restaurants of the Zoo. Today I perceive
what gave this flow its elemental force. For the city dweller

there was no higher school of flirtation than this, surrounded by the sandy precincts of gnus and zebras, the bare trees and clefts where vultures and condors nested, the stinking enclosures of wolves, and the hatcheries of pelicans and herons. The calls and screeches of these animals mingled with the noise of drums and percussion. This was the air in which the glance of a boy fell for the first time on a passing girl, while he talked all the more zealously to his friend. And such were his efforts to betray himself neither by his eyes nor his voice that he saw nothing of her.

At that time the Zoological Garden still had an entrance by the Lichtenstein Bridge. Of the three gates it was the least frequented, and gave access to the park's most deserted quarter: an avenue that, with the milk-white orbs of its candelabras, resembled some deserted promenade at Wiesbaden or Pyrmont; and before the economic crisis had so depopulated these resorts that they seemed more antique than Roman spas, this dead corner of the Zoological Garden was an image of what was to come, a prophesying place. It must be considered certain that there are such places; indeed, just as there are plants that primitive peoples claim confer the power of clairvoyance, so there are places endowed with such power: they may be deserted promenades, or treetops, particularly in towns, seen against walls, railway level-crossings, and above all the thresholds that mysteriously divide the districts of a town. The Lichtenstein gate was really such a threshold, between the two West End parks. It was as if in both, at the point where they were nearest, life paused. And this daily desertion was the more keenly felt by one who remembered the dazzling approach to be seen on festal nights for a number of years from a doorway of the Adler ballrooms, which has fallen now into just such disuse as has this long-closed gate.

Language shows clearly that memory is not an instrument for exploring the past but its theater. It is the medium of past experience, as the ground is the medium in which dead cities lie interred. He who seeks to approach his own buried past must conduct himself like a man digging. This confers the tone and bearing of genuine reminiscences. He must not be afraid to return again and again to the same matter; to scatter it as one scatters earth, to turn it over as one turns over soil. For the matter itself is only a deposit, a stratum, which yields only to the most meticulous examination what constitutes the real treasure hidden within the earth: the images, severed from all earlier associations, that stand—like precious fragments or torsos in a collector's gallery—in the prosaic rooms of our later understanding. True, for successful excavations a plan is needed. Yet no less indispensable is the cautious probing of the spade in the dark loam, and it is to cheat oneself of the richest prize to preserve as a record merely the inventory of one's discoveries, and not this dark joy of the place of the finding itself. Fruitless searching is as much a part of this as succeeding, and consequently remembrance must not proceed in the manner of a narrative or still less that of a report, but must, in the strictest epic and rhapsodic manner, assay its spade in ever-new places, and in the old ones delve to ever-deeper layers.

It is true that countless façades of the city stand exactly as they stood in my childhood. Yet I do not encounter my childhood in their contemplation. My gaze has brushed them too often since, too often they have been the *décor* and theater of my walks and concerns. And the few exceptions to this rule —above all St. Matthew's Church on St. Matthew's Square— are perhaps only apparently so. For did I as a child really frequent the remote corner where it stands, did I even know it? I cannot tell. What it says to me today it owes solely to the edifice itself: the church with the two pointed, gabled roofs over its two side aisles, and the yellow-and-ocher brick of which it is built. It is an old-fashioned church, of which the same is true as of many an old-fashioned building: although they were not young with us and perhaps did not even know us when we were children, they have much knowledge of our childhood, and for this we love them. But I should confront myself at that age in quite a different way had I the courage to enter a certain front door that I have passed thousands upon thousands of times. A front door in the old West End. True, my eyes no longer see it, or the façade of the house. My soles would doubtless be the first to send me word, once I had closed the door behind me, that on this worn staircase they trod in ancient tracks, and if I no longer cross the threshold of that house it is for fear of an encounter with this stairway interior, which has conserved in seclusion the power to recognize me that the façade lost long ago. For with its columned windows it has stayed the same, even if within the living quarters all is changed. Bleak verses filled the intervals between our heartbeats, when we paused exhausted on the landings between floors. They glimmered or shone from panes in which a woman with nut-brown eyebrows floated aloft with a goblet from a niche, and while the straps of my satchel cut into my shoulders I was forced to read, "Industry adorns the burgher, blessedness is toil's reward." Outside it may have been raining. One of the colored windows was open, and to the beat of raindrops the upward march resumed.

> Motto: O brown-baked column of victory
> With children's sugar from the winter days.

I never slept on the street in Berlin. I saw sunset and dawn, but between the two I found myself a shelter. Only those for whom poverty or vice turns the city into a landscape in which they stray from dark till sunrise know it in a way denied to me. I always found quarters, even though sometimes tardy and also unknown ones that I did not revisit and where I was not alone. If I paused thus late in a doorway, my legs had become entangled in the ribbons of the streets, and it was not the cleanest of hands that freed me.

Reminiscences, even extensive ones, do not always amount to an autobiography. And these quite certainly do not, even for the Berlin years that I am exclusively concerned with here. For autobiography has to do with time, with sequence and what makes up the continuous flow of life. Here, I am talking of a space, of moments and discontinuities. For even if months and years appear here, it is in the form they have at the moment of recollection. This strange form—it may be called fleeting or eternal—is in neither case the stuff that life is made of. And this is shown not so much by the role that my own life plays here, as by that of the people closest to me in Berlin—whoever and whenever they may have been. The atmosphere of the city that is here evoked allots them only a brief, shadowy existence. They steal along its walls like beggars, appear wraithlike at windows, to vanish again, sniff at thresholds like a *genius loci,* and even if they fill whole quarters with their names, it is as a dead man's fills his gravestone. Noisy, matter-of-fact Berlin, the city of work and the metropolis of business, nevertheless has more, rather than less, than some others, of those places and moments when it bears witness to the dead, shows itself full of dead; and the obscure awareness of these moments, these places, perhaps more than anything else, confers on childhood memories a quality that makes them at once as evanescent and as alluringly tormenting as half-forgotten dreams. For childhood, knowing no preconceived opinions, has none about life. It is as dearly attached (though with just as strong reservations) to the realm of the dead, where it juts into that of the living, as to life itself. How far a child has access to the past is difficult to tell, and depends on many things—time, environment, its nature and education. The limitation of my own feeling for the Berlin that is not circumscribed by a few facts about the Stratau Fair and Frederick in 1848—that is, for the topographical tradition representing the connection with the dead of this ground—results entirely from the circumstance that neither of my parents' families were natives of Berlin. That sets a limit to the child's memory—and it is this limit, rather than childhood experience itself, that is manifest in what follows. Wherever this boundary may have been drawn, however, the second half of the nineteenth century certainly lies within it, and to it belong the following images, not in the manner of general representations, but of images that, according to the teaching of Epicurus, constantly detach themselves from things and determine our perception of them.

First of all, let no one think we were talking of a *Markt-Halle* [covered market]. No: it was pronounced "*Mark-Talle*," and just as these words were eroded by the habit of speech until none retained its original "sense," so by the habit of this walk all the images it offered were worn away, so that none of them conforms to the original concept of buying and selling.

Behind us lay the forecourt, with its dangerous, heavy swing doors on their whiplash springs, and we had now set foot on the flagstones, slippery with fish water or swill, on which you could so easily slip on carrots or lettuce leaves. Behind wire partitions, each bearing a number, were ensconced the ponderous ladies, priestesses of Venal Ceres, purveyors of all the fruits of field and tree, and of all edible birds, fishes, and mammals, procuresses, untouchable wool-clad colossi exchanging vibrant signs from booth to booth with a flash of their large mother-of-pearl buttons or a slap on their booming black aprons or their money-filled pouches. Did it not bubble and seethe below the hems of their skirts, and was this not the truly fertile ground? Did not a god of the market himself cast the goods into their laps: berries, crustaceans, mushrooms, chunks of meat and cabbage, invisibly cohabiting with those who abandoned themselves as they languidly and mutely eyed the unsteady procession of housewives who, laden with baskets and bags, laboriously drove their brood before them along these slippery alleyways of ill repute. But if in winter the gas lamps went on in the early evening, you had at once a feeling of sinking, becoming aware, in this gentle gliding, of the depths of sea below the surface that heaved opaque and sluggish in the glassy waters.

The more frequently I return to these memories, the less fortuitous it seems to me how slight a role is played in them by people: I think of an afternoon in Paris to which I owe insights into my life that came in a flash, with the force of an illumination. It was on this very afternoon that my biographical relationships to people, my friendships and comradeships, my passions and love affairs, were revealed to me in their most vivid and hidden intertwinings. I tell myself it had to be in Paris, where the walls and quays, the places to pause, the collections and the rubbish, the railings and the squares, the arcades and the kiosks, teach a language so singular that our relations to people attain, in the solitude encompassing us in our immersion in that world of things, the depths of a sleep in which the dream image waits to show the people their true faces. I wish to write of this afternoon because it made so apparent what kind of regimen cities keep over imagination, and why the city, where people make the most ruthless demands on one another, where appointments and telephone calls, sessions and visits, flirtations and the struggle for existence grant the individual not a single moment of contemplation, indemnifies itself in memory, and why the veil it has covertly woven out of our lives shows the images of people less than those of the sites of our encounters with others or ourselves. Now on the afternoon in question I was sitting inside the Café des Deux Magots at St.-Germain-des-Prés, where I was waiting—I forget for whom. Suddenly, and with compelling force, I was struck by the idea of drawing a diagram of my life, and knew at the same moment exactly how it was to be done. With a very simple question I interro-

gated my past life, and the answers were inscribed, as if of
their own accord, on a sheet of paper that I had with me. A
year or two later, when I lost this sheet, I was inconsolable.
I have never since been able to restore it as it arose before
me then, resembling a series of family trees. Now, however,
reconstructing its outline in thought without directly repro-
ducing it, I should, rather, speak of a labyrinth. I am not
concerned here with what is installed in the chamber at its
enigmatic center, ego or fate, but all the more with the many
entrances leading into the interior. These entrances I call
primal acquaintances; each of them is a graphic symbol of
my acquaintance with a person whom I met, not through
other people, but through neighborhood, family relationships,
school comradeship, mistaken identity, companionship on
travels, or other such—hardly numerous—situations. So many
primal relationships, so many entrances to the maze. But
since most of them—at least those that remain in our memory
—for their part open up new acquaintances, relations to new
people, after some time they branch off these corridors (the
male may be drawn to the right, female to the left). Whether
cross-connections are finally established between these systems
also depends on the intertwinements of our path through life.
More important, however, are the astonishing insights that a
study of this plan provides into the differences among individual lives. What part is played in the primal acquaintance-
ships of different people's lives by profession and school, family and travel? And above all: is the formation of the many
offshoots governed in individual existence by hidden laws?
Which ones start early and which late in life? Which are
continued to the end of life and which peter out? "If a man
has character," says Nietzsche, "he will have the same experience over and over again." Whether or not this is true on a
large scale, on a small one there are perhaps paths that lead
us again and again to people who have one and the same function for us: passageways that always, in the most diverse periods of life, guide us to the friend, the betrayer, the beloved,

the pupil, or the master. This is what the sketch of my life
revealed to me as it took shape before me on that Paris afternoon. Against the background of the city, the people who had
surrounded me closed together to form a figure. It was many
years earlier, I believe at the beginning of the war, that in
Berlin, against the background of the people then closest to
me, the world of things contracted to a symbol similarly profound. It was an emblem of four rings. This takes me to one
of the old Berlin houses on the Kupfergraben. With their
plain, genteel façades and their wide hallways, they may have
stemmed from the Schinkel period. In one of them lived at
that time a prominent antique dealer. He had no display window. You had to go into his apartment to admire, in a number of showcases, a selection of prehistoric brooches and
clasps, Lombard earrings, late Roman neck chains, medieval
coins, and many similar valuables. How my friend A. C.* had
tracked him down I do not know. But I remember distinctly
the engrossment with which, under the impression of Alois
Riegl's *Late Roman Art Industry,* which I had recently studied, I contemplated the breastplates made from sheet gold
and garnet-adorned bracelets. There were, if I am not mistaken, three of us: my friend, his fiancée at that time or Frau
Dorothea J., and me. C. asked to see rings—Greek and Renaissance cameos, rings from the imperial period, usually work
carved in semiprecious stone. Each of the four that he finally
purchased is imprinted unforgettably on my mind. Except for
one that I have lost sight of, they are still today with those
for whom they were intended that morning. One, a bright-
yellow smoky topaz, was chosen by Dorothea J. The workman-
ship was Grecian and depicted in a tiny space Leda receiving
the swan between her parted thighs. It was most graceful. I
was less able to admire the amethyst that the donor, Ernst
S[choen], selected for our mutual friend: a fifteenth- or six-
teenth-century Italian had carved a profile in it which Lederer
claimed to be that of Pompey. I was quite differently affected,

* Alfred Cohn.—ED.

however, by the last two rings. One was intended for me, but only as a very temporary owner; it was really destined to reach, through me, my then fiancée, Grete R[adt]. It was the most fascinating ring I have ever seen. Cut in a dark, solid garnet, it portrayed a Medusa's head. It was a work of the Roman imperial period. The proustite mounting was not the original. Worn on the finger, the ring seemed merely the most perfect of signet rings. You only entered its secret by taking it off and contemplating the head against the light. As the different strata of the garnet were unequally translucent, and the thinnest so transparent that it glowed with rose hues, the somber bodies of the snakes seemed to rise above the two deep, glowing eyes, which looked out from a face that, in the purple-black portions of the cheeks, receded once more into the night. Later I tried more than once to seal with this stone, but it proved easy to crack and in need of the utmost care. Shortly after giving it away, I broke off my relationship with its new owner. My heart had already gone with the last of the four rings, which the giver had reserved for his sister. And certainly this girl was the true center of the circle's fate, though years were to elapse before we realized it. For apart from her beauty—itself not dazzling, but inconspicuous and without luster—she had nothing that seemed to destine her for the center of the stage. And in fact she never was the center of people but, in the strictest sense, of fates, as if her plantlike passivity and inertia had arranged the latter—which, of all human things, seem the most subject to vegetal laws— concentrically about her. Many years were needed before what at that time was in part beginning to unfold in its seed, and in part still dormant, emerged in its ramifications to the light of day: the fate by virtue of which she, who stood in a relation to her brother that by its tenderness filled to the very edge the limits of sisterly love, was to form a liaison with her brother's two closest friends—with the recipient of the ring with the head of Pompey and with me—to find her husband finally in the brother of the woman who married her own brother as her second husband*—and she it was, on the day I am speaking of, who received from me the ring with the Medusa's head. It cannot have been many days later that I sent after the lapis lazuli with the lute wreathed in foliage engraved in it—after the fourth ring and to its wearer—this sonnet: To your finger constantly encircled†

The treasure-dispensing giant‡ in the green pine forest or the fairy who grants one wish—they appear to each of us at least once in a lifetime. But only Sunday's children remember the wish they made, and so it is only a few who recognize its fulfillment in their own lives. I know of such a wish that was fulfilled for me, and would not claim it to be wiser than those of children in fairy tales. It goes back to my early childhood, and arose in me in connection with the lamp that on dark winter mornings at half past six was carried through my doorway and cast the shadow of our nursemaid on the ceiling. The fire was lit in the stove and soon, amid reddish reflections, the grating was marked out on the bare floor. When the temperature—the nightly warmth from my bed and the morning warmth from the fire—had made me doubly drowsy, it was time to get up. Then I had no other wish than to finish my sleep. This wish accompanied me throughout the whole of my school days. Its inseparable attendant, however, was fear of being late. I can still feel today, when I pass the Savignyplatz, the dread with which, stepping into Carmerstrasse, where I lived, I read my judgment in the spellbound space between the ten and the twelve on the repulsive clock-face. The wish that animated me on such winter days, and even later, when, in an extremity of fatigue, I rose from the

* Jula Cohn married Fritz Radt, whose sister, Grete Radt, became the wife of Alfred Cohn.—ED.
† The sentence breaks off without punctuation at the end of a page, and the continuation is no doubt missing. The sonnet is likely to have been by Benjamin but has not been preserved.—ED.
‡ See Hauff's fairy tale, "The Cold Heart."—ED.

couch in the afternoon because of a gymnastics class, had been fulfilled. Only I did not always recognize this fulfillment when yet another of my attempts to find a place of work, in the bourgeois sense of the word, had come to grief.

There is one other sound that, thanks to the decades in which it neither passed my lips nor reached my ears, has preserved the unfathomable mystery that certain words from the language of adults possess for children. It was not long ago that I rediscovered it, and indeed a number of indivisible finds of this nature have played a large part in my decision to write down these memories. My parents being wealthy, we moved every year, before I went to school and perhaps later, too, notwithstanding other occasional summer trips, into summer residences not far from home. First it was Potsdam, later Neubabelsberg. Whereas the latter period still survives in a number of images, of which I may perhaps have more to tell —the night of the great burglary when my parents locked themselves in my room, the hours I stood fishing beside my father on the bank of Lake Griebnitz, the visit to Peacock Island that brought the first great disappointment of my life, because I could not find the peacock feathers in the grass as I had been promised—by contrast, the summer months in Potsdam have wholly vanished, unless I may situate the asparagus cutting—my first and only agricultural passion—as far back as the garden on the Brauhausberg. And I have thus divulged the word in which, like countless rose petals in a drop of Rose Malmaison, hundreds of summer days, forfeiting their form, their color, and their multiplicity, are preserved in their scent. The word is Brauhausberg. To approach what it enfolds is almost impossible. These words that exist on the frontier between two linguistic regions, of children and of adults, are comparable to those of Mallarmé's poems, which the conflict between the poetic and the profane word has as it were consumed and made evanescent, airy. Likewise the word Brauhausberg has lost all heaviness, no longer contains a trace of a brewery [*Brauhaus*], and is at the most a hill swathed in blue that rose up each summer to give lodging to me and my parents.

The economic basis on which the finances of my parents rested was surrounded, long past my childhood and adolescence, by deepest secrecy. Probably not only for me, the eldest child, but also for my mother. And it is certain that such a state of affairs was the rule in a Jewish family, and no doubt in very many Christian ones as well. More curious is the fact that consumption, too, was wrapped in some of the mystery that so deeply shrouded income and fortune. I remember, at any rate, that the mention of certain suppliers—"sources," as they were called—always took place with the solemnity befitting an initiation. There are, it is true, distinctions to be drawn. The purveyors who met the daily household needs no more belonged to that secret circle than did the Berlin firms of long-standing repute that my mother visited when she took me and the younger children "to town." On such occasions it was as certain that our suits would be bought at Arnold Müller's, shoes at Stiller's, and suitcases at Mädler's, as that at the end of these commissions our hot chocolate with whipped cream would be ordered at Hillbrich's. These shopping places were strictly preordained by tradition—quite unlike the connections with traders, which were my father's responsibility. My father possessed at base, along with a number of inhibitions stemming not only from his decency but also from a certain civic worthiness, the entrepreneurial nature of a big-business man. Unfavorable influences brought about his very premature retirement from an enterprise that was probably by no means ill-suited to his capacities, the Lepke art auction, in which he was a partner. When he had relinquished his share in the firm, he concerned himself increasingly with speculative investments of his capital, and it would not surprise me if the interest he took in household transactions was far keener from this time on. What is certain is that the suppliers he henceforth searched out were indirectly connected with his investments. If, therefore, from my mother's shopping excursions, a traditional and as it were official image of the Berlin commercial world emerged, the hints and instructions of my father gave rise to an unknown and slightly sinister one, the prestige of which derived as much from the authoritarian resonance that these names carried at the family table as from the fact that these firms, unlike the others, were never seen by me. At their head, so to speak, was the Lepke auction room itself, with which my father not only had connections but from which, from time to time, he also brought home a purchase. I doubt that this commerce was an altogether happy one, with the exception perhaps of his carpet buying. Shortly before his death he told me that he could distinguish the qualities of a pile with the ball of his foot, if his soles were suitably thin. In my childhood, however, what impressed me most was to imagine the gavel blows with which my father accompanied the auction. Later, when he had withdrawn from Lepke's, this gavel always lay on his desk. Even if I never heard the rap of this gavel, there is another sound that became indissoluble from the image of my father's power and grandeur—or, rather, from those of a man in his profession. It is, implausible as it may seem, the noise made by the knife that my mother used to spread the rolls that my father took to his work in the morning, when it was scraped for the last time, to remove the butter still adhering to it, against the crisp surface of the cut roll. This signal preluding the labor of my father's day was no less exciting to me than, in later years, the sound of the bell that announced the start of a performance at the theater. Apart from this, the real token of my father's profession in our apartment was a Moor, almost life-size, who stood on a gondola reduced to one-thirtieth of its size, holding with one hand an oar that could be taken out, and lifting on the other a golden bowl. This work of art was made of wood, the Moor black, the gondola and oar glowing in many colors beneath the varnish. The whole, however, was so urgently oriented toward its companion piece that I cannot tell today whether a second Moor, whom I imagine with it, really stood there originally or is a creature of my imagination. So much for Lepke's art auction. There was, besides, a further purveyor of artwork—at least as far as bronzes were concerned; it was the firm of Gladenbeck. Whether the choice was affected here, too, by more intimate commercial ties, I do not know. Such was certainly the case, however, with our supply of mouthwash, hydrogen peroxide obtained in huge bottles from the "Medicinal Stores," of which my father was a director. Less transparent, on the other hand, was the state of affairs regarding the Stabernack firm, which for years held an uncontested monopoly of installations in our apartment. Here the intermediate party was perhaps a certain company of building contractors, one of whose directors, Herr Altgelt, filled the role of partner in countless telephone conversations with my father, and whose name has stayed in my memory because his son was a member, and one of the most inglorious, of my class. Leaving aside mealtime conversations, it was only the telephone that intimated to us the occult world of business and traders. My father telephoned a great deal. He, whose outward manner seems to have been almost always courteous and pliable, possessed perhaps only on the telephone the bearing and decisiveness corresponding to his sometimes great wealth. In conversations with mediating agencies this energy not infrequently grew vociferous, and the "serious side of life," which was embodied tangibly in my father's activity, found in the altercations with the telephone operators its true symbol. The telephone first came into use during my childhood. I have therefore known it nailed in some corner of the corridor, whence, shrilling from the darkness, it augmented the terrors of that Berlin apartment with the endless passage leading from the half-lit dining room to the back bedrooms. It became a truly infernal machine when my school friends phoned in the prohibited period between two and four. But not all my father's mysterious transactions were carried out by telephone. From earliest times he had had—like many husbands who do not always find life easy in marriage—a tendency to address himself independently to certain branches of the domestic economy. Thus he had connections in the provinces, principally in the vicinity of Hamburg, which frequently called him away on business. The house was regularly plied from this source with Holstein butter, and in autumn with teal. Wine, on the other hand, was catered for by a Berlin firm, whose share certificates were also in my father's possession: this was the Central Wine Distributors, who were trying out new methods of calculation in the wine business. Finally these names became entwined, in the parental discussions, with others in which the traditions of the middle-class Berlin of that time converged from both sides: for notarial attestation Oberneck was consulted, operations were performed by Rinne, dancing instruction was entrusted to Quaritsch, the family doctor was Renvers, at least as long as he lived in the same building,* Joseph Goldschmidt was our banker. But as for me, I was most lastingly affected by a reckless attempt that my father embarked upon one evening to bring even the family's amusements into the harmony with his business enterprises that he had been able to establish for all its other needs. For when, about 1910, on Lutherstrasse in the West End, a consortium erected the building that now houses the Scala as an "Ice Palace," my father, with a sizable stake, was among their number. Now one evening, I do not know whether it was the opening date or later, my father conceived the idea of taking me there. The Ice Palace, however, was not only the first artificial ice rink to be seen in Berlin, but also a thriving nightclub. So it happened that my attention was held far less by the convolutions in the arena than by the apparitions at the bar, which I was able to survey at my ease from a box in the circle. Among these was a prostitute in a very tight-fitting

* Professor R. Renvers lived at 24 Nettelbeckstrasse.—ED.

white sailor's suit, who, without my having been able to exchange a word with her, determined my erotic fantasies for
years to come.

In those early years I got to know the "town" only as the
theater of purchases, on which occasions it first became apparent how my father's money could cut a path for us between
the shop counters and assistants and mirrors, and the apprais-
ing eyes of our mother, whose muff lay on the counter. In the
ignominy of a "new suit" we stood there, our hands peeping
from the sleeves like dirty price tags, and it was only in the
confectioner's that our spirits rose with the feeling of having
escaped the false worship that humiliated our mother before
idols bearing the names of Mannheimer, Herzog and Israel,
Gerson, Adam, Esders and Mädler, Emma Bette, Bud and
Lachmann. An impenetrable chain of mountains, no, caverns
of commodities—that was "the town."

There are people who think they find the key to their des-
tinies in heredity, others in horoscopes, others again in education. For my part, I believe that I should gain numerous
insights into my later life from my collection of picture postcards, if I were able to leaf through it again today. The main
contributor to this collection was my maternal grandmother, a
decidedly enterprising lady, from whom I believe I have inherited two things: my delight in giving presents and my love of
travel. If it is doubtful what the Christmas holidays—which
cannot be thought of without the Berlin of my childhood—
meant for the first of these passions, it is certain that none of
my boys' adventure books kindled my love of travel as did the
postcards with which she supplied me in abundance from her
farflung travels. And because the longing we feel for a place
determines it as much as does its outward image, I shall say
something about these postcards. And yet—was what they
awakened in me longing? Did they not have far too magnetic
an attraction to leave room for a wish to travel to the places

they showed? For I was there—in Tabarz, Brindisi, Madonna di Campiglio, Westerland, when I gazed, unable to tear myself away, at the wooded slopes of Tabarz covered with glowing red berries, the yellow-and-white-daubed quays at Brindisi, the cupolas of Madonna di Campiglio printed bluish on blue, and the bows of the "Westerland" slicing high through the waves. Visiting the old lady in her carpeted window alcove, ornamented with a little balustrade and looking out onto the Blumeshof, it was hard to imagine how she had undertaken long sea voyages or even camel rides under the direction of Stangel's Travel Bureau. She was a widow; three of her daughters were already married when I was small. I can tell nothing about the fourth, but a good deal about the room that she occupied in her mother's apartment. But perhaps I must first say something about the apartment as a whole. With what words am I to circumscribe the almost immemorial feeling of bourgeois security that emanated from these rooms? Paradoxical as it may sound, the idea of that particular protectedness seems to relate most directly to their shortcomings. The inventory that filled these many rooms—twelve or fourteen—could today be accommodated without incongruity in the shabbiest of secondhand furniture shops. And if these ephemeral forms were so much more solid than those of the *art nouveau* that superseded them—what made you feel at home, at ease, comfortable, and comforted in them was the nonchalance with which they attached themselves to the sauntering passage of years and days, entrusting their future to the durability of their material alone, and nowhere to rational calculation. Here reigned a species of things that was, no matter how compliantly it bowed to the minor whims of fashion, in the main so wholly convinced of itself and its permanence that it took no account of wear, inheritance, or moves, remaining forever equally near to and far from its ending, which seemed the ending of all things. Poverty could have no place in these rooms where even death had none. They had no space for dying—which is why their owners died in a sanatorium, while the furniture went straight to the secondhand dealer. Death was not provided for in them—that is why they were so cozy by day, and by night the theater of our most oppressive dreams. It is for this reason that, when I think of this house—it was number 10 or 12 Blumeshof—in which were spent so many of my childhood's happiest hours, such as when I was allowed, to the sound of piano études, to browse in *Darling's Diversions* in an armchair—I am met on its threshold by a nightmare. My waking existence has preserved no image of the staircase. But in my memory it remains today the scene of a haunting dream that I once had in just those happy years. In this dream the stairway seemed under the power of a ghost that awaited me as I mounted, though without barring my way, making its presence felt when I had only a few more stairs to climb. On these last stairs it held me spellbound. The rooms in this apartment on the Blumeshof were not only numerous but also in some cases very large. To reach my grandmother at her window I had to cross the huge dining room and attain the farthest end of the living room. Only feast days, and above all Christmas Day, could give an idea of the capaciousness of these rooms. But if, when this day came, it seemed as though it had been awaited all the year long in the front rooms, there were other occasions that brought other parts of the apartment to life: a visit by a married daughter unlocked a long-disused wardrobe; another back room opened to us children when the grownups wished to take their afternoon nap at the front of the house, and another part again was animated by the piano lessons received by the last daughter to remain at home. The most important of these remote, less-frequented rooms, however, was the loggia. Perhaps this was because, being the least furnished, it was least suited to the sojourn of adults, or because muted street noises came in, or finally because it opened onto the back courtyards with children, domestic servants, hurdy-gurdy men, and porters. But of these it was more often the voices than the forms that were to be described from the loggia. Moreover, the courtyards of a residential quarter as

genteel as this never really bustled with activity; something of
the composure of the rich people whose work was being done
there seemed to have permeated this work itself, and everything seemed to await the Sleeping Beauty slumber that descended here on Sundays. For this reason Sunday was properly
the day of the loggia—Sunday, which none of the other rooms
could ever quite contain, as if they were damaged. Sunday
seeped out of them; only the loggia, looking out onto the yard
with the carpet rails and the other loggias with their bare walls
of Pompeian red, could hold it, and not a chime of the cargo
of bells with which the churches—the Twelve Apostles, St.
Matthew's, and the Emperor William Memorial Church—
slowly loaded it throughout the afternoon, slipped over its
balustrade; all remained piled high till evening. As I have already indicated, my grandmother did not die in the Blumeshof; nor did the other, who lived opposite her in the same
street and was older and more severe, my father's mother. So
the Blumeshof has become for me an Elysium, an indefinite
realm of the shades of deceased but immortal grandmothers.
And just as imagination, having once cast its veil over a district, is apt to adorn its edges with incomprehensible, capri-
cious frills, so, in the course of decades and to this day it made
of a long-established grocer's store situated near this house
but on Magdeburgerstrasse, to one driving past without ever
having set foot inside, a monument to an early-departed grand-
father, solely because the first name of its owner, like his, was
Georg.

But is not this, too, the city: the strip of light under the bedroom door on evenings when we were "entertaining." Did not
Berlin itself find its way into the expectant childhood night,
as later the world of William Tell or Julius Caesar invaded the
night of an audience? The dream ship that came to fetch us
on those evenings must have rocked at our bedside on the
waves of conversation, or under the spray of clattering plates,
and in the early morning it set us down on the ebb of the

carpet beating that came in at the window with the moist air on rainy days and engraved itself more indelibly in the child's memory than the voice of the beloved in that of the man, the carpet beating that was the language of the nether world, of servant girls, the real grownups, a language that sometimes took its time, languid and muted under the gray sky, breaking at others into an inexplicable gallop, as if the servants were pursued by phantoms. The courtyard was one of the places where the city opened itself to the child; others, admitting him or letting him go, were railway stations. On departure, their openings were a panorama, the frame of a *fata morgana*. No distance was more remote than the place where the rails converged in the mist. Returning home, however, all was different. For the lamps still burned in us that had shone in isolation from courtyard windows often without curtains, from staircases bristling with filth, from cellar windows hung with rags. These were the back yards that the city showed me as I returned from Hahnenklee or Sylt, only to close upon them once more, never to let me see or enter them. But those five last fearful minutes of the journey before everyone got out have been converted into the gaze of my eyes, and there are those perhaps who look into them as into courtyard windows in damaged walls, in which at early evening a lamp stands.

Among the postcards in my album there are a number of which the written side has lasted better in my memory than the picture. All bear the handsome, legible signature "Helene Pufahl." She was my first teacher. Long before I knew of classes at school, I was brought by her into close relationship to the children of my "class," in the sense of the word that I was to become acquainted with only two decades later. And that it was high on the social scale I can infer from the names of the two girls from the little circle that remain in my memory: Ilse Ullstein and Luise von Landau. What order of nobility these Landaus belonged to I do not know. But their name had an immense attraction for me and—I have grounds to suppose—for my parents. Yet this is hardly the reason why their name has remained undimmed in my mind until today; rather, it is the circumstance that this was the first name on which I consciously heard fall the accent of death. That was, as far as I know, not long after I had grown out of the little private circle. Later, each time I passed the Lützow Ufer, my eyes sought her house, and when, toward the end of my school days, I wrote my first philosophical essay, with the title "Reflections on the Nobility," beside that of Pindar with which I started, the alluring name of my first schoolmate stood unuttered. Fraülein Pufahl was succeeded by Herr Knoche, whom I had to confront quite alone. He was the preschool teacher from the school for which my parents later intended me. His instruction does not appear to have entirely agreed with me. At any rate, I performed on occasion magical rites directed against his person, and I still remember the feeling of omnipotence that came over me one day on the Herkules Bridge on receiving the news that Herr Knoche had canceled the next day's class. At that time I knew to what I might attribute this, but today, sadly, I have forgotten the magic formula. More than in his private appearances, Herr Knoche impressed me in the classroom lessons I had with him later, when I had started school. They were enlivened by frequent intermezzi for thrashing. Herr Knoche was a zealous exponent of the cane. He was also entrusted with our singing instruction. And it was in a singing lesson that he showed me one of the shut gates that we all know from our childhood, behind which, we were assured, the way to later, real life lay open. We were practicing the cuirassier's song from *Wallenstein's Camp*. "To horse, trusty friends, to horse and away/to the field of freedom and valiance,/ where a man's worth more than dust and clay/and the heart's still weighed in the balance." Herr Knoche wanted the class to tell him what these last words actually meant. No one, of course, could give an answer. It was one of those artful questions that make children obtuse. Our discomfiture seemed most agreeable to Herr Knoche, who said pointedly, "You'll understand that when you are grown up." Now I am grown up; I am today inside the gate that Herr Knoche showed me; but it is still firmly shut. I was not to make my entrance through that portal.

As lights on a foggy night have around them gigantic rings, my earliest theatrical impressions emerge from the mist of my childhood with great aureoles. At the very beginning is a "monkey theater" that played perhaps on Unter den Linden and at which I appeared, as I remember, heavily escorted, as neither parents nor grandmother was prepared to forgo witnessing the effect on me of my first theatrical performance. True, the source of the light, the actual happening on the stage, I can no longer discern in so much luminous haze. A pinkish-gray cloud of seats, lights, and faces has obliterated the pranks of the poor little monkeys on the stage. And while I can recount the sequence of theatrical events in the following six or seven years, I can say nothing more of them—neither of the *Ladies' Man* I saw at the Spa Theater at Suderode; nor of the *William Tell* that, as is customary, initiated me to the Berlin stage; nor of the *Fiesco,* with Matkowsky, that I saw at the Schauspielhaus or the *Carmen,* with Destinn, at the Opera. The latter two performances my grandmother had taken under her wing; hence not only the dazzling program but also the imposing circle seats. And yet more fondly than to them, my mind goes back to the *William Tell,* because of the event that preceded it, the highly hermetic nature of which is still undimmed, while nothing remains in my memory of the same evening's performance. It must have been in the afternoon that a difference of opinion arose between myself and my mother. Something was to be done that I did not like. Finally, my mother had recourse to coercion. She threatened that unless I did her bidding I should be left at home in the evening. I obeyed. But the feeling with which I did so, or rather, with which, the threat hardly uttered, I measured the two opposed forces and instantaneously perceived how enormous was the preponderance of the other side, and thus my silent indignation at so crude and brutal a procedure, which put at stake something totally disproportionate to the end—for the end was momentary whereas the stake, the gratitude for the evening that my mother was about to give me, as I know today and anticipated then, was deep and permanent—this feeling of misused and violated trust has outlived in me all that succeeded it that day. Many years afterward it was proved a second time how much more significant and enduring the anticipation of an event can be than what actually ensues. As a boy I longed for nothing more than to see Kainz. But his guest performances in Berlin were during school time. As the advance bookings in the morning offered the only possibility of procuring seats at prices commensurate with my pocket money, my wish was denied for years. My parents, at any rate, did nothing to advance its fulfillment. One day—whether because the advance bookings were on a Sunday or for another reason—I was able after all to be one of the first at the ticket office, which was already that of the theater at the Nollendorf-platz. I see myself standing at the box office and—as if memory wanted to prelude the approaching main theme—waiting there, sure enough, but not buying my ticket. At this point memory pauses, and only picks up its thread again when I am mounting the stairs to the circle in the evening, before the performance of *Richard II*. What is it that imposes once again on memory, at the door of the auditorium, a "so far and no further"? True, I see before me a scene from the drama, but entirely cut off, without my knowing whether it is really from this performance or from another, any more than I know whether I saw Kainz or not; whether his appearance was canceled or whether the disappointment of finding him less great than I had believed him annulled, with the image of his acting, the whole evening. So I confront uncertainty wherever I follow my earliest theatrical memories, and in the end I can no longer even distinguish dream from reality. This is true of a dark winter evening when I went with my mother to a production of *The Merry Wives of Windsor*. I really saw this opera, in a kind of people's theater. It was a noisy, cheerful evening, but all the more silent was the journey there, through a snow-covered, unknown Berlin spreading about me in the gaslight. It stood in the same relation to the city I knew as that most jealously guarded of my postcards, the depiction of the Halle Gate in pale blue on a darker blue background. The Belle-Allianceplatz was to be seen with the houses that frame it; the full moon was in the sky. From the moon and the windows in the façades, however, the top layer of card had been removed; their contrasting white disrupted the picture, and one had to hold it against a lamp or a candle to see, by the light of windows and a lunar surface parading in exactly the same illumination, the whole scene regain its composure. Perhaps that evening the opera we were approaching was the source of light that made the city suddenly gleam so differently, but perhaps it was only a dream that I had later of this walk, the memory of which has displaced what previously stood in for reality.

The architect of the Kaiser Friedrich School must have had something on the order of Brandenburg brick Gothic in mind. At any rate, it is constructed in red brick work and displays a preference of motifs commonly found at Stendal or Tangermünde. The whole, however, gives a narrow-chested, high-shouldered impression. Rising close by the precincts of the municipal railway, the building exudes a sad, spinsterish primness. Even more than to the experiences I had within, it is probably to this exterior that I should attribute the fact that I have not retained a single cheerful memory of it. Nor, since leaving, have I ever had the idea of going back. Of the walk to school I have already spoken. But if the portal had been reached just in time, or there was no longer sufficient time— and the nightmarish things to come did not weigh too heavily —to allow me to buy at the adjoining stationer's another piece of plasticine, a protractor, or, at the very beginning, wafers and the little ribbons used to attach blotting sheets to exercise-book covers—if finally the wrought-iron door, which the janitor was allowed to open only ten minutes before school started, was still closed—how melancholy and oppressed must this wait at the door have been, under the arch of the municipal railway, which crossed Knesebeckstrasse at this point, if nothing of it comes back to me besides the compulsion incessantly to remove my cap, to pay attention to myself, when another of the teachers passed, who were permitted to enter, of course, at any time they pleased.

Only today, it seems to me, am I able to appreciate how much hatefulness and humiliation lay in the obligation to raise my cap to teachers. The necessity of admitting them by this gesture into the sphere of my private existence seemed presumptuous. I should have had no objection to a less intimate, and in some way military display of respect. But to greet a teacher as one would a relation or a friend seemed inordinately unfitting, as if they had wanted to hold school in my home. From this alone it can be seen how little school was ever able to win me over. And if I experienced the antiquated forms of school discipline—caning, change of seats, or detention—only in the lower forms, nevertheless the terror and the pall they placed me under in those years never lifted from me. I find this not only in the importance attached to promotion to the next form and to the four reports brought home each year, but also in smaller but more telling details. Above all in the unfathomable shock or, rather, bewilderment into which I was plunged by interruptions in the continuity of teaching—such as excursions to the country, games, and above all the great annual competition between the schools of Greater Berlin to decide the best team at prisoner's base. Needless to say, I never belonged to the school team, which seldom met with success. But in the mobilization of the whole school that took place on such occasions, I, too, was involved. The matches were normally played in May or June, on some field or drill ground in the vicinity of the Lehrter station. As a rule, the weather was blazing hot. Nervously I alighted at the Lehrter station, uncertainly I set off in the direction I vaguely remembered, and found myself at last, with mixed feelings of relief and repugnance, amid some alien troop of schoolboys. From now on bewilderment was uninterrupted: whether I had to look for my own school party, or sought a resting place in the shade, whether I had to reach a stall without crossing the field in order to buy fruit for breakfast, or congregate, while avoiding any appearance of indifference, around one of the gentlemen who made known the day's results, or finally, although I had not understood these results, exchange with my school fellows during the homeward journey observations on the course of the game. Yet what made these sporting occasions most hated and most repellent of all was not their multitudinous attendance but their site. The broad, unfrequented avenues leading to it were flanked by barracks, barracks bordered the playing field, the field was a parade ground. And on those days the feeling never left me that if for only a moment I relaxed my vigilance, permitted myself only the briefest well-being in the shade of a tree or before a sausage vendor's stand, I should fall in ten years' time irredeemably into the power of this place: I should have to become a soldier. The Kaiser Friedrich School stands close by the municipal railway yard at the Savignyplatz. At the Savignyplatz station you can look down into its playground. And because, once liberated from it, I frequently took the opportunity to do this, it now stands before me quite uselessly, similar to one of those Mexican temples that were excavated much too early and inexpertly, their frescoes having been long effaced by rain by the time the excavation of the ceremonial implements and papyri, which might have thrown some light on these images, could at last seriously begin. So I have to make do with what is resurrected only today, isolated pieces of interior that have broken away and yet contain the whole within them, while the whole, standing out there before me, has lost its details without trace. The first fragment to reappear is what was certainly, throughout my whole time at school, the idlest of my perceptions: the molding, crowned

with crenelations, above the classrooms. And perhaps that is
not so difficult to explain. For everything else that came within
my visual field sooner or later became of use to me, became
associated with a thought or a notion that swept it along into
the sea of oblivion. Only this narrow molding, cast out innumerable times by the healthy beat of everyday waves until
it was left stranded like a shell on the shore of my daydreaming. And there I now come across it. I pick it up and question
it like Hamlet addressing the skull. It is, as I have said, a molding representing a row of battlements. What is visible between
them, therefore, is not empty space but the same wood, only
beveled and notched. The intention was certainly to remind
the onlooker of a castle. What he was to do with the recollection was another question. In any event, this molding reinforced the idea of the dense mass divined in the morning behind the closed doors: the class at lessons. Over the doors
leading to the arts-and-crafts rooms it became the emblem of a
certain guildlike solidity. On the classroom cupboard I encountered it again, but how much more emphasis it had on the
identically shaped cupboards standing along the faculty-room
wall. In the first, second, and third forms, in the vicinity of the
many little coats and caps on their racks, its impact was lost;
but in the upper classes it acquired an allusion to the *Abitur*
that was soon to crown the labors of their members. Yet never
more than a shadow of meaning and reason passed across it in
such places, and it remained, with the unspeakable gray-green
ornaments adorning the wall of the hall, and with the absurd
bosses and scrolls of the cast-iron balustrades, the refuge of all
my minutes of terror and my nightmares. Nothing, however,
could compare with the molding, unless it were the bell that
shrilly marked the beginning and end of lessons and breaks.
The timbre and duration of this signal never varied. And yet
how different it sounded at the beginning of the first and at
the end of the last period—to circumscribe this difference
would be to lift the veil that seven years of school cast ever
more tightly over each of the days that composed them. In the

winter the lamps were often still on when it rang, but it was
bereft of coziness, offering as little shelter as the light the
dentist shines into the mouth on which he is about to operate.
Between two peals of the bell lay the break, the second pre-
cipitating the shuffling, chattering uproar with which the mass
of pupils, streaming through only two doors, surged up the
narrow stairway from floor to floor. These staircases I have always hated: hated when forced to climb them in the midst of
the herd, a forest of calves and feet before me, defenselessly
exposed to the bad odors emanating from all the bodies pressing so closely against mine, hated no less when, arriving late,
passing deserted corridors, I hastened up them quite alone to
the very top, arriving breathless in the classroom. If that happened before the teacher's hand was on the door handle, even
though he might be quite near, you got in unseen. But woe if
the door was already shut—however wide open those next to
it might still be, and even if above or below some time passed
before the bang of a shutting door announced the start of a
lesson, and no matter how harmlessly the eye of a strange
teacher approaching along the corridor brushed you—the judgment was ineluctable within, once you had plucked up courage
to open it.

In one of the streets I passed along on my endless wander-
ings I was surprised, many years earlier, by the first stirring of
my sexual urge, under the oddest circumstances. It was on the
Jewish New Year's Day, and my parents had made arrangements for me to attend some divine celebration. Probably it
was a service at the reformed synagogue, which my mother, on
grounds of a family tradition, held in some sympathy, whereas
my father's upbringing inclined him more to the orthodox rite.
However, he had to give way. For this visit to the synagogue I
had been entrusted to a relative whom I had to fetch on my
way. But whether because I had forgotten his address or because I was unfamiliar with the district, it grew later and later
without my drawing nearer to my goal. To make my way inde-

pendently to the synagogue was out of the question, since I had no idea where it was. This bewilderment, forgetfulness, and embarrassment were doubtless chiefly due to my dislike of the impending service, in its familial no less than its divine aspect. While I was wandering thus, I was suddenly and simultaneously overcome, on the one hand, by the thought "Too late, time was up long ago, you'll never get there"—and, on the other, by a sense of the insignificance of all this, of the benefits of letting things take what course they would; and these two streams of consciousness converged irresistibly in an immense pleasure that filled me with blasphemous indifference toward the service, but exalted the street in which I stood as if it had already intimated to me the services of procurement it was later to render to my awakened drive.

We had our "summer residences" first at Potsdam, then at Babelsberg. They were outside, from the point of view of the city; but from that of the summer, inside: we were ensconced within it, and I must disengage my memories of it, like moss that one plucks at random in the dark from the walls of a cave, from its sultry, humid glimmer. There are memories that are especially well preserved because, although not themselves affected, they are isolated by a shock from all that followed. They have not been worn away by contact with their successors and remain detached, self-sufficient. The first such memory appears when I speak of these summer days: it is an evening in my seventh or eighth year. One of our maidservants stands a long while at the wrought-iron gate, which opens onto I know not what tree-lined walk. The big garden, where I have been roaming in overgrown border regions, is already closed to me. It is time to go to bed. Perhaps I have sated myself with my favorite game, shooting with the rubber bolts of my "Eureka" pistol, somewhere in the bushes by the wire fence, at the wooden birds, which, struck by a bolt, fell backward out of the painted foliage to which they were attached by strings. The whole day I had been keeping a secret to myself: the dream of

the previous night. It had been an eerie one. A ghost had appeared to me. The site of its operations did not, in exact truth,
really exist, but had nevertheless a very strong resemblance to
one known, tantalizing, and inaccessible to me, namely the
corner of my parents' bedroom that was separated from the
rest of the chamber by an arch hung with a heavy, faded-violet
curtain, and in which my mother's dressing gowns, house
dresses, and shawls were suspended. The darkness behind the
curtain was impenetrable, and this corner was the sinister,
nocturnal counterpart of that bright, beatific realm that
opened occasionally with my mother's linen cupboard, in
which, piled up on the shelves, edged with white trimming and
bearing a blue-embroidered text from Schiller's "The Bell,"
lay the sheets, tablecloths, napkins, and pillowcases. A sweet
lavender scent came from the brightly colored silk sachets
hanging on the inside of the cupboard doors. These were the
hell and paradise into which the ancient magic of hearth and
home, which had once been lodged in the spinning wheel, had
been sundered. Now my dream had risen from the evil world:
a ghost busying itself at a trestle draped with a profusion of
silken fabrics, one covering another. These silks the ghost was
stealing. It did not snatch them up or carry them away, it did
nothing with or to them that was actually visible and distin-
guishable, and yet I knew it stole them, just as in legends people who discover a spirits' banquet know that these dead beings
are feasting, without seeing them eat or drink. It was this
dream that I had kept secret. And in the night that followed
it I noticed, half asleep, my mother and father coming quietly
into my room at an unusual hour. I did not see them lock
themselves in; when I got up next morning there was nothing
for breakfast. The house had been stripped of everything. At
midday my grandmother arrived from Berlin with the bare
necessities. A numerous band of burglars had descended on the
house in the night. Fortunately the noise they made gave an
indication of their number, so that my mother had succeeded
in restraining my father, who, armed only with a pocketknife,

had wanted to confront them. The dangerous visit had lasted almost until morning. In vain my parents had stood at the window in the first light, signaling to the outside world: the band had departed at their leisure with the baskets. Much later they were caught, and it emerged that their organizer, a murderer and criminal with many previous convictions, was a deaf-mute. It made me proud that I was questioned about the events of the previous evening—for a complicity was suspected between the housebreakers and the maidservant who had stood at the gate. What made me even prouder, however, was the question why I had kept silent about my dream, which I now, of course, narrated at length as a prophecy.

What my first books were to me—to remember this I should first have to forget all other knowledge of books. It is certain that all I know of them today rests on the readiness with which I then opened myself to books; but whereas now content, theme, and subject matter are extraneous to the book, earlier they were solely and entirely in it, being no more external or independent of it than are today the number of its pages or its paper. The world that revealed itself in the book and the book itself were never, at any price, to be divided. So with each book its content, too, its world, was palpably there, at hand. But, equally, this content and world transfigured every part of the book. They burned within it, blazed from it; located not merely in its binding or its pictures, they were enshrined in chapter headings and opening letters, paragraphs and columns. You did not read books through; you dwelt, abided between their lines, and, reopening them after an interval, surprised yourself at the spot where you had halted. The rapture with which you received a new book, scarcely venturing a fleeting glance between its pages, was that of the guest invited for a few weeks to a mansion and hardly daring to dart a glance of admiration at the long suites of state rooms through which he must pass to reach his quarters. He is all the more impatient to be allowed to withdraw. And so each year scarcely had I found the latest volume of the *New Companion of German Youth* when I retreated completely behind the ramparts of its cover, which was adorned with coats of arms, and felt my way into the spy or hunting story in which I was to spend the first night. There was nothing finer than to sniff out, on this first tentative expedition into the labyrinth of stories, the various drafts, scents, brightnesses, and sounds that came from its different chambers and corridors. For in reality the longer stories, interrupted many times to reappear as continuations, extended through the whole like subterranean passages. And what did it matter if the aromas that rose from the tunnels high into the air, where we saw globes or waterwheels glisten, mingled with the smell of the gingerbread, or if a Christmas carol wove its halo around the head of Stephenson glimpsed between two pages like an ancestral portrait through a door crack, or if the smell of the gingerbread joined with that of a Sicilian sulfur mine that suddenly burst upon us in a full-page illustration as in a fresco. But if I had sat for a while immersed in my book and then went back to the table bearing the presents, it no longer stood almost imperiously over me as it had when I first entered the Christmas room; rather, I seemed to be walking on a small platform that led down to it from my fairy castle.

Anyone can observe that the duration for which we are exposed to impressions has no bearing on their fate in memory. Nothing prevents our keeping rooms in which we have spent twenty-four hours more or less clearly in our memory, and forgetting others in which we passed months. It is not, therefore, due to insufficient exposure time if no image appears on the plate of remembrance. More frequent, perhaps, are the cases when the half-light of habit denies the plate the necessary light for years, until one day from an alien source it flashes as if from burning magnesium powder, and now a snapshot transfixes the room's image on the plate. Nor is this very mysterious, since such moments of sudden illumination are at the same time moments when we are beside ourselves, and while our waking, habitual, everyday self is involved actively or passively in what is happening, our deeper self rests in another place and is touched by the shock, as is the little heap of magnesium powder by the flame of the match. It is to this immolation of our deepest self in shock that our memory owes its most indelible images. So the room in which I slept at the age of six would have been forgotten had not my father come in one night—I was already in bed—with the news of a death. It was not, really, the news itself that so affected me: the deceased was a distant cousin. But in the way in which my father told me, there lay [text breaks off]

With the joy of remembering, however, another is fused: that of possession in memory. Today I can no longer distinguish them: it is as if it were only a part of the gift of the moment I am now relating, that it, too, received the gift of never again being wholly lost to me—even if decades have passed between the seconds in which I think of it.

The first great disappointment of my life reached me one afternoon on Peacock Island. I had been told on the way there that I should find peacock feathers in the grass. Scarcely had I heard this when, with the speed of a spark leaping between two charged systems, a close connection must have been formed in me between the name of these islands and the peacock feathers. It was not that the spark took a roundabout path by way of the image of the peacock. This had no part in the process. And so my reproachful dismay as I scoured the turf so vainly was not directed against the peacocks that I saw strutting up and down, but, rather, against the soil of the island itself, which was a peacock island yet bore no peacock earth. Had I found the feather I craved in the grass, I should have felt as if I were expected and welcome at this spot. Now the island seemed to have broken a promise. Certainly the peacocks could not console me. Were they not there for everybody to see? And I was to have had something intended only for me, concealed from all others, to be found in the grass only by me. This disappointment would not have been so great had it not been Mother Earth herself who had inflicted it on me. Similarly, the bliss at having, after much toil, at last learned to ride a bicycle would have been less sweet had not Mother Earth herself let me feel her praise. One learned to ride in those days —it was the heyday of bicycle racing—in large halls specially established for the purpose. These halls did not however, have the snobbish character of the later ice palaces or indoor tennis courts; rather, they resembled skating rinks or gymnasiums, and bespoke a mentality for which sport and open air were not inseparable as they are today. It was the era of "sporting costumes" that, unlike our present track suits, did not yet seek to adapt the body to immediate needs, but, rather, to define the particular sport as sharply as possible and isolate it from all others, just as those halls cut it off from nature and other exercises. The sport, as it was practiced in those halls, still had about it all the eccentricities of its beginnings. On the asphalted floor, moving under the supervision of trainers among the ordinary tricycles for gentlemen, ladies, and children, were constructions with front wheels ten times larger than their small rear wheels, their airy seats probably occupied by artistes rehearsing a number. The orchard at Glienicke, the broad, ceremonious promenade of Schloss Babelsberg, the narrow, concealed pathways of our summer garden, the shady ways through the foliage leading down to Lake Griebnitz at the places where there were jetties—all this I annexed to my domain, completing in an instant in fantasy the work of countless walks, games, and outings, kneeling in my nuptials with the ground as a dynast conquers endless territories by means of a single felicitous union.

I have talked of the courtyards. Even Christmas was fundamentally a festival of the courtyards. There it began with the barrel organs, which stretched the week before the festival with chorales, and there it ended with the Christmas trees, which, bereft of feet, leaned in the snow or glistened in the rain. But Christmas came, and all at once, before the eyes of the bourgeois child, it divided his city into two mighty camps. These were not the genuine ones, in which the exploited and their rulers lie irreconcilably opposed. No, it was a camp posed and arranged almost as artificially as the cribs composed of paper or wooden figures, but also as old and as honorable: Christmas came and divided the children into those who shuffled past the booths on Potsdam Square and those who, alone, indoors, offered their dolls and farm animals for sale to children of their age. Christmas came and with it a whole, unknown world of wares, [breaks off]

The *déjà vu* effect has often been described. But I wonder whether the term is actually well chosen, and whether the metaphor appropriate to the process would not be far better taken from the realm of acoustics. One ought to speak of events that reach us like an echo awakened by a call, a sound that seems to have been heard somewhere in the darkness of past life. Accordingly, if we are not mistaken, the shock with which moments enter consciousness as if already lived usually strikes us in the form of a sound. It is a word, tapping, or a rustling that is endowed with the magic power to transport us into the cool tomb of long ago, from the vault of which the present seems to return only as an echo. But has the counterpart of this temporal removal ever been investigated, the shock with which we come across a gesture or a word as we suddenly find in our house a forgotten glove or reticule? And just as they cause us to surmise a stranger who has been there, there are words or gestures from which we infer that invisible stranger, the future, who left them in our keeping. I was perhaps five years old. One evening—I was already in bed—my father appeared, probably to say good night. It was half against his will, I thought, that he told me the news of a relative's death. The deceased was a cousin, a grown man who scarcely concerned me. But my father gave the news with details, took the opportunity to explain, in answer to my question, what a heart attack was, and was communicative. I did not take in much of the explanation. But that evening I must have memorized my room and my bed, as one observes exactly a place where one feels dimly that one will later have to search for something one has forgotten there. Many years afterward I discovered what I had "forgotten," a part of the news that my father had broken to me in that room: that the illness was called syphilis.

One-Way Street

(SELECTION)

This street is named
Asja Lacis Street
after her who
as an engineer
cut it through the author

FILLING STATION

The construction of life is at present in the power of facts far more than of convictions, and of such facts as have scarcely ever become the basis of convictions. Under these circumstances true literary activity cannot aspire to take place within a literary framework—this is, rather, the habitual expression of its sterility. Significant literary work can only come into being in a strict alternation between action and writing; it must nurture the inconspicuous forms that better fit its influence in active communities than does the pretentious, universal gesture of the book—in leaflets, brochures, articles, and placards. Only this prompt language shows itself actively equal to the moment. Opinions are to the vast apparatus of social existence what oil is to machines: one does not go up to a turbine and pour machine oil over it; one applies a little to hidden spindles and joints that one has to know.

BREAKFAST ROOM

A popular tradition warns against recounting dreams on an empty stomach. In this state, though awake, one remains under the sway of the dream. For washing brings only the surface of the body and the visible motor functions into the light, while in the deeper strata, even during the morning ablution, the gray penumbra of dream persists and, indeed, in the solitude of the first waking hour, consolidates itself. He who shuns contact with the day, whether for fear of his fellow men or for the sake of inward composure, is unwilling to eat and disdains his breakfast. He thus avoids a rupture between the nocturnal and the daytime worlds—a precaution justified only by the combustion of dream in a concentrated morning's work, if not in prayer, but otherwise a source of confusion between vital rhythms. The narration of dreams brings calamity, because a person still half in league with the dream world betrays it in his words and must incur its revenge. Expressed in more modern terms: he betrays himself. He has outgrown the protection of dreaming naïveté, and in laying clumsy hands on his dream visions he surrenders himself. For only from the far bank, from broad daylight, may dream be recalled with impunity. This further side of dream is only attainable through a cleansing analogous to washing yet totally different. By way of the stomach. The fasting man tells his dream as if he were talking in his sleep.

NO. 113

The hours that hold the figure and the form
Have run their course within the house of dream.

Cellar. We have long forgotten the ritual by which the house of our life was erected. But when it is under assault and enemy bombs are already taking their toll, what enervated, perverse antiquities do they not lay bare in the foundations. What things were interred and sacrificed amid magic incantations, what horrible cabinet of curiosities lies there below, where the deepest shafts are reserved for what is most commonplace. In a night of despair I dreamed I was with my first friend from my school days, whom I had not seen for decades and had scarcely ever remembered in that time, tempestuously renewing our friendship and brotherhood. But when I awoke it became clear that what despair had brought to light like a detonation was the corpse of that boy, who had been immured as a warning: that whoever one day lives here may in no respect resemble him.

Vestibule. A visit to Goethe's house. I cannot recall having seen rooms in the dream. It was a perspective of whitewashed corridors like those in a school. Two elderly English lady visitors and a curator are the dream's extras. The curator requests us to sign the visitors' book lying open on a desk at the farthest end of a passage. On reaching it, I find as I turn the pages my name already entered in big, unruly, childish characters.

Dining Hall. In a dream I saw myself in Goethe's study. It bore no resemblance to the one in Weimar. Above all, it was very small and had only one window. The side of the writing desk abutted on the wall opposite the window. Sitting and writing at it was the poet, in extreme old age. I was standing to one side when he broke off to give me a small vase, an urn from antiquity, as a present. I turned it between my hands. An immense heat filled the room. Goethe rose to his feet and accompanied me to an adjoining chamber, where a table was set for my relatives. It seemed prepared, however, for many more than their number. Doubtless there were places for my ancestors, too. At the end, on the right, I sat down beside Goethe. When the meal was over, he rose with difficulty, and by gesturing I sought leave to support him. Touching his elbow, I began to weep with emotion.

FOR MEN
To convince is to conquer without conception.

STANDARD CLOCK

To great writers, finished works weigh lighter than those fragments on which they work throughout their lives. For only the more feeble and distracted take an inimitable pleasure in conclusions, feeling themselves thereby given back to life. For the genius each caesura, and the heavy blows of fate, fall like gentle sleep itself into his workshop labor. About it he draws a charmed circle of fragments. "Genius is application."

COME BACK! ALL IS FORGIVEN

Like someone performing the giant swing on the horizontal bar, each boy spins for himself the wheel of fortune from which, sooner or later, the momentous lot shall fall. For only that which we knew or practiced at fifteen will one day constitute our attraction. And one thing, therefore, can never be made good: having neglected to run away from home. From forty-eight hours' exposure in those years, as in a caustic solution, the crystal of life's happiness forms.

MANORIALLY FURNISHED TEN-ROOM APARTMENT

The furniture style of the second half of the nineteenth century has received its only adequate description, and analysis, in a certain type of detective novel at the dynamic center of which stands the horror of apartments. The arrangement of the furniture is at the same time the site plan of deadly traps, and the suite of rooms prescribes the fleeing victim's path. That this kind of detective novel begins with Poe—at a time when such accommodations hardly yet existed—is no counterargument. For without exception the great writers perform their combinations in a world that comes after them, just as the Paris streets of Baudelaire's poems, as well as Dostoyevsky's characters, only existed after 1900. The bourgeois interior of the 1860's to the 1890's, with its gigantic sideboards distended with carvings, the sunless corners where palms stand, the balcony embattled behind its balustrade, and the long corridors with their singing gas flames, fittingly houses only the corpse. "On this sofa the aunt cannot but be murdered." The soulless luxuriance of the furnishings becomes true comfort only in the presence of a dead body. Far more interesting than the Oriental landscapes in detective novels is that rank Orient inhabiting their interiors: the Persian carpet and the ottoman, the hanging lamp and the genuine Caucasian dagger. Behind the heavy, gathered Khilim tapestries the master of the house has orgies with his share certificates, feels himself the Eastern merchant, the indolent pasha in the caravanserai of otiose enchantment, until that dagger in its silver sling above the divan puts an end, one fine afternoon, to his siesta and himself. This character of the bourgeois apartment, tremulously awaiting the nameless murderer like a lascivious old lady her gallant, has been penetrated by a number of authors who, as writers of "detective stories"—and perhaps also because in their works part of the bourgeois pandemonium is exhibited—have been denied the reputation they deserve. The quality in question has been captured in isolated writings by Conan Doyle and in a major production by A. K. Green; and with *The Phantom of the Opera,* one of the great novels about the nineteenth century, Gaston Leroux has brought the genre to its apotheosis.

CHINESE CURIOS
These are days when no one should rely unduly on his "competence." Strength lies in improvisation. All the decisive blows are struck left-handed.

At the beginning of the long downhill lane that leads to the house of ——, whom I visited each evening, is a gate.

After she moved, the opening of its archway stood henceforth before me like an ear that has lost the power of hearing.

Ho!

A child in his nightshirt cannot be prevailed upon to greet an arriving visitor. Those present, invoking a higher moral standpoint, admonish him in vain to overcome his prudery. A few minutes later he reappears, now stark naked, before the visitor. In the meantime he has washed.

The power of a country road is different when one is walking along it from when one is flying over it by airplane. In the same way, the power of a text is different when it is read from when it is copied out. The airplane passenger sees only how the road pushes through the landscape, how it unfolds according to the same laws as the terrain surrounding it. Only he who walks the road on foot learns of the power it commands, and of how, from the very scenery that for the flier is only the unfurled plain, it calls forth distances, belvederes, clearings, prospects at each of its turns like a commander deploying soldiers at a front. Only the copied text thus commands the soul of him who is occupied with it, whereas the mere reader never discovers the new aspects of his inner self that are opened by the text, that road cut through the interior jungle forever closing behind it: because the reader follows the movement of his mind in the free flight of daydreaming, whereas the copier submits it to command. The Chinese practice of copying books was thus an incomparable guarantee of literary culture, and the transcript a key to China's enigmas.

GLOVES

In an aversion to animals the predominant feeling is fear of being recognized by them through contact. The horror that stirs deep in man is an obscure awareness that in him something lives so akin to the animal that it might be recognized. All disgust is originally disgust at touching. Even when the feeling is mastered, it is only by a drastic gesture that over-leaps its mark: the nauseous is violently engulfed, eaten, while the zone of finest epidermal contact remains taboo. Only in this way is the paradox of the moral demand to be met, exact-ing simultaneously the overcoming and the subtlest elabora-tion of man's sense of disgust. He may not deny his bestial relationship with animals, the invocation of which revolts him: he must make himself its master.

MEXICAN EMBASSY

> *Je ne passe jamais devant un fétiche de bois, un Bouddha doré, une idole mexicaine sans me dire: c'est peut-être le vrai dieu.* (I never pass by a wooden fetish, a gilded Buddha, a Mexi-can idol without reflecting: per-haps it is the true God.)
> —Charles Baudelaire

I dreamed I was a member of an exploring party in Mexico. After crossing a high, primeval jungle, we came upon a system of aboveground caves in the mountains where an order had survived from the time of the first missionaries till now, its monks continuing the work of conversion among the natives. In an immense central grotto with a Gothically pointed roof, Mass was celebrated according to the most ancient rites. We joined the ceremony and witnessed its climax: toward a wooden bust of God the Father fixed high on a wall of the cave, a priest raised a Mexican fetish. At this the divine head turned thrice in denial from right to left.

TO THE PUBLIC: PLEASE PROTECT AND
PRESERVE THESE NEW PLANTINGS

What is "solved"? Do not all the questions of our lives, as we live, remain behind us like foliage obstructing our view? To uproot this foliage, even to thin it out, does not occur to us.

We stride on, leave it behind, and from a distance it is indeed open to view, but indistinct, shadowy, and all the more enigmatically entangled.

Commentary and translation stand in the same relation to the text as style and mimesis to nature: the same phenomenon considered from different aspects. On the tree of the sacred text both are only the eternally rustling leaves; on that of the profane, the seasonally falling fruits.

He who loves is attached not only to the "faults" of the beloved, not only to the whims and weaknesses of a woman. Wrinkles in the face, moles, shabby clothes, and a lopsided walk bind him more lastingly and relentlessly than any beauty. This has long been known. And why? If the theory is correct that feeling is not located in the head, that we sentiently experience a window, a cloud, a tree not in our brains but, rather, in the place where we see it, then we are, in looking at our beloved, too, outside ourselves. But in a torment of tension and ravishment. Our feeling, dazzled, flutters like a flock of birds in the woman's radiance. And as birds seek refuge in the leafy recesses of a tree, feelings escape into the shaded wrinkles, the awkward movements and inconspicuous blemishes of the body we love, where they can lie low in safety. And no passer-by would guess that it is just here, in what is defective and censurable, that the fleeting darts of adoration nestle.

CONSTRUCTION SITE

Pedantic brooding over the production of objects—visual aids, toys, or books—that are supposed to be suitable for children is folly. Since the Enlightenment this has been one of the mustiest speculations of the pedagogues. Their infatuation with psychology keeps them from perceiving that the world is full of the most unrivaled objects for childish attention and use. And the most specific. For children are particularly fond of haunting any site where things are being visibly worked upon. They are irresistibly drawn by the detritus generated by building, gardening, housework, tailoring, or carpentry. In waste products they recognize the face that the world of things turns directly and solely to them. In using these things they do not so much imitate the works of adults as bring together, in the artifact produced in play, materials of widely differing kinds in a new, intuitive relationship. Children thus produce their own small world of things within the greater one. The norms of this small world must be kept in mind if one wishes to create things specially for children, rather than let one's adult activity, through its requisites and instruments, find its own way to them.

MINISTRY OF THE INTERIOR

The more antagonistic a person is toward the traditional order, the more inexorably he will subject his private life to the norms that he wishes to elevate as legislators of a future society. It is as if these laws, nowhere yet realized, placed him under obligation to enact them in advance at least in the confines of his own existence. The man, on the other hand, who knows himself to be in accord with the most ancient heritage of his class or nation will sometimes bring his private life into ostentatious contrast to the maxims that he unrelentingly asserts in public, secretly approving his own behavior, without the slightest qualms, as the most conclusive proof of the unshakable authority of the principles he puts on display. Thus are distinguished the types of the anarcho-socialist and the conservative politician.

FLAG . . .

How much more easily the leave-taker is loved! For the flame burns more purely for those vanishing in the distance, fueled by the fleeting scrap of material waving from the ship or railway window. Separation penetrates the disappearing person like a pigment and steeps him in gentle radiance.

. . . AT HALF-MAST
If a person very close to us is dying, there is something in the months to come that we dimly apprehend—much as we should have liked to share it with him—could only happen through his absence. We greet him at the last in a language that he no longer understands.

IMPERIAL PANORAMA
A Tour of German Inflation
1. In the stock of phraseology that lays bare the amalgam of stupidity and cowardice constituting the mode of life of the German bourgeois, the locution referring to impending catastrophe—that "things can't go on like this"—is particularly noteworthy. The helpless fixation on notions of security and property deriving from past decades keeps the average citizen from perceiving the quite remarkable stabilities of an entirely new kind that underlie the present situation. Because the relative stabilization of the prewar years benefited him, he feels compelled to regard any state that dispossesses him as unstable. But stable conditions need by no means be pleasant conditions, and even before the war there were strata for whom stabilized conditions amounted to stabilized wretchedness. To decline is no less stable, no more surprising, than to rise. Only a view that acknowledges downfall as the sole reason for the present situation can advance beyond enervating amazement at what is daily repeated, and perceive the phenomena of decline as stability itself and rescue alone as extraordinary, verging on the marvelous and incomprehensible. People in the

national communities of Central Europe live like the inhabitants of an encircled town whose provisions and gunpowder are running out and for whom deliverance is, by human reasoning, scarcely to be expected—a case in which surrender, perhaps unconditional, should be most seriously considered. But the silent, invisible power that Central Europe feels opposing it does not negotiate. Nothing, therefore, remains but to direct the gaze, in the perpetual expectation of the final onslaught, on nothing except the extraordinary event in which alone salvation now lies. But this necessary state of intense and uncomplaining attention could, because we are in mysterious contact with the powers besieging us, really call forth a miracle. Conversely, the assumption that things cannot go on like this will one day find itself apprised of the fact that for the suffering of individuals as of communities there is only one limit beyond which things cannot go: annihilation.

2. A curious paradox: people have only the narrowest private interest in mind when they act, yet they are at the same time more than ever determined in their behavior by the instincts of the mass. And more than ever mass instincts have become confused and estranged from life. Whereas the obscure impulse of the animal—as innumerable anecdotes relate —detects, as danger approaches, a way of escape that still seems invisible, this society, each of whose members cares only for his own abject well-being, falls victim, with animal insensibility but without the insensate intuition of animals, as a blind mass, to even the most obvious danger, and the diversity of individual goals is immaterial in face of the identity of the determining forces. Again and again it has been shown that society's attachment to its familiar and long-since-forfeited life is so rigid as to nullify the genuinely human application of intellect, forethought, even in dire peril. So that in this society the picture of imbecility is complete: uncertainty, indeed perversion of vital instincts, and impotence, indeed de-

cay of the intellect. This is the condition of the entire German bourgeoisie.

3. All close relationships are lit up by an almost intolerable, piercing clarity in which they are scarcely able to survive. For on the one hand, money stands ruinously at the center of every vital interest, but on the other, this is the very barrier before which almost all relationships halt; so, more and more, in the natural as in the moral sphere, unreflecting trust, calm, and health are disappearing.

4. Not without reason is it customary to speak of "naked" want. What is most damaging in the display of it, a practice started under the dictates of necessity and making visible only a thousandth part of the hidden distress, is not the pity or the equally terrible awareness of his own impunity awakened in the onlooker, but his shame. It is impossible to remain in a large German city, where hunger forces the most wretched to live on the bank notes with which passers-by seek to cover an exposure that wounds them.

5. "Poverty disgraces no man." Well and good. But *they* disgrace the poor man. They do it, and then console him with the little adage. It is one of those that may once have held good but have long since degenerated. The case is no different with the brutal "If a man does not work, neither shall he eat." When there was work that fed a man, there was also poverty that did not disgrace him, if it arose from deformity or other misfortune. But this deprivation, into which millions are born and hundreds of thousands are dragged by impoverishment, does indeed disgrace. Filth and misery grow up around them like walls, the work of invisible hands. And just as a man can endure much in isolation, but feels justifiable shame when his wife sees him bear it or suffers it herself, so he may tolerate much as long as he is alone, and everything as long as he conceals it. But no one may ever make peace

with poverty when it falls like a gigantic shadow upon his countrymen and his house. Then he must be alert to every humiliation done to him and so discipline himself that his suffering becomes no longer the downhill road of grief, but the rising path of revolt. But of this there is no hope so long as each blackest, most terrible stroke of fate, daily and even hourly discussed by the press, set forth in all its illusory causes and effects, helps no one uncover the dark powers that hold his life in thrall.

6. To the foreigner cursorily acquainted with the pattern of German life who has even briefly traveled about the country, its inhabitants seem no less bizarre than an exotic race. A witty Frenchman has said: "A German seldom understands himself. If he has once understood himself, he will not say so. If he says so, he will not make himself understood." This comfortless distance was increased by the war, but not merely through the real and legendary atrocities that Germans are reported to have committed. Rather, what completes the isolation of Germany in the eyes of other Europeans, what really engenders the attitude that they are dealing with Hottentots in the Germans (as it has been aptly put), is the violence, incomprehensible to outsiders and wholly imperceptible to those imprisoned by it, with which circumstances, squalor, and stupidity here subjugate people entirely to collective forces, as the lives of savages alone are subjected to tribal laws. The most European of all accomplishments, that more or less discernible irony with which the life of the individual asserts the right to run its course independently of the community into which he is cast, has completely deserted the Germans.

7. The freedom of conversation is being lost. If it was earlier a matter of course in conversation to take interest in one's partner, this is now replaced by inquiry into the price of his shoes or his umbrella. Irresistibly intruding on any convivial exchange is the theme of the conditions of life, of

money. What this theme involves is not so much the concerns
and sorrows of individuals, in which they might be able to
help one another, as the overall picture. It is as if one were
trapped in a theater and had to follow the events on the stage
whether one wanted to or not, had to make them again and
again, willingly or unwillingly, the subject of one's thought
and speech.

8. Anyone who does not simply refuse to perceive decline
will hasten to claim a special justification for his own continued presence, his activity and involvement in this chaos.
As there are many insights into the general failure, so there
are many exceptions for one's own sphere of action, place of
residence, and moment of time. A blind determination to
save the prestige of personal existence, rather than, through
an impartial disdain for its impotence and entanglement, at
least to detach it from the background of universal delusion,
is triumphing almost everywhere. That is why the air is so
thick with life theories and world views, and why in this
country they cut so presumptuous a figure, for almost always
they finally serve to sanction some wholly trivial private situation. For just the same reason the air is so full of phantoms,
mirages of a glorious cultural future breaking upon us overnight in spite of all, for everyone is committed to the optical
illusions of his isolated standpoint.

9. The people cooped up in this country no longer discern
the contours of human personality. Every free man appears
to them as an eccentric. Let us imagine the peaks of the High
Alps silhouetted not against the sky but against folds of dark
drapery. The mighty forms would show up only dimly. In
just this way a heavy curtain shuts off Germany's sky, and we
no longer see the profiles of even the greatest men.

10. Warmth is ebbing from things. The objects of daily use
gently but insistently repel us. Day by day, in overcoming the

sum of secret resistances—not only the overt ones—that they put in our way, we have an immense labor to perform. We must compensate for their coldness with our warmth if they are not to freeze us to death, and handle their spines with infinite dexterity, if we are not to perish by bleeding. From our fellow men we should expect no succor. Bus conductors, officials, workmen, salesmen—they all feel themselves to be the representatives of a refractory matter whose menace they take pains to demonstrate through their own surliness. And in the degeneration of things, with which, emulating human decay, they punish humanity, the country itself conspires. It gnaws at us like the things, and the German spring that never comes is only one of countless related phenomena of decomposing German nature. Here one lives as if the weight of the column of air supported by everyone had suddenly, against all laws, become in these regions perceptible.

11. Any human movement, whether it springs from an intellectual or even a natural impulse, is impeded in its unfolding by the boundless resistance of the outside world. Shortage of houses and the rising cost of travel are in the process of annihilating the elementary symbol of European freedom, which existed in certain forms even in the Middle Ages: freedom of domicile. And if medieval coercion bound men to natural associations, they are now chained together in unnatural community. Few things will further the ominous spread of the cult of rambling as much as the strangulation of the freedom of residence, and never has freedom of movement stood in greater disproportion to the abundance of means of travel.

12. Just as all things, in a perpetual process of mingling and contamination, are losing their intrinsic character while ambiguity displaces authenticity, so is the city. Great cities—whose incomparably sustaining and reassuring power encloses those at work within them in the peace of a fortress and lifts from them, with the view of the horizon, awareness of the ever-

vigilant elemental forces—are seen to be breached at all points by the invading countryside. Not by the landscape, but by what in untrammeled nature is most bitter: plowed land, highways, night sky that the veil of vibrant redness no longer conceals. The insecurity of even the busy areas puts the city dweller in the opaque and truly dreadful situation in which he must assimilate, along with isolated monstrosities from the open country, the abortions of urban architectonics.

13. Noble indifference to the spheres of wealth and poverty has quite forsaken manufactured things. Each stamps its owner, leaving him only the choice of appearing a starveling or a racketeer. For while even true luxury can be permeated by intellect and conviviality and so forgotten, the luxury goods swaggering before us now parade such brazen solidity that all the mind's shafts break harmlessly on their surface.

14. The earliest customs of peoples seem to send us a warning that in accepting what we receive so abundantly from nature we should guard against a gesture of avarice. For we are able to make Mother Earth no gift of our own. It is therefore fitting to show respect in taking, by returning a part of all we receive before laying hands on our share. This respect is expressed in the ancient custom of the libation. Indeed, it is perhaps this immemorial practice that has survived, transformed, in the prohibition on gathering forgotten ears of corn or fallen grapes, these reverting to the soil or to the ancestral dispensers of blessings. An Athenian custom forbade the picking up of crumbs at the table, since they belonged to the heroes. If society has so degenerated through necessity and greed that it can now receive the gifts of nature only rapaciously, that it snatches the fruit unripe from the trees in order to sell it most profitably, and is compelled to empty each dish in its determination to have enough, the earth will be impoverished and the land yield bad harvests.

CAUTION: STEPS
Work on good prose has three steps: a musical stage when it is composed, an architectonic one when it is built, and a textile one when it is woven.

ATTESTED AUDITOR OF BOOKS
Just as this time is the antithesis of the Renaissance in general, it contrasts in particular to the situation in which the art of printing was discovered. For whether by coincidence or not, its appearance in Germany came at a time when the book in the most eminent sense of the word, the book of books, had through Luther's translation become the people's property. Now everything indicates that the book in this traditional form is nearing its end. Mallarmé, who in the crystalline structure of his certainly traditionalist writing saw the true image of what was to come, was in the "*Coup de dés*" the first to incorporate the graphic tensions of the advertisement in the printed page. The typographical experiments later undertaken by the Dadaists stemmed, it is true, not from constructive principles but from the precise nervous reactions of these literati, and were therefore far less enduring than Mallarmé's, which grew out of the inner nature of his style. But they show up for this very reason the topicality of what Mallarmé, monadically, in his hermetic room, had discovered through a pre-established harmony with all the decisive events of our times in economics, technology, and public life. Printing, having found in the book a refuge in which to lead an autonomous existence, is pitilessly dragged out onto the street by advertisements and subjected to the brutal heteronomies of economic chaos. This is the hard schooling of its new form. If centuries ago it began gradually to lie down, passing from the upright inscription to the manuscript resting on sloping desks before finally taking to bed in the printed book, it now

begins just as slowly to rise again from the ground. The newspaper is read more in the vertical than in the horizontal plane, while film and advertisement force the printed word entirely into the dictatorial perpendicular. And before a child of our time finds his way clear to opening a book, his eyes have been exposed to such a blizzard of changing, colorful, conflicting letters that the chances of his penetrating the archaic stillness of the book are slight. Locust swarms of print, which already eclipse the sun of what is taken for intellect for city dwellers, will grow thicker with each succeeding year. Other demands of business life lead further. The card index marks the conquest of three-dimensional writing, and so presents an astonishing counterpoint to the three-dimensionality of script in its original form as rune or knot notation. (And today the book is already, as the present mode of scholarly production demonstrates, an outdated mediation between two different filing systems. For everything that matters is to be found in the card box of the researcher who wrote it, and the scholar studying it assimilates it into his own card index.) But it is quite beyond doubt that the development of writing will not indefinitely be bound by the claims to power of a chaotic academic and commercial activity; rather, quantity is approaching the moment of a qualitative leap when writing, advancing ever more deeply into the graphic regions of its new eccentric figurativeness, will take sudden possession of an adequate factual content. In this picture writing, poets, who will now as in earliest times be first and foremost experts in writing, will be able to participate only by mastering the fields in which (quite unobtrusively) it is being constructed: the statistical and technical diagram. With the foundation of an international moving script they will renew their authority in the life of peoples, and find a role awaiting them in comparison to which all the innovative aspirations of rhetoric will reveal themselves as antiquated daydreams.

TEACHING AID
Principles of the Weighty Tome, or How to Write Fat Books.

1. The whole composition must be permeated with a protracted and wordy exposition of the initial plan.

2. Terms are to be included for conceptions that, except in *Ha* ¹ this definition, appear nowhere in the whole book.

3. Conceptual distinctions laboriously arrived at in the text are to be obliterated again in the relevant notes.

4. For concepts treated only in their general significance, examples should be given; if, for example, machines are mentioned, all the different kinds of machines should be enumerated.

5. Everything that is known a priori about an object is to be consolidated by an abundance of examples.

6. Relationships that could be represented graphically must be expounded in words. Instead of being represented in a genealogical tree, for example, all family relationships are to be enumerated and described.

7. A number of opponents all sharing the same argument should each be refuted individually.

The typical work of modern scholarship is intended to be read like a catalogue. But when shall we actually write books like catalogues? If the deficient content were thus to determine the outward form, an excellent piece of writing would result, in which the value of opinions would be marked without their being thereby put on sale.

The typewriter will alienate the hand of the man of letters from the pen only when the precision of typographic forms has directly entered the conception of his books. One might suppose that new systems with more variable typefaces would then be needed. They will replace the pliancy of the hand with the innervation of commanding fingers.

A period that, constructed metrically, afterward has its rhythm upset at a single point yields the finest prose sentence imaginable. In this way a ray of light falls through a chink in the wall of the alchemist's cell, to light up gleaming crystals, spheres, and triangles.

GERMANS, DRINK GERMAN BEER!

The mob, impelled by a frenetic hatred of the life of the mind, has found a sure way to annihilate it in the counting of bodies. Whenever given the slightest opportunity, they form ranks and advance into artillery barrages and price rises in marching order. No one sees further than the back before him, and each is proud to be thus exemplary for the eyes behind. Men have been adept at this for centuries in the field, but the march-past of penury, standing in line, is the invention of women.

POST NO BILLS

The Writer's Technique in Thirteen Theses.

1. Anyone intending to embark on a major work should be lenient with himself and, having completed a stint, deny himself nothing that will not prejudice the next.

2. Talk about what you have written, by all means, but do not read from it while the work is in progress. Every gratification procured in this way will slacken your tempo. If this regime is followed, the growing desire to communicate will become in the end a motor for completion.

3. In your working conditions avoid everyday mediocrity. Semirelaxation, to a background of insipid sounds, is degrading. On the other hand, accompaniment by an étude or a cacophony of voices can become as significant for work as the perceptible silence of the night. If the latter sharpens the inner ear, the former acts as touchstone for a diction ample enough to bury even the most wayward sounds.

4. Avoid haphazard writing materials. A pedantic adherence to certain papers, pens, inks is beneficial. No luxury, but an abundance of these utensils is indispensable.

5. Let no thought pass incognito, and keep your notebook as strictly as the authorities keep their register of aliens.

6. Keep your pen aloof from inspiration, which it will then attract with magnetic power. The more circumspectly you delay writing down an idea, the more maturely developed it will be on surrendering itself. Speech conquers thought, but writing commands it.

7. Never stop writing because you have run out of ideas. Literary honor requires that one break off only at an appointed moment (a mealtime, a meeting) or at the end of the work.

8. Fill the lacunae of inspiration by tidily copying out what is already written. Intuition will awaken in the process.

9. *Nulla dies sine linea*—but there may well be weeks.

10. Consider no work perfect over which you have not once sat from evening to broad daylight.

11. Do not write the conclusion of a work in your familiar study. You would not find the necessary courage there.

12. Stages of composition: idea—style—writing. The value of the fair copy is that in producing it you confine attention to calligraphy. The idea kills inspiration, style fetters the idea, writing pays off style.

13. The work is the death mask of its conception.

ORDNANCE

I had arrived in Riga to visit a woman friend. Her house, the town, the language were unfamiliar to me. Nobody was expecting me, no one knew me. For two hours I walked the streets in solitude. Never again have I seen them so. From every gate a flame darted, each cornerstone sprayed sparks, and every streetcar came toward me like a fire engine. For she might have stepped out of the gateway, around the corner, been sitting in the streetcar. But of the two of us I had to be, at any price, the first to see the other. For had she touched me with the match of her eyes, I should have gone up like a magazine.

FIRST AID
A highly embroiled quarter, a network of streets that I had avoided for years, was disentangled at a single stroke when one day a person dear to me moved there. It was as if a searchlight set up at this person's window dissected the area with pencils of light.

INTERIOR DECORATION
The tract is an Arabic form. Its exterior is undifferentiated and unobtrusive, like the façades of Arabian buildings, the articulation of which begins only in the courtyard. So, too, the articulated structure of the tract is invisible from outside, revealing itself only from within. If it is formed by chapters, they have not verbal headings but numbers. The surface of its deliberations is not pictorially enlivened, but covered with unbroken, proliferating arabesques. In the ornamental density of this presentation the distinction between thematic and excursive expositions is abolished.

ANTIQUES
Medallion.   In everything that is with reason called beautiful, appearance has a paradoxical effect.

Fan. The following experience will be familiar: if one is in love, or just intensely preoccupied with another, his portrait will appear in almost every book. Moreover, he appears as both protagonist and antagonist. In stories, novels, and novellas he is encountered in endless metamorphoses. And from this it follows that the faculty of imagination is the gift of interpolating into the infinitely small, of inventing, for every intensity, an extensiveness to contain its new, compressed fullness, in short, of receiving each image as if it were that of the folded fan, which only in spreading draws breath and flourishes, in its new expanse, the beloved features within it.

Relief. One is with the woman one loves, speaks with her. Then, weeks or months later, separated from her, one thinks again of what was talked of then. And now the motif seems banal, tawdry, shallow, and one realizes that it was she alone, bending low over it with love, who shaded and sheltered it before us, so that the thought was alive in all its folds and crevices like a relief. Alone, as now, we see it lie flat, bereft of comfort and shadow, in the light of our knowledge.

LOST-PROPERTY OFFICE

Articles lost. What makes the very first glimpse of a village, a town, in the landscape so incomparable and irretrievable is the rigorous connection between foreground and distance. Habit has not yet done its work. As soon as we begin to find our bearings, the landscape vanishes at a stroke like the façade of a house as we enter it. It has not yet gained preponderance through a constant exploration that has become habit. Once we begin to find our way about, that earliest picture can never be restored.

Articles found. The blue distance that never gives way to foreground or dissolves at our approach, which is not revealed spread-eagle and long-winded when reached but only looms more compact and threatening, is the painted distance of a backdrop. It is what gives stage sets their incomparable atmosphere.

FIRE ALARM

The notion of the class war can be misleading. It does not refer to a trial of strength to decide the question "Who shall win, who be defeated?," or to a struggle the outcome of which is good for the victor and bad for the vanquished. To think in this way is to romanticize and obscure the facts. For whether the bourgeoisie wins or loses the fight, it remains doomed by the inner contradictions that in the course of development will become deadly. The only question is whether its downfall will come through itself or through the proletariat. The continuance or the end of three thousand years of cultural development will be decided by the answer. History knows nothing of the evil infinity contained in the image of the two wrestlers locked in eternal combat. The true politician reckons only in dates. And if the abolition of the bourgeoisie is not completed by an almost calculable moment in economic and technical development (a moment signaled by inflation and poison-gas warfare), all is lost. Before the spark reaches the dynamite, the lighted fuse must be cut. The interventions, dangers, and tempi of politicians are technical—not chivalrous.

TRAVEL SOUVENIRS

Atrani. The gently rising, curved baroque staircase leading to the church. The railing behind the church. The litanies of the old women at the "Ave Maria": preparing to die first-class. If you turn around, the church verges like God Himself on the sea. Each morning the Christian Era crumbles the rock, but between the walls below, the night falls always into the four old Roman quarters. Alleyways like air shafts. A well in the marketplace. In the late afternoon women about it. Then, in solitude: archaic plashing.

Navy. The beauty of the tall sailing ships is unique. Not only has their outline remained unchanged for centuries, but also they appear in the most immutable landscape: at sea, silhouetted against the horizon.

POLYCLINIC

The author lays his idea on the marble table of the café. Lengthy meditation, for he makes use of the time before the arrival of his glass, the lens through which he examines the patient. Then, deliberately, he unpacks his instruments: fountain pens, pencil, and pipe. The numerous clientele, arranged as in an amphitheater, make up his clinical audience. Coffee, carefully poured and consumed, puts the idea under chloroform. What this idea may be has no more connection with the matter at hand than the dream of an anesthetized patient with the surgical intervention. With the cautious lineaments of handwriting the operator makes incisions, displaces internal accents, cauterizes proliferations of words, inserts a foreign term as a silver rib. At last the whole is finely stitched together with punctuation, and he pays the waiter, his assistant, in cash.

THIS SPACE FOR RENT

Fools lament the decay of criticism. For its day is long past. Criticism is a matter of correct distancing. It was at home in a world where perspectives and prospects counted and where it was still possible to take a standpoint. Now things press too closely on human society. The "unclouded," "innocent" eye has become a lie, perhaps the whole naïve mode of expression sheer incompetence. Today the most real, the mercantile gaze into the heart of things is the advertisement. It abolishes the space where contemplation moved and all but hits us between the eyes with things as a car, growing to gigantic proportions, careens at us out of a film screen. And just as the film does not present furniture and façades in completed forms for critical inspection, their insistent, jerky nearness alone being sensational, the genuine advertisement hurtles things at us with the tempo of a good film. Thereby "matter-of-factness" is finally dispatched, and in face of the huge images across the walls of houses, where toothpaste and cosmetics lie handy for giants, sentimentality is restored to health and liberated in American style, just as people whom nothing moves or touches any longer are taught to cry again by films. For the man in the street, however, it is money that affects him in this way, brings him into perceived contact with things. And the paid critic, manipulating paintings in the dealer's exhibition room, knows more important if not better things about them than the art lover viewing them in the showroom window. The warmth of the subject is communicated to him, stirs sentient springs. What, in the end, makes advertisements so superior to criticism? Not what the moving red neon sign says—but the fiery pool reflecting it in the asphalt.

"AUGEAS" SELF-SERVICE RESTAURANT

This is the weightiest objection to the mode of life of the confirmed bachelor: he eats by himself. Taking food alone tends to make one hard and coarse. Those accustomed to it must lead a Spartan life if they are not to go downhill. Hermits have observed, if for only this reason, a frugal diet. For it is only in company that eating is done justice; food must be divided and distributed if it is to be well received. No matter by whom: formerly a beggar at the table enriched each banquet. The splitting up and giving are all-important, not sociable conversation. What is surprising, on the other hand, is that without food conviviality grows precarious. Playing host levels differences, binds together. The Count of Saint-Germain fasted before loaded tables, and by this alone dominated conversation. When all abstain, however, rivalries and conflict ensue.

TAX ADVICE

Beyond doubt: a secret connection exists between the measure of goods and the measure of life, which is to say, between money and time. The more trivial the content of a lifetime, the more fragmented, multifarious, and disparate are its moments, while the grand period characterizes a superior existence. Very aptly, Lichtenberg suggests that time whiled away should be seen as made smaller, rather than shorter, and he also observes, "A few dozen million minutes make up a life of forty-five years, and something more." When a currency is in use a few million units of which are insignificant, life will have to be counted in seconds, rather than years, if it is to appear a respectable sum. And it will be frittered away like a bundle of bank notes: Austria cannot break the habit of thinking in florins.

Money and rain belong together. The weather itself is an index of the state of this world. Bliss is cloudless, knows no weather. There also comes a cloudless realm of perfect goods, on which no money falls.

A descriptive analysis of bank notes is needed. The unlimited satirical force of such a book would be equaled only by its objectivity. For nowhere more naïvely than in these documents does capitalism display itself in solemn earnest. The innocent cupids frolicking about numbers, the goddesses holding tablets of the law, the stalwart heroes sheathing their swords before monetary units, are a world of their own: ornamenting the façade of hell. If Lichtenberg had found paper money in circulation, the plan of this work would not have escaped him.

LEGAL PROTECTION FOR THE NEEDY

Publisher: My expectations have been most rudely disappointed. Your work makes no impression on the public; you do not have the slightest pulling power. And I have not spared expenses. I have incurred advertising costs. You know how highly I think of you, despite all this. But you cannot hold it against me if even I now have to listen to my commercial conscience. If there is anyone who does what he can for authors, I am he. But, after all, I also have a wife and children to look after. I do not mean, of course, that I hold you accountable for the losses of the past years. But a bitter feeling of disappointment will remain. I regret that I am at present absolutely unable to support you further.

Author: Sir, why did you become a publisher? We shall have the answer by return mail. But permit me to say one thing in advance. I figure in your archive as number 27. You have published five of my books; in other words, you have put your money five times on number 27. I am sorry that number 27 did not prove a winner. Incidentally, you only took coupled bets. Only because I come next to your lucky number 28. Now you know why you became a publisher. You might just as well have entered an honest profession, like your esteemed father. But never a thought for the morrow—such is youth. Continue to indulge your habits. But avoid posing as an honest businessman. Do not feign innocence when you have gambled everything away; do not talk about your eight-hour working day, or the night when you hardly get any rest, either. "Truth and fidelity before all else, my child." And don't start making scenes with your numbers! Otherwise you will be bounced.

MADAME ARIANE—
SECOND COURTYARD ON THE LEFT
He who asks fortunetellers the future unwittingly forfeits an inner intimation of coming events that is a thousand times more exact than anything they may say. He is impelled by inertia, rather than curiosity, and nothing is more unlike the

submissive apathy with which he hears his fate revealed than the alert dexterity with which the man of courage lays hands on the future. For presence of mind is an extract of the future, and precise awareness of the present moment more decisive than foreknowledge of the most distant events. Omens, presentiments, signals pass day and night through our organism like wave impulses. To interpret them or to use them, that is the question. The two are irreconcilable. Cowardice and apathy counsel the former, lucidity and freedom the latter. For before such prophecy or warning has been mediated by word or image it has lost its vitality, the power to strike at our center and force us, we scarcely know how, to act accordingly. If we neglect to do so, and only then, the message is deciphered. We read it. But it is now too late. Hence, when you are taken unawares by an outbreak of fire or the news of a death, there is in the first mute shock a feeling of guilt, the indistinct reproach: did you really not know of this? Did not the dead person's name, the last time you uttered it, sound differently in your mouth? Do you not see in the flames a sign from yesterday evening, in a language you only now understand? And if an object dear to you has been lost, was there not, hours, days before, an aura of mockery or mourning about it that gave the secret away? Like ultraviolet rays memory shows to each man in the book of life a script that invisibly and prophetically glosses the text. But it is not with impunity that these intentions are exchanged, that unlived life is handed over to cards, spirits, stars, to be in an instant squandered, misused, and returned to us disfigured; we do not go unpunished for cheating the body of its power to meet the fates on its own ground and triumph. The moment is the Caudine Yoke beneath which fate must bow to the body. To turn the threatening future into a fulfilled now, the only desirable telepathic miracle, is a work of bodily presence of mind. Primitive epochs, when such demeanor was part of man's daily husbandry, provided him, in the naked body, with the most reliable instrument of divination. Even the ancients knew of this true practice, and Scipio, stumbling as he set foot on Carthaginian soil, cried out, spreading his arms wide as he fell, the watchword of victory, *"Teneo te, terra Africana!"* What would have become a portent of disaster he binds bodily to the moment, making himself the factotum of his body. In just such mastery the ancient ascetic exercises of fasting, chastity, and vigil have for all time celebrated their greatest victories. Each morning the day lies like a fresh shirt on our bed; this incomparably fine, incomparably tightly woven tissue of pure prediction fits us perfectly. The happiness of the next twenty-four hours depends on our ability, on waking, to pick it up.

COSTUME WARDROBE

A bearer of news of death appears to himself as very important. His feeling—even against all reason—makes him a messenger from the realm of the dead. For the community of all the dead is so immense that even he who only reports death is aware of it. *Ad plures ire* was the Latins' expression of dying.

At Bellinzona I noticed three priests in the station waiting room. They were sitting on a bench diagonally opposite mine. In rapt attention I observed the gestures of the one seated in the middle, who was distinguished from his brothers by a red skullcap. While he speaks to them, his hands are folded in his lap, and only now and then is one or the other very slightly raised and moved. I think to myself: his right hand must always know what the left is doing.

Is there anyone who has not once been stunned, emerging from the Métro into the open air, to step into brilliant sunlight? And yet the sun shone a few minutes earlier, when he went down, just as brightly. So quickly has he forgotten the weather of the upper world. And as quickly the world in its turn will forget him. For who can say more of his own existence than that it has passed through the lives of two or three others as gently and closely as the weather?

Again and again, in Shakespeare, in Calderón, battles fill the last act, and kings, princes, attendants and followers "enter, fleeing." The moment in which they become visible to spectators brings them to a standstill. The flight of the *dramatis personae* is arrested by the stage. Their entry into the visual field of nonparticipating and truly impartial persons allows the harassed to draw breath, bathes them in new air. The appearance on stage of those who enter "fleeing" takes from this its hidden meaning. Our reading of this formula is imbued with expectation of a place, a light, a footlight glare, in which our flight through life may be likewise sheltered in the presence of onlooking strangers.

BETTING OFFICE
Bourgeois existence is the regime of private affairs. The more important the nature and implications of a mode of behavior, the further removed it is from observation here. Political conviction, financial situation, religion—all these seek hideouts, and the family is the rotten, dismal edifice in whose closets and crannies the most ignominious instincts are deposited. Mundane life proclaims the total subjugation of eroticism to privacy. So wooing becomes a silent, dead-serious transaction between two persons alone, and this thoroughly private wooing, severed from all responsibility, is what is really new in "flirting." In contrast, the proletarian and the feudal type of men resemble each other in that in wooing it is much less the woman than their competitors that they overcome. In this they respect the woman far more deeply than in her freedom, being at her command without cross-examining her. The shift of erotic emphasis to the public sphere is both feudal and proletarian. To be seen with a woman on such-and-such an occasion can mean more than to sleep with her. Thus in marriage, too,

value does not lie in the sterile "harmony" of the partners: it is as the eccentric offshoot of their struggles and rivalries enacted elsewhere that, like the child, the spiritual force of marriage is manifest.

NO VAGRANTS!

All religions have honored the beggar. For he proves that in a matter at the same time as prosaic and holy, banal and regenerating as the giving of alms, intellect and morality, consistency and principles are miserably inadequate.

We deplore the beggars in the South, forgetting that their persistence in front of our noses is as justified as a scholar's before a difficult text. No shadow of hesitation, no slightest wish or deliberation in our faces escapes their notice. The telepathy of the coachman who, by accosting us, makes known to us our previously unsuspected inclination to board his vehicle, and of the shopkeeper who extracts from his junk the single chain or cameo that could delight us, is of the same order.

TO THE PLANETARIUM

If one had to expound the doctrine of antiquity with utmost brevity while standing on one leg, as did Hillel that of the Jews, it could only be in this sentence: "They alone shall possess the earth who live from the powers of the cosmos." Nothing distinguishes the ancient from the modern man so much as the former's absorption in a cosmic experience scarcely known to later periods. Its waning is marked by the flowering of astronomy at the beginning of the modern age. Kepler, Copernicus, and Tycho Brahe were certainly not driven by scientific impulses alone. All the same, the exclusive emphasis on an optical connection to the universe, to which astronomy very quickly led, contained a portent of what was to come. The ancients' intercourse with the cosmos had been different: the ecstatic trance. For it is in this experience alone that we gain certain knowledge of what is nearest to us and what is remotest to us, and never of one without the other. This means, however, that man can be in ecstatic contact with the cosmos only communally. It is the dangerous error of modern men to regard this experience as unimportant and avoidable, and to consign it to the individual as the poetic rapture of starry nights. It is not; its hour strikes again and again, and then neither nations nor generations can escape it, as was made terribly clear by the last war, which was an attempt at a new and unprecedented commingling with the cosmic powers. Human multitudes, gases, electrical forces were hurled into the open country, high-frequency currents coursed through the landsape, new constellations rose in the sky, aerial space and ocean depths thundered with propellers, and everywhere sacrificial shafts were dug in Mother Earth. This immense wooing of the cosmos was enacted for the first time on a planetary scale, that is, in the spirit of technology. But because the lust for profit of the ruling class sought satisfaction through it, technology betrayed man and turned the bridal bed into a bloodbath. The mastery of nature, so the imperialists teach, is the purpose of all technology. But who would trust a cane wielder who proclaimed the mastery of children by adults to be the purpose of education? Is not education above all the indispensable ordering of the relationship between generations and therefore mastery, if we are to use this term, of that relationship and not of children? And likewise technology is not the mastery of nature but of the relation between nature and man. Men as a species completed their development thousands of years ago; but mankind as a species is just beginning his. In technology a *physis* is being organized through which mankind's contact with the cosmos takes a new and different form from that which it had in nations and families. One need recall only the experience of velocities by virtue of which mankind is now preparing to embark on incalculable journeys into the interior of time, to encounter there rhythms from which

the sick shall draw strength as they did earlier on high mountains or at Southern seas. The "Lunaparks" are a prefigura-
tion of sanatoria. The paroxysm of genuine cosmic experience
is not tied to that tiny fragment of nature that we are accustomed to call "Nature." In the nights of annihilation of the
last war the frame of mankind was shaken by a feeling that
resembled the bliss of the epileptic. And the revolts that followed it were the first attempt of mankind to bring the new
body under its control. The power of the proletariat is the
measure of its convalescence. If it is not gripped to the very
marrow by the discipline of this power, no pacifist polemics
will save it. Living substance conquers the frenzy of destruction only in the ecstasy of procreation.

TWO

Moscow

————

1

More quickly than Moscow itself, one gets to know Berlin through Moscow. For someone returning home from Russia the city seems freshly washed. There is no dirt, but no snow, either. The streets seem in reality as desolately clean and swept as in the drawings of Grosz. And how true-to-life his types are has become more obvious. What is true of the image of the city and its people applies also to the intellectual situation: a new perspective of this is the most undoubted gain from a stay in Russia. However little one may know Russia, what one learns is to observe and judge Europe with the conscious knowledge of what is going on in Russia. This is the first benefit to the intelligent European in Russia. But, equally, this is why the stay is so exact a touchstone for foreigners. It obliges everyone to choose his standpoint. Admittedly, the only real guarantee of a correct understanding is to have chosen your position before you came. In Russia above all, you can only see if you have already decided. At the turning point in historical events that is indicated, if not constituted, by the fact of "Soviet Russia," the question at issue is not which reality is better, or which has greater potential. It is only: which reality is inwardly convergent with truth? Which truth is inwardly preparing itself to converge with the real? Only he who clearly answers these questions is "objective." Not toward his contemporaries (which is unimportant) but toward events (which is decisive). Only he who, by decision, has made his dialectical peace with the world can grasp the concrete. But someone who wishes to decide "on the basis of facts" will find no basis in the facts. Returning home, he will discover above all that Berlin is a deserted city. People and groups moving in its streets have solitude about them. Berlin's luxury seems unspeakable. And it begins on the asphalt, for the breadth of the pavements is princely. They make of the poorest wretch a *grand seigneur* promenading on the terrace of his mansion. Princely solitude, princely desolation hang over the streets of Berlin. Not only in the West End. In Moscow there are three or four places where it is possible to make headway without that strategy of shoving and weaving that one learns in the first week (at the same time, therefore, as the technique of achieving locomotion on sheet ice). Stepping onto the Stolechnikov one breathes again: here at last one may stop without compunction in front of shopwindows and go on one's way without partaking in the loitering, serpentine gait to which the narrow pavements have accustomed most people. But what fullness has this street that overflows not only with people, and how deserted and empty is Berlin! In Moscow goods burst everywhere from the houses, they hang on fences, lean against railings, lie on pavements. Every fifty steps stand women with cigarettes, women with fruit, women with sweets. They have their wares in a laundry basket next to them, sometimes a little sleigh as well. A brightly colored woolen cloth protects apples or oranges from the cold, with two prize examples lying on top. Next to them are sugar figures, nuts, candy. One thinks: before leaving her house a grandmother must have looked around to see what she could take to surprise her grandchildren. Now she had stopped on the way to have a short rest in the street. Berlin streets know no such places with sleighs, sacks, little carts, and baskets. Compared to those of Moscow, they are like a freshly swept, empty racecourse on which a field of six-day cyclists hastens comfortlessly on.

2

The city seems to deliver itself at the outset, at the station. Kiosks, arc lamps, buildings crystallize into figures that are never to return. Yet this is dispelled as soon as I seek words. I must be on my way. . . . At first there is nothing to be seen but snow, the dirty snow that has already installed itself, and the clean slowly moving up behind. The instant one arrives, the childhood stage begins. On the thick sheet ice of the streets walking has to be relearned. The jungle of houses is so impenetrable that only brilliance strikes the eye. A transparency with the inscription *"Kefir"* glows in the evening. I notice it as if the Tverskaia, the old road to Tver on which I now am, were really still the open road, with nothing to be seen far and wide except the plain. Before I discovered Moscow's real landscape, its real river, found its real heights, each thoroughfare became for me a contested river, each house number a trigonometric signal, and each of its gigantic squares a lake. For every step one takes here is on named ground. And where one of these names is heard, in a flash imagination builds a whole quarter about the sound. This will long defy the later reality and remain brittly embedded in it like glass masonry. In the first phase the city still has barriers at a hundred frontiers. Yet one day the gate, the church that were the boundary of a district become without warning its center. Now the city turns into a labyrinth for the newcomer. Streets that he had located far apart are yoked together by a corner like a pair of horses in a coachman's fist. The whole exciting sequence of topographical dummies that deceives him could only be shown by a film: the city is on its guard against him, masks itself, flees, intrigues, lures him to wander its circles to the point of exhaustion. (This could be approached in a very practical way; during the tourist season in great cities, "orientation films" would run for foreigners.) But in the end, maps and plans are victorious: in bed at night, imagination juggles with real buildings, parks, and streets.

3

Moscow in winter is a quiet city. The immense bustle on the streets takes place softly. This is because of the snow, but also because of the backwardness of the traffic. Car horns dominate the orchestra of great cities. But in Moscow there are only a few cars. They are used only for weddings and funerals and for accelerated government. True, in the evening they switch on brighter lights than are permitted in any other great city. And the cones of light they project are so dazzling that anyone caught in them stands helplessly rooted to the spot. In the blinding light before the Kremlin gate the guards stand in their brazen ocher furs. Above them shines the red signal that regulates the traffic passing through the gate. All the colors of Moscow converge prismatically here, at the center of Russian power. Beams of excessive brilliance from the car headlights race through the darkness. The horses of the cavalry, who have a large drill ground in the Kremlin, shy in their light. Pedestrians force their way between cars and unruly horses. Long rows of sleighs transport snow away. Single horsemen. Silent swarms of ravens have settled in the snow. The eye is infinitely busier than the ear. The colors do their utmost against the white. The smallest colored rag glows out of doors. Picture books lie in the snow; Chinese sell artfully made paper fans, and still more frequently, paper kites in the form of exotic deep-sea fish. Day in, day out, children's festivals are provided for. There are men with baskets full of wooden toys, carts and spades; the carts are yellow and red, yellow or red the children's shovels. All these carved wooden utensils are more simply and solidly made than in Germany, their peasant origin being clearly visible. One morning, at the side of the road stand tiny houses that have never been seen before, each with shining windows and a fence around the front garden: wooden toys from the Vladimir government. That is to say, a new consignment of goods has arrived. Serious, sober utensils become audacious in street trading. A basket seller with all kinds of brightly colored wares, such as can be bought everywhere in Capri, two-handled baskets with plain square patterns, carries at the end of his pole glazed-paper cages with glazed-paper birds inside them. But a real parrot, too, a white ara can sometimes be seen. In the Miasnitskaia stands a woman with linen goods, the bird perching on her tray or shoulder. A picturesque background for such animals must be sought elsewhere, at the photographer's stand. Under the bare trees of the boulevards are screens showing palms, marble staircases, and southern seas. And something else, too, reminds one of the South. It is the wild variety of the street trade. Shoe polish and writing materials, handkerchiefs, dolls' sleighs, swings for children, ladies' underwear, stuffed birds, clothes hangers—all this sprawls on the open street, as if it were not twenty-five degrees below zero but high Neapolitan summer. I was for a long time mystified by a man who had in front of him a densely lettered board. I wanted to see a soothsayer in him. At last I succeeded in watching him at work: I saw him sell two of his letters and fix them as initials to his customer's galoshes. Then the wide sleighs with three compartments for peanuts, hazelnuts, and *semitchky* (sunflower seeds, which now, according to a ruling of the Soviet, may no longer be chewed in public places). Cookshop owners gather in the neighborhood of the labor exchange. They have hot cakes to sell, and sausage fried in slices. But all this goes on silently; calls like those of every trader in the South are unknown. Rather, the people address the passer-by with words, measured if not whispered words, in which there is something of the humility of beggars. Only one caste parades noisily through the streets here, the rag-and-bone men with sacks on their backs; their melancholy cry rings one or more times a week in every quarter. Street trading is in part illegal and therefore avoids attracting attention. Women, each with a piece of meat, a chicken, or a leg of pork resting on a layer of straw in her open hand, stand offering it to passers-by. These are vendors without permits. They are too poor to pay the duty for a stall and have no time to stand in line many hours at an office for a weekly concession. When a member of the militia approaches, they simply run away. The street trade culminates in the large markets, on the Smolenskaia and the Arbat. And on the Sucharevskaia. This, the most famous of all, is situated at the foot of a church that rises with blue domes above the booths. First one passes the quarter of the scrap-iron dealers. The people simply have their wares lying in the snow. One finds old locks, meter rulers, hand tools, kitchen utensils, electrical goods. Repairs are carried out on the spot; I saw someone soldering over a pointed flame. There are no seats anywhere, everyone stands up, gossiping or trading. At this market the architectonic function of wares is perceptible: cloth and fabric form buttresses and columns; shoes, *valenki*, hanging threaded on strings across the counters, become the roof of the booth; large *garmoshkas* (accordions) form sounding walls, therefore in a sense Memnos walls. Whether, at the few stalls with pictures of saints, one can still secretly buy those strange icons that it was already punishable under tsarism to sell, I do not know. There was the Mother of God with three hands. She is half naked. From her navel rises a strong, well-formed hand. At right and left the two others spread in the gesture of blessing. This threesome of hands is deemed a symbol of the Holy Trinity. There was another devotional picture of the Mother of God that shows her with open belly; clouds come from it instead of entrails; in their midst dances the Christ child holding a violin in his hand. Since the sale of icons is considered a branch of the paper and picture trade, these booths with pictures of saints stand next to those with paper goods, so that they are always flanked by portraits of Lenin, like a prisoner between two policemen. The street life does not cease entirely even at night. In dark gateways you stumble against furs built like houses. Night watchmen huddle inside on chairs, from time to time bestirring themselves ponderously.

4

In the street scene of any proletarian quarter the children are important. They are more numerous there than in other districts, and move more purposefully and busily. Moscow swarms with children everywhere. Even among them there is a Communist hierarchy. The "Komsomoltsy," as the eldest, are at the top. They have their clubs in every town and are really trained as the next generation of the Party. The younger children become—at six—"Pioneers." They, too, are united in clubs, and wear a red tie as a proud distinction. *"Oktiabr"* ("Octobrists"), lastly—or "Wolves"—is the name given to little babies from the moment they are able to point to the picture of Lenin. But even now one also comes across the derelict, unspeakably melancholy *besprizornye,* war orphans. By day they are usually seen alone; each one on his own warpath. But in the evening they join up before the lurid façades of movie houses to form gangs, and foreigners are warned against meeting such bands alone when walking home. The only way for the educator to understand these thoroughly savage, mistrustful, embittered people was to go out on the street himself. In each of Moscow's districts, children's centers have been installed for years already. They are supervised by a female state employee who seldom has more than one assistant. Her task is, in one way or another, to make contact with the children of her district. Food is distributed, games are played. To begin with, twenty or thirty children come to the center, but if a superintendent does her work properly, it may be filled with hundreds of children after two weeks. Needless to say, traditional pedagogical methods never made much impression on these infantile masses. To get through to them at all, to be heard, one has to relate as directly and clearly as possible to the catchwords of the street itself, of the whole collective life. Politics, in the organization of crowds of such children, is not tendentious, but as natural a subject, as obvious a visual aid, as the toy shop or dollhouse for middle-class children. If one also bears in mind that a superintendent has to look after the children, to occupy and feed them, and in addition to keep a record of all expenses for milk, bread, and materials, that she is responsible for all this, it must become drastically clear how much room such work leaves for the private life of the person performing it. But amid all the images of childhood destitution that is still far from having been overcome, an attentive observer will perceive one thing: how the liberated pride of the proletariat is matched by the emancipated bearing of the children. Nothing is more pleasantly surprising on a visit to Moscow's museums than to see how, singly or in groups, sometimes around a guide, children and workers move easily through these rooms. Nothing is to be seen of the forlornness of the few proletarians who dare to show themselves to the other visitors in our museums. In Russia the proletariat has really begun to take possession of bourgeois culture, whereas on such occasions in our country they have the appearance of planning a burglary. Admittedly, there are collections in Moscow in which workers and children can quickly feel themselves at home. There is the Polytechnic Museum, with its many thousands of experiments, pieces of apparatus, documents, and models relating to the history of primary production and manufacturing industry. There is the admirably run toy museum, which under its director, Bartram, has brought together a precious, instructive collection of Russian toys, and serves the scholar as much as the children who walk about for hours in these rooms (about midday there is also a big, free puppet show, as fine as any in the Luxembourg). There is the famous Tretiakov Gallery in which one understands for the first time what genre painting means and how especially appropriate it is to the Russians. Here the proletarian finds subjects from the history of his movement: *A Conspirator Surprised by the Police, The Return from Exile in Siberia, The Poor Governess Enters Service in a Rich Merchant's House.* And the fact that such scenes are still painted entirely in the spirit of bourgeois art not only does no harm—it actually brings them closer to this public. For education in art (as Proust explains very well from time to time) is not best promoted by the contemplation of "masterpieces." Rather, the child or the proletarian who is educating himself rightly acknowledges very different works as masterpieces from those selected by the collector. Such pictures have for him a very transitory but solid meaning, and a strict criterion is necessary only with regard to the topical works that relate to him, his work, and his class.

5

Begging is not aggressive as in the South, where the importunity of the ragamuffin still betrays some remnant of vitality. Here it is a corporation of the dying. The street corners of some quarters are covered with bundles of rags—beds in the vast open-air hospital called Moscow. Long, beseeching speeches are addressed to people. There is one beggar who always begins, at the approach of a promising-looking passer-by, to emit a soft, drawn-out howling; this is directed at foreigners who cannot speak Russian. Another has the exact posture of the pauper for whom Saint Martin, in old pictures, cuts his cloak in two with his sword: he kneels with both arms outstretched. Shortly before Christmas, two children sat day after day in the snow against the wall of the Museum of the Revolution, covered with a scrap of material, and whimpering. (But outside the English Club, the most genteel in Moscow, to which this building earlier belonged, even that would not have been possible.) One ought to know Moscow as such beggar children know it. They know of a corner beside the door of a certain shop where, at a particular time, they are allowed to warm themselves for ten minutes, they know where one day each week at a certain hour they can fetch themselves crusts, and where a sleeping place among stacked sewage pipes is free. They have developed begging to a high art with a hundred schematisms and variations. They watch the customers of a pastry cook on a busy street corner, approach one, and accompany him, whining and pleading, until he has relinquished to them a piece of his hot pie. Others keep station at a streetcar terminus, board a vehicle, sing a song, and collect kopecks. And there are places, admittedly only a few, where even street trading has the appearance of begging. A few Mongols stand against the wall of

Kitai Gorod. One stands no more than five paces from the next, selling leather briefcases, each with exactly the same article as his neighbor. There must be some agreement behind this, for they cannot seriously intend such hopeless competition. Probably in their homeland the winter is no less harsh and their ragged furs are no worse than those of the natives. Nevertheless they are the only people in Moscow whom one pities on account of the climate. Even priests who go begging for their churches are still to be seen. But one very seldom sees anyone give. Begging has lost its strongest foundation, the bad social conscience, which opens purses so much wider than does pity. Beyond this it appears as an expression of the unchanging wretchedness of these beggars; perhaps, too, it is only the result of judicious organization that, of all the institutions of Moscow, they alone are dependable, remaining unchanged in their place while everything around them shifts.

6

Each thought, each day, each life lies here as on a laboratory table. And as if it were a metal from which an unknown substance is by every means to be extracted, it must endure experimentation to the point of exhaustion. No organism, no organization, can escape this process. Employees in their factories, offices in buildings, pieces of furniture in the apartments are rearranged, transferred, and shoved about. New ceremonies for christening and marriage are presented in the clubs as at research institutes. Regulations are changed from day to day, but streetcar stops migrate, too, shops turn into restaurants and a few weeks later into offices. This astonishing experimentation—it is here called *remonte*—affects not only Moscow, it is Russian. In this ruling passion there is as much naïve desire for improvement as there is boundless curiosity and playfulness. Few things are shaping Russia more powerfully today. The country is mobilized day and night, most of all, of course, the Party. Indeed, what distinguishes the Bolshevik, the Russian Commu-

nist, from his Western comrade is this unconditional readiness
for mobilization. The material basis of his existence is so
slender that he is prepared, year in, year out, to decamp. He
would not otherwise be a match for this life. Where else is it
conceivable that a distinguished military leader should one day
be made director of a great state theater? The present director
of the Theater of the Revolution is a former general. True: he
was a man of letters before he became a victorious commander.
Or in which other country can one hear stories like those told
me by the commissionaire of my hotel? Until 1924 he was employed in the Kremlin. Then one day he was afflicted by severe
sciatica. The Party had him treated by their best doctors, sent
him to the Crimea, had him take mud baths and try radiation
treatment. When all proved in vain he was told, "You need a
job in which you can look after yourself, keep warm, and not
move!" The next day he was a hotel porter. When he is cured
he will go back to the Kremlin. Ultimately, even the health of
comrades is a prized possession of the Party, which, against the
person's wishes if necessary, takes such measures as are needed
to conserve it. So it is presented, at any rate, in an excellent
novella by Boris Pilniak. Against his will a high official undergoes an operation that has a fatal outcome. (A very famous
name is mentioned here among the dead of the last few years.)
There is no knowledge and no faculty that are not somehow
appropriated by collective life and made to serve it. The specialist is a spearhead of this increasingly practical approach
and the only citizen who, outside the political sphere, has any
status. At times the respect for this type verges on fetishism.
Thus the red Military Academy employed as a teacher a general who is notorious for his part in the civil war. He had
every captured Bolshevik unceremoniously hanged. For Europeans such a point of view, which intransigently subordinates
the prestige of ideology to practical demands, is barely comprehensible. But this incident is also characteristic of the opposing
side. For it is not only the military of the tsarist empire who, as
is known, placed themselves at the service of the Bolsheviks.

Intellectuals, too, return in time as specialists to the posts they sabotaged during the civil war. Opposition, as we should like to imagine it in the West—intellectuals holding themselves aloof and languishing under the yoke—does not exist, or, better, no longer exists. It has—with whatever reservations— accepted the truce with the Bolsheviks, or it has been annihilated. There is in Russia—particularly outside the Party—only the most loyal opposition. For this new life weighs on no one more heavily than on the outsider observing from a distance. To endure this existence in idleness is impossible because, in each smallest detail, it becomes beautiful and comprehensible only through work. To the integration of personal thoughts with the pre-existing field of forces, with the mandate, however virtual, for organized, guaranteed contact with comrades—to this, life here is so tightly bound that anyone who abstains or cannot achieve it degenerates intellectually as if through years of solitary confinement.

7

Bolshevism has abolished private life. The bureaucracy, political activity, the press are so powerful that no time remains for interests that do not converge with them. Nor any space. Apartments that earlier accommodated single families in their five to eight rooms now often lodge eight. Through the hall door one steps into a little town. More often still, an army camp. Even in the lobby one can encounter beds. Indoors one only camps, and usually the scanty inventory is only a residue of petit-bourgeois possessions that have a far more depressing effect because the room is so sparsely furnished. An essential feature of the petit-bourgeois interior, however, was completeness: pictures must cover the walls, cushions the sofa, covers the cushions, ornaments fill the mantelpiece, colored glass the windows. (Such petit-bourgeois rooms are battlefields over which the attack of commodity capital has advanced victoriously; nothing human can flourish there again.) Of all that, only a part here or there has been indiscriminately preserved. Weekly the furniture in the bare rooms is rearranged—that is the only luxury indulged in with them, and at the same time a radical means of expelling "coziness," along with the melancholy with which it is paid for, from the house. People can bear to exist in it because they are estranged from it by their way of life. Their dwelling place is the office, the club, the street. Of the mobile army of officials only the baggage train is to be found here. Curtains and partitions, often only half the height of the walls, have had to multiply the number of rooms. For each citizen is entitled by law to only thirteen square meters of living space. For his accommodations he pays according to his income. The state—all house ownership is nationalized—charges the unemployed one ruble monthly for the same area for which the better-off pay sixty or more. Anyone who lays claim to more than this prescribed area must, if he cannot justify his claim professionally, make manifold amends. Every step away from the preordained path meets with an immeasurable bureaucratic apparatus and with impossible costs. The member of a trade union who produces a certificate of illness and goes through the prescribed channels can be admitted to the most modern sanatorium, sent to health resorts in the Crimea, can enjoy expensive radiation treatment, without paying a penny for it. The outsider can go begging and sink into penury if he is not in a position, as a member of the new bourgeoisie, to buy all this for thousands of rubles. Anything that cannot be based on the collective framework demands a disproportionate expenditure of effort. For this reason there is no "homeliness." But nor are there any cafés. Free trade and the free intellect have been abolished. The cafés are thereby deprived of their public. There remain, therefore, even for private affairs, only the office and the club. Here, however, transactions are under the aegis of the new *byt*—the new environment for which nothing counts except the function of the producer in the collective. The new Russians call *milieu* the only reliable educator.

8

For each citizen of Moscow the days are full to the brim. Meetings, committees are fixed at all hours in offices, clubs, factories, and often have no site of their own, being held in corners of noisy editorial rooms, at the cleared table of a canteen. There is a kind of natural selection and a struggle for existence between these meetings. Society projects them to some extent, plans them, they are convened. But how often must this be repeated until finally one of the many is successful, proves viable, is adapted, takes place. That nothing turns out as was intended and expected—this banal expression of the reality of life here asserts itself in each individual case so inviolably and intensely that Russian fatalism becomes comprehensible. If civilizing calculation slowly establishes itself in the collective, this will, in the first place, only complicate matters. (One is better provided for in a house that has only candles than where electric light is installed but the supply of current is interrupted hourly.) A feeling for the value of time, notwithstanding all "rationalization," is not met with even in the capital of Russia. "Trud," the trade-union institute for the study of work, under its director, Gastiev, launched a poster campaign for punctuality. From earliest times a large number of clockmakers have been settled in Moscow. They are crowded, in the manner of medieval guilds, in particular streets, on the Kuznetsky Bridge, on Ulitsa Gertsena. One wonders who actually needs them. "Time is money"—for this astonishing statement posters claim the authority of Lenin, so alien is the idea to the Russians. They fritter everything away. (One is tempted to say that minutes are a cheap liquor of which they can never get enough, that they are tipsy with time.) If on the street a scene is being shot for a film, they forget where they are going and why, and follow the camera for hours, arriving at the office distraught. In his use of time, therefore, the Russian will remain "Asiatic" longest of all. Once I needed to be wakened at seven in the morning: "Please knock tomorrow at seven." This elicited from the hotel porter the following Shakespearean monologue: "If we think of it we shall wake you, but if we do not think of it we shall not wake you. Actually we usually do think of it, and then we wake people. But to be sure, we also forget sometimes when we do not think of it. Then we do not wake people. We are under no obligation, of course, but if it crosses our mind, we do it. When do you want to be wakened? At seven? Then we shall write that down. You see, I am putting the message there where he will find it. Of course, if he does not find it, then he will not wake you. But usually we do wake people." The real unit of time is the *seichas*. That means "at once." You can hear it ten, twenty, thirty times, and wait hours, days, or weeks until the promise is carried out. Just as you seldom hear the answer "no." Negative replies are left to time. Time catastrophes, time collisions are therefore as much the order of the day as the *remonte*. They make each hour superabundant, each day exhausting, each life a moment.

9

Travel by streetcar in Moscow is above all a tactical experience. Here the newcomer learns perhaps most quickly of all to adapt himself to the curious tempo of this city and to the rhythm of its peasant population. And the complete interpenetration of technological and primitive modes of life, this world-historical experiment in the new Russia, is illustrated in miniature by a streetcar ride. The conductresses stand fur-wrapped at their places like Samoyed women on a sleigh. A tenacious shoving and barging during the boarding of a vehicle usually overloaded to the point of bursting takes place without a sound and with great cordiality. (I have never heard an angry word on these occasions.) Once everyone is inside, the migration begins in earnest. Through the ice-covered windows you can never make out where the vehicle has just stopped. If you do find out, it is of little avail. The way to the exit is blocked by a human wedge. Since you must board at the rear but alight at the front, you have to thread your way through this mass. However, conveyance usually occurs in batches; at important stops the vehicle is almost completely emptied. Thus even the traffic in Moscow is to a large extent a mass phenomenon. So one can encounter whole caravans of sleighs blocking the streets in a long row because loads that require a truck are being stacked on five or six large sleighs. The sleighs here take the horse into consideration first and then the passenger. They do not know the slightest superfluity. A feeding sack for the nags, a blanket for the passenger—and that is all. There is room for not more than two on the narrow bench, and as it has no back (unless you are willing so to describe a low rail), you must keep a good balance on sharp corners. Everything is based on the assumption of the highest velocity; long journeys in the cold are hard to bear and distances in this gigantic village immeasurable. The *izvozshchik* drives his vehicle close to the sidewalk. The passenger is not enthroned high up; he looks out on the same level as everyone else and brushes the passers-by with his sleeve. Even this is an incomparable experience for the sense of touch. Where Europeans, on their rapid journeys, enjoy superiority, dominance over the masses, the Muscovite in the little sleigh is closely mingled with people and things. If he has a box, a child, or a basket to take with him—for all this the sleigh is the cheapest means of transport—he is truly wedged into the street bustle. No condescending gaze: a tender, swift brushing along stones, people, and horses. You feel like a child gliding through the house on its little chair.

10

Christmas is a feast of the Russian forest. With pines, candles, tree decorations, it settles for many weeks in the streets, for

the advent of Greek Orthodox Christians overlaps the Christmas of those Russians who celebrate the feast by the Western,
that is the new, official calendar. Nowhere does one see Christmas trees more beautifully decorated. Little boats, birds, fishes,
houses, and fruit crowd the street stalls and shops, and every
year about this time the Kustarny Museum for Regional Art
holds a kind of trade fair for all this. At a crossroads I found
a woman selling tree decorations. The glass balls, yellow and
red, glinted in the sun; it was like an enchanted apple basket
in which red and yellow were divided among different fruit.
Pines are drawn through the streets on slow sleighs. The
smaller ones are trimmed only with silk bows; little pines
with blue, pink, and green ribbons stand on the corners. But
to the children the Christmas toys, even without a Santa Claus,
tell how they come from deep in the forests of Russia. It is as
if only under Russian hands does wood put forth such luxuri-
ant greenness. It turns green—and then reddens and puts on
a coat of gold, flares sky-blue and petrifies black. "Red" and
"beautiful" are in [old] Russian *one* word. Certainly the glowing logs in the stove are the most magical metamorphosis of
the Russian forest. Nowhere does the hearth seem to glow
with such splendor as here. But radiance is captured in all
the wood that the peasant carves and paints. And when var-
nished, it is fire frozen in all colors. Yellow and red on the
balalaika, black and green on the little *garmoshka* for children, and every shade in the thirty-six eggs that fit one inside
another. But forest night, too, lives in the wood. There are
the heavy little boxes with scarlet interiors: on the outside, on
a gleaming-black background, a picture. Under the tsars this
industry was on the point of extinction. Now, besides new
miniatures, the old, gold-embellished images are again emerging from peasant life. A *troika* with its three horses races
through the night, or a girl in a sea-blue dress stands at night
beside green flaring bushes, waiting for her lover. No night of
terror is as dark as this durable lacquer night in whose womb
all that appears in it is enfolded. I saw a box with a picture

of a seated woman selling cigarettes. Beside her stands a child who wants to take one. Pitch-black night here, too. But on the right a stone and on the left a leafless tree are discernible. On the woman's apron is the word *Mossel'prom*. She is the Soviet "Madonna with the Cigarettes."

11

Green is the supreme luxury of the Moscow winter. But it shines from the shop in the Petrovka not half as beautifully as the paper bunches of artificial carnations, roses, lilies on the street. In markets they are the only wares to have no fixed stall and appear now among groceries, now among textile goods and crockery stalls. But they outshine everything, raw meat, colored wool, and gleaming dishes. Other bouquets are seen at New Year's. On the Strastnaia Square I saw as I passed long twigs with red, white, blue, green blooms stuck to them, each stalk of a different color. When talking of Moscow flowers one must not forget the heroic Christmas roses, nor the gigantically tall hollyhock made of lampshades that the trader carries through the streets. Or the glass cases full of flowers with the heads of saints looking out among them. Nor what the frost here inspires, the peasant cloths with patterns, embroidered in blue wool, imitating ice ferns on windows. Finally, the glistening candy-icing flower beds on cakes. The Pastry Cook from children's fairy tales seems to have survived only in Moscow. Only here are there structures made of nothing but spun sugar, sweet icicles with which the tongue indemnifies itself against the bitter cold. Most intimately of all, snow and flowers are united in candy icing; there at last the marzipan flora seems to have fulfilled entirely Moscow's dream, to bloom out of whiteness.

12

Under capitalism power and money have become commensurable qualities. Any given amount of money may be converted into a specific power, and the market value of all power can be calculated. So things stand on a large scale. We can only speak of corruption where the process is handled too hastily. It has in the smooth interplay of press, boards, and trusts a switchgear within the limits of which it remains entirely legal. The Soviet state has severed this communication between money and power. It reserves power for the Party, and leaves money to the NEP man.* In the eyes of any Party functionary, even the highest, to put something aside, to secure the "future," even if only "for the children," is quite unthinkable. To its members the Communist Party guarantees the bare minimum for material existence—it does so practically, without actual obligation. On the other hand, it controls their further earnings and sets an upper limit of two hundred and fifty rubles on their monthly income. This can be increased solely through literary activity alongside one's profession. To such discipline the life of the ruling class is subjected. However, the power of the ruling authorities is by no means identical with their possessions. Russia is today not only a class but also a caste state. Caste state—that means that the social status of a citizen is determined not by the visible exterior of his existence—his clothes or living place—but exclusively by his relations to the Party. This is also decisive for those who do not directly belong to it. To them, too, jobs are open to the extent that they do not overtly repudiate the regime. Between them, too, the most precise distinctions are made. But however exaggerated—or obsolete—the European conception of the official suppression of nonconformists in Russia may on the one hand be, on the other, no one living abroad has any idea of the terrible social ostracism to which the NEP man is here subjected. The silence, the mistrust, perceptible not only between strangers, could not otherwise be explained. If you ask a superficial acquaintance here about his impressions of however unimportant a play, however trivial a film, you may expect stock phrases in reply: "We say

* NEP—New Economic Policy.—ED.

here..." or "The conviction is prevalent here..." A judgment is weighed innumerable times before being uttered to more distant contacts. For at any time the Party can casually, unobtrusively change its line in *Pravda,* and no one likes to see himself disavowed. Because a reliable political outlook, if not the only good, is for most people the only guarantee of other goods, everyone uses his name and his voice so cautiously that the citizen with a democratic turn of mind cannot understand him. Two close acquaintances are having a conversation. In the course of it one of them says: "That fellow Mikhailovich was in my office yesterday looking for a job. He said he knew you." "He is an excellent comrade, punctual and hardworking." They change the subject. But as they part the first says, "Would you be kind enough to give me a few words on that Mikhailovich in writing?" Class rule has adopted symbols that serve to characterize the opposing class. And of them jazz is perhaps the most popular. That people also enjoy listening to it in Russia is not surprising. But dancing to it is forbidden. It is kept behind glass, as it were, like a brightly colored, poisonous reptile, and so appears as an attraction in revues. Yet always a symbol of the "bourgeois." It is one of the crude stage sets with the aid of which, for propaganda purposes, a grotesque image of the bourgeois type is constructed. In reality the image is often merely ridiculous, the discipline and competence of the adversary being overlooked. In this distorted view of the bourgeois a nationalistic moment is present. Russia was the possession of the tsar (indeed, anyone walking past the endlessly piled-up valuables in the Kremlin collections is tempted to say, "*a* possession"). The people, however, have become overnight his immeasurably wealthy heirs. They now set about drawing up a grand inventory of their human and territorial wealth. And they undertake this work in the consciousness of having already performed unimaginably difficult tasks, and built up, against the hostility of half the world, the new system of power. In admiration for this national achievement all Russians are united. It is this reversal of the power structure that makes life here so heavy with content. It is as complete in itself and rich in events, as poor, and in the same breath as full of prospects, as a gold digger's life on the Klondike. From early till late people dig for power. All the combinations of our leading figures are meager in comparison to the countless constellations that here confront the individual in the course of a month. True, a certain intoxication can result, so that a life without meetings and committees, debates, resolutions, and votes (and all these are wars or at least maneuvers of the will to power) can no longer be imagined. What does it matter—Russia's next generation will be adjusted to this existence. Its health, however, is subject to one indispensable condition: that never (as one day happened even to the Church) should a black market of power be opened. Should the European correlation of power and money penetrate Russia, too, then perhaps not the country, perhaps not even the Party, but Communism in Russia would be lost. People here have not yet developed European consumer concepts and consumer needs. The reasons for this are above all economic. Yet it is possible that in addition an astute Party stratagem is involved: to equal the level of consumption in Western Europe, the trial by fire of the Bolshevik bureaucracy, at a freely chosen moment, steeled and with the absolute certainty of victory.

13

In the Red Army Club at the Kremlin, a map of Europe hangs on the wall. Beside it is a handle. When this handle is turned, the following is seen: one after the other, at all the places through which Lenin passed in the course of his life, little electric lights flash. At Simbirsk, where he was born, at Kazan, Petersburg, Geneva, Paris, Cracow, Zurich, Moscow, up to the place of his death, Gorki. Other towns are not marked. The contours of this wooden relief map are rectilinear, angular, schematic. On it Lenin's life resembles a cam-

paign of colonial conquest across Europe. Russia is beginning
to take shape for the man of the people. On the street, in the
snow, lie maps of the SFSR,* piled up by street vendors who
offer them for sale. Meyerhold uses a map in *D.E. (Here with
Europe!)*—on it the West is a complicated system of little
Russian peninsulas. The map is almost as close to becoming
the center of the new Russian iconic cult as Lenin's portrait.
Quite certainly the strong national feeling that Bolshevism
has given all Russians without distinction has conferred a new
reality on the map of Europe. They want to measure, compare, and perhaps enjoy that intoxication with grandeur
which is induced by the mere sight of Russia; citizens can only
be urgently advised to look at their country on the map of
neighboring states, to study Germany on a map of Poland,
France, or even Denmark; but all Europeans ought to see, on
a map of Russia, their little land as a frayed, nervous territory
far out to the west.

14

What figure does the man of letters cut in a country where
his employer is the proletariat? The theoreticians of Bolshevism stress how widely the situation of the proletariat in Russia after this successful revolution differs from that of the
bourgeoisie in 1789. At that time the victorious class, before
it attained power, had secured for itself in struggles lasting
decades the control of the cultural apparatus. Intellectual organization, education, had long been pervaded by the ideas
of the third estate, and the mental struggle for emancipation
was fought out before the political. In present-day Russia it
is quite different. For millions upon millions of illiterates, the
foundations of a general education have yet to be laid. This
is a national, Russian task. Prerevolutionary education in Russia was, however, entirely unspecific, European. The European

* Soviet Federated Socialist Republic.—ED.

moment in higher education, and the national on the elementary level, are in Russia seeking an accommodation. That is one side of the educational question. On the other the victory of the Revolution has in many areas accelerated the process of Europeanization. There are writers like Pilniak who see in Bolshevism the crowning of the work of Peter the Great. In the technical area this tendency, despite all the adventures of its earliest years, is presumably sure of victory sooner or later. Not so in the intellectual and scientific areas. It is now apparent in Russia that European values are being popularized in just the distorted, desolating form that they owe finally to imperialism. The second academic theater—a state-supported institution—is putting on a performance of the *Oresteia* in which a dusty antiquity struts about the stage as untruthfully as in a German Court theater. And as the marble-stiff gesture is not only corrupt in itself, but also a copy of Court acting in revolutionary Moscow, it has a still more melancholy effect than in Stuttgart or Anhalt. The Russian Academy of Science has for its part made a man like Walzel—an average specimen of the modern academic *bel esprit*—a member. Probably the only cultural conditions in the West for which Russia has a lively enough understanding for disagreement with it to be profitable, are those of America. In contrast, cultural *rapprochement* as such (without the foundation of the most concrete economic and political community) is an interest of the pacifist variety of imperialism, benefits only gossiping busybodies, and is for Russia a symptom of restoration. The country is isolated from the West less by frontiers and censorship than by the intensity of an existence that is beyond all comparison with the European. Stated more precisely: contact with the outside world is through the Party and primarily concerns political questions. The old bourgeoisie has been annihilated; the new is neither materially nor intellectually in a position to establish external relations. Undoubtedly Russians know far less about the outside world than foreigners (with the possible exception of the Romantic countries) know about Russia. If an influential Russian mentions Proust and Bronnen in the same breath as authors who take their subject matter from the area of sexual problems, this shows clearly the foreshortened perspective in which European matters appear from here. But if one of Russia's leading authors, in conversation, quotes Shakespeare as one of the great poets who wrote before the invention of printing, such a lack of training can only be understood from the completely changed conditions affecting Russian writing as a whole. Theses and dogmas that in Europe—admittedly only for the last two centuries—have been regarded as alien to art and beneath discussion by men of letters are decisive in literary criticism and production in the new Russia. Message and subject matter are declared of primary importance. Formal controversies still played a not inconsiderable part at the time of the civil war. Now they have fallen silent. Today it is official doctrine that subject matter, not form, decides the revolutionary or counterrevolutionary attitude of a work. Such doctrines cut the ground from under the writer's feet just as irrevocably as the economy has done on the material plane. In this Russia is ahead of Western developments—but not as far ahead as is believed. For sooner or later, with the middle classes who are being ground to pieces by the struggle between capital and labor, the "freelance" writer must also disappear. In Russia the process is complete: the intellectual is above all a functionary, working in the departments of censorship, justice, finance, and, if he survives, participating in work—which, however, in Russia means power. He is a member of the ruling class. Of his various organizations the most prominent is the general association of proletarian writers in Russia. It supports the notion of dictatorship even in the field of intellectual creation. In this it takes account of Russian reality. The transfer of the mental means of production into public ownership can be distinguished only fictitiously from that of the material means. To begin with, the proletarian can be trained in the use of both only under the protection of dictatorship.

15

Now and again one comes across streetcars painted all over with pictures of factories, mass meetings, red regiments, Communist agitators. These are gifts from the personnel of a factory to the Moscow Soviet. These vehicles carry the only political posters still to be seen in Moscow, but they are by far the most interesting. For nowhere are more naïve commercial posters to be seen than here. The wretched level of pictorial advertising is the only similarity between Paris and Moscow. Countless walls around churches and monasteries offer on all sides the finest surfaces for posters. But the constructivists, suprematists, abstractivists who under wartime Communism put their graphic propaganda at the service of the Revolution have long since been dismissed. Today only banal clarity is demanded. Most of these posters repel the Westerner. But Moscow shops are inviting; they have something of the tavern about them. The shop signs point at right angles into the street, as otherwise only old inn signs do, or golden barbers' basins, or a top hat before a hatter's. Also, the last charming, unspoiled motifs that remain are most likely to be found here. Shoes falling out of a basket; a Pomeranian running away with a sandal in his mouth. Pendants before the entrance of a Turkish kitchen: gentlemen, each with a fez adorning his head and each at his own little table. Catering to a primitive taste, advertising is still tied to narrative, example, or anecdote. In contrast, the Western advertisement convinces first and foremost by the expense of which it shows the firm capable. Here almost every ad also specifies the commodity in question. The grand, showy device is alien to commerce. The city, so inventive in abbreviations of all kinds, does not yet possess the simplest—brand names. Often Moscow's evening sky glows in frightening blue: one has unwittingly looked at it through one of the gigantic pairs of blue spectacles that project from opticians' shops like signposts. From the gateways, on the frames of front doors, in black, blue, yellow, and red letters of varying sizes—as an arrow, a picture of boots or freshly-ironed washing, a worn step or a solid staircase—a silently determined, contentious life accosts the passer-by. One must ride through the streets on the streetcar to perceive how this struggle is continued upward through the various stories, finally to reach its decisive phase on the roof. That height only the strongest, youngest slogans and signs attain. Only from an airplane does one have a view of the industrial élite of the city, the film and automobile industries. Mostly, however, the roofs of Moscow are a lifeless wasteland, having neither the dazzling electric signs of Berlin, nor the forest of chimneys of Paris, nor the sunny solitude of the rooftops of great cities in the South.

16

Anyone entering a Russian classroom for the first time will stop short in surprise. The walls are crammed with pictures, drawings, and pasteboard models. They are temple walls to which the children daily donate their own work as gifts to the collective. Red predominates; they are pervaded by Soviet emblems and heads of Lenin. Something similar is to be seen in many clubs. Wall newspapers are for grownups schemata of the same collective form of expression. They came into being under the pressure of the civil war, when in many places neither newspaper nor printing ink was available. Today they are an obligatory part of the public life of factories. Every Lenin niche has its wall newspaper, which varies its style among factories and authors. The only thing common to all is the naïve cheerfulness: colorful pictures interspersed with prose and verses. The newspaper is the chronicle of the collective. It gives statistical reports but also jocular criticism of comrades mingled with suggestions for improving the factory or appeals for communal aid. Notices, warning signs, and didactic pictures cover the walls of the Lenin niche elsewhere, too. Even inside a factory everyone is as if surrounded by

colored posters all exorcising the terrors of the machine. One
worker is portrayed with his arm forced between the spokes
of a driving wheel, another, drunk, causing an explosion with
a short circuit, a third with his knee caught between two
pistons. In the lending room of the Red Army bookshop hangs
a notice, its short text clarified by many charming drawings,
showing how many ways there are of ruining a book. In hundreds of thousands of copies a poster introducing the weights
and measures normal in Europe is disseminated throughout
the whole of Russia. Meters, liters, kilograms, etc., must be
stuck up in every pub. In the reading room of the peasant
club on Trubnaia Square the walls are covered with visual
aids. The village chronicle, agricultural development, production technique, cultural institutions are graphically recorded
in lines of development, along with components of tools,
machine parts, retorts containing chemicals displayed everywhere on the walls. Out of curiosity I went up to a shelf from
which two Negro faces grimaced at me. But as I came nearer,
they turned out to be gas masks. Earlier, the building occupied
by this club was one of the leading restaurants in Moscow.
The erstwhile *séparées* are today bedrooms for the peasants of
both sexes who have received a *komandirovka* to visit the city.
There they are conducted through collections and barracks,
and attend courses and educational evenings. From time to
time there is also pedagogical theater in the form of "legal
proceedings." About three hundred people, sitting and standing, fill the red-draped room to its farthest corners. In a niche
a bust of Lenin. The proceedings take place on a stage in
front of which, on the right and the left, painted proletarian
types—a peasant and an industrial worker—symbolize the
smychka, the clasping together of town and country. The hearing of evidence has just finished, an expert is called on to
speak. He and his assistant have one table, opposite him is
the table of the defense, both facing sideways to the public.
In the background, frontally, the judge's table. Before it,
dressed in black, with a thick branch in her hand, sits the

defendant, a peasant woman. She is accused of medical incompetence with fatal results. Through incorrect treatment she caused the death of a woman in childbirth. The argumentation now circles around this case in monotonous, simple trains of thought. The expert gives his report: to blame for the mother's death was the incorrect treatment. The defense counsel, however, pleads against harshness; in the country there is a lack of sanitary aid and hygienic instruction. The final word of the defendant: *nichevo,* people have always died in childbirth. The prosecution demands the death penalty. Then the presiding judge turns to the assembly: Are there any questions? But only a Komsomol appears on the stage, to demand severe punishment. The court retires to deliberate. After a short pause comes the judgment, for which everyone stands up: two years' imprisonment with recognition of mitigating circumstances. Solitary confinement is thus ruled out. In conclusion, the president points to the necessity of establishing centers of hygiene and instruction in rural areas. Such demonstrations are carefully prepared; there can be no question of improvisation. For mobilizing the public on questions of Bolshevik morality in accordance with Party wishes there can be no more effective means. On one occasion, alcoholism will be disposed of in this way, on others fraud, prostitution, hooliganism. The austere forms of such educational work are entirely appropriate to Soviet life, being precipitates of an existence that requires that a stand be taken a hundred times each day.

17

In the streets of Moscow there is a curious state of affairs: the Russian village is playing hide-and-seek in them. If you step through one of the high gateways—they often have wrought-iron gates, but I never found them closed—you stand on the threshold of a spacious settlement. Opening before you, broad and expansive, is a farmyard or a village, the ground is uneven, children ride about in sleighs, sheds for wood and tools fill the corners, trees stand here and there, wooden staircases give the backs of houses, which look like city buildings from the front, the appearance of Russian farmhouses. Frequently churches stand in these yards, just as on a large village green. So the street is augmented by the dimension of landscape. Nor is there any Western city that, in its vast squares, looks so rurally formless and perpetually sodden from bad weather, thawing snow or rain. Scarcely one of these broad spaces bears a monument. (In contrast, there is hardly one in Europe whose secret structure was not profaned and destroyed by a monument in the nineteenth century.) Like every other city, Moscow builds up with names a little world within itself. There is a casino called Alcazar, a hotel named Liverpool, a Tirol boardinghouse. From there it still takes half an hour to reach the centers of urban winter sport. True, skaters and skiers are encountered throughout the city, but the toboggan track is closer to the center. There sleighs of the most diverse construction are used: from a board that runs at the front on sleigh rails and at the back drags in the snow, to the most comfortable bobsleds. Nowhere does Moscow look like the city itself; at the most it resembles its outskirts. The wet ground, the wooden booths, long convoys carrying raw materials, cattle being driven to the slaughterhouse, and indigent taverns are found in the busiest parts. The city is still interspersed with little wooden buildings in exactly the same Slavonic style as those found everywhere in the surroundings of Berlin. What looks so desolate in Brandenburg stone attracts here with the lovely colors of warm wood. In the suburban streets leading off the broad avenues, peasant huts alternate with *art-nouveau* villas or with the sober façades of eight-story blocks. Snow lies deep, and if all of a sudden silence falls, one can believe oneself in a village in midwinter, deep in the Russian interior. Nostalgia for Moscow is engendered not only by the snow, with its starry luster by night and its flowerlike crystals by day, but also by the sky. For between low roofs the horizon of the broad plains is constantly entering the city. Only toward evening does it become invisible. But then the shortage of housing in Moscow produces its most astonishing effect. If you wander the streets in the dusk you see in the large and small houses almost every window brightly lit. If the light coming from them were not so unsteady, you would believe you had a festive illumination before your eyes.

18

The churches are almost mute. The city is as good as free of the chimes that on Sundays spread such deep melancholy over our cities. But there is still perhaps not a single spot in Moscow from which at least *one* church is not visible. More exactly: at which one is not watched by at least *one* church. The subject of the tsars was surrounded in this city by more than four hundred chapels and churches, which is to say by two thousand domes, which hide in the corners everywhere, cover one another, spy over walls. An architectural *okhrana* was around him. All these churches preserve their incognito. Nowhere do high towers jut into the sky. Only with time does one become accustomed to putting together the long walls and crowds of low domes into complexes of monastery churches. It then also becomes clear why in many places Moscow looks as tightly sealed as a fortress. The monasteries still bear traces today of their old defensive purpose. Here Byzantium with its thousand domes is not the wonder that the European dreams it to be. Most of the churches are built on an insipid, sickly-sweet pattern: their blue, green, and golden domes are a candied Orient. If you enter one of these churches you first find a spacious anteroom with a few sparse portraits of saints. It is gloomy, the half-light lending itself to conspiracy. In such rooms one can discuss the most dubious business, even pogroms if the occasion demands. Adjoining the anteroom is the only room for worship. In the background it has a few small steps leading to a narrow, low platform along which one advances past pictures of saints to the iconostasis. At short intervals, altar succeeds altar, a glimmering red light denoting each. The side walls are occupied by large pictures of saints. All parts of the wall that are not thus covered with pictures are lined with shining gold-colored tin plate. From the trashily painted ceiling hangs a crystal chandelier. Nevertheless the room is always lit only by candles, a drawing room with sanctified walls against which the ceremony unrolls. The large pictures are greeted by making the sign of the cross and kneeling down to touch the ground with the forehead; then, with renewed signs of the cross, the worshiper, praying or doing penance, goes on to the next. Before small, glass-covered pictures lying in rows or singly on desks the genuflection is omitted. One bends over them and kisses the glass. On such desks, beside the most precious old icons, series of the gaudiest oil paintings are displayed. Many pictures of saints have taken up positions outside on the façade and look down from the highest cornices under the tinny eaves like birds sheltering there. From their inclined, retort-shaped heads affliction speaks. Byzantium seems to have no church-window form of its own. A magical but uncanny impression: the profane, drab windows looking out onto the street from the assembly rooms and towers of the church as if from a living room. Behind them the Orthodox priest is ensconced like the Buddhist monk in his pagoda. The lower part of the Basilius Cathedral might be the ground floor of a fine boyar house. However, if you enter Red Square from the west, its domes gradually rise into the sky like a pack of fiery suns. This building always holds something back, and could only be surprised by a gaze coming from an airplane, against which the builders forgot to take precautions. The inside has been not just emptied but evis-cerated like a shot deer. (And it could hardly have turned out differently, for even in 1920 people still prayed here with fanatical fervor.) With the removal of all the furniture, the colorful vegetal convolutions that proliferate as murals in all the corridors and vaults are hopelessly exposed, distorting with a sad rococo playfulness the much older decoration that sparingly preserves in the interior the memory of the colorful spirals of the domes. The vaulted passageways are narrow, suddenly broadening into altar niches or circular chapels into which so little light falls from the high windows above that isolated devotional objects that have been left standing are scarcely discernible. Many churches remain as untended and as empty. But the glow that now shines only occasionally from the altars into the snow has been well preserved in the wooden cities of booths. In their snow-covered, narrow alleyways it is quiet. One hears only the soft jargon of the Jewish clothiers in their stalls next to the junk of the paper dealer, who, enthroned in concealment behind silver chains, has drawn tinsel and cotton-wool-tufted Father Christmases across her face like an oriental veil.

19

Even the most laborious Moscow weekday has two coordinates that define each of its moments sensuously as expectation and fulfillment. One is the vertical coordinate of mealtimes, crossed by the evening horizontal of the theater. One is never very far from either. Moscow is crammed with pubs and theaters. Sentries with sweets patrol the street, many of the large grocery stores do not close until about eleven at night, and on the corners tearooms and beerhouses open. *Chainaia, pivnaia*—but usually both are painted on a background where a dull green from the upper edge gradually and sullenly merges into a dirty yellow. Beer is served with curious condiments: tiny pieces of dried white and black bread baked over with a salt crust, and dried peas in salt water. In certain taverns one can dine in this way and enjoy in addition a primitive *intsenirovka*. This is the term for an epic or lyrical subject that has been adapted for the theater. It is often a folk song crudely divided for a choir. In the orchestra of such folk music, alongside accordions and violins, abacuses used as instruments are sometimes to be heard. (They can be found in every shop and office. The smallest calculation is unthinkable without them.) The intoxicating warmth that overcomes the guest on entering these taverns, on drinking the hot tea and enjoying the sharp *zakuska*, is Moscow's most secret winter lust. Therefore no one knows the city who has not known it in snow. Or each district must be visited during the season in which its climatic extreme falls, for to this it is primarily adapted, and it can be understood only through this adaptation. In Moscow, life in winter is richer by a dimension. Space literally changes according to whether it is hot or cold. People live on the street as if in a frosty chamber of mirrors, each pause to think is unbelievably difficult. It needs half a day's resolution even to mail an already addressed letter, and despite the severe cold it is a feat of will power to go into a shop and buy something. Yet when you have finally found a restaurant, no matter what is put on the table—vodka (which is here spiced with herbs), cakes, or a cup of tea—warmth makes the passing time itself an intoxicant. It flows into the weary guest like honey.

20

On the anniversary of Lenin's death many wear black arm bands. For at least three days, flags throughout the city are at half-mast. Many of the black-veiled pennants, however, once hanging, are left out for a few weeks. Russia's mourning for a dead leader is certainly not comparable to the attitudes adopted by other peoples on such days. The generation that was active in the civil wars is growing old in vitality if not in years. It is as if stabilization had admitted to their lives the calm, sometimes even the apathy, that is usually brought only by old age. The halt the Party one day called to wartime Communism with the NEP had a terrible backlash, which felled many of the movement's fighters. At that time many returned their membership books to the Party. Cases are known of such total demoralization that trusty pillars of the Party became defrauders within a few weeks. The mourning for Lenin is, for Bolsheviks, also mourning for heroic Communism. The few years since its passing are for Russian consciousness a long time. Lenin's activity so accelerated the course of events in his era that he recedes swiftly into the past, his image grows quickly remote. Nevertheless, in the optic of history—opposite in this to that of space—movement in the distance means enlargement. Today other orders are in force than those of Lenin's time, admittedly slogans that he himself suggested. Now it is made clear to every Communist that the revolutionary work of this hour is not conflict, not civil war, but canal construction, electrification, and factory building. The revolutionary nature of true technology is emphasized ever more clearly. Like everything else, this (with reason) is done in Lenin's name. His name grows and grows. It is significant that the report of the English trade-union delegation, a sober document sparing with prognoses, thought it worth mentioning the possibility "that, when the memory of Lenin has found its place in history, this great Russian revolutionary reformer will even be pronounced a saint." Even today the cult of his picture has assumed immeasurable proportions. It hangs in the vestibule of the armory in the Kremlin, as in formerly godless places the cross was erected by converted heathens. It is also gradually establishing its canonical forms. The well-known picture of the orator is the most common, yet another speaks perhaps more intensely and directly: Lenin at a table bent over a copy of *Pravda*. When he is thus immersed in an ephemeral newspaper, the dialectical tension of his nature appears: his gaze turned, certainly, to the far horizon, but the tireless care of his heart to the moment.

Marseilles

The street...the only valid field of experience.
—*André Breton*

Marseilles—the yellow-studded maw of a seal with salt water running out between the teeth. When this gullet opens to catch the black and brown proletarian bodies thrown to it by ship's companies according to their timetables, it exhales a stink of oil, urine, and printer's ink. This comes from the tartar baking hard on the massive jaws: newspaper kiosks, lavatories, and oyster stalls. The harbor people are a bacillus culture, the porters and whores products of decomposition with a resemblance to human beings. But the palate itself is pink, which is the color of shame here, of poverty. Hunchbacks wear it, and beggarwomen. And the discolored women of rue Bouterie are given their only tint by the sole pieces of clothing they wear: pink shifts.

"*Les bricks*," the red-light district is called, after the barges moored a hundred paces away at the jetty of the old harbor. A vast agglomeration of steps, arches, bridges, turrets, and cellars. It seems to be still awaiting its designated use, but it already has it. For this depot of worn-out alleyways is the prostitutes' quarter. Invisible lines divide the area up into sharp, angular territories like African colonies. The whores are strategically placed, ready at a sign to encircle hesitant visitors, and to bounce the reluctant guest like a ball from one side of the street to the other. If he forfeits nothing else in this game, it is his hat. Has anyone yet probed deeply enough into this refuse heap of houses to reach the innermost place

in the gynaeceum, the chamber where the trophies of manhood—boaters, bowlers, hunting hats, trilbies, jockey caps—
hang in rows on consoles or in layers on racks? From the interiors of taverns the eye meets the sea. Thus the alleyway
passes between rows of innocent houses as if shielded by a
bashful hand from the harbor. On this bashful, dripping hand,
however, shines a signet ring on a fishwife's hard finger, the
old Hôtel de Ville. Here, two hundred years ago, stood pa-
tricians' houses. The high-breasted nymphs, the snake-ringed
Medusa's heads over their weather-beaten doorframes have
only now become unambiguously the signs of a professional
guild. Unless, that is, signboards were hung over them as the
midwife Bianchamori has hung hers, on which, leaning against
a pillar, she turns a defiant face to all the brothel keepers of
the quarter, and points unruffled to a sturdy baby in the act
of emerging from an egg.

Noises. High in the empty streets of the harbor district they
are as densely and loosely clustered as butterflies on a hot
flower bed. Every step stirs a song, a quarrel, a flapping of wet
linen, a rattling of boards, a baby's bawling, a clatter of
buckets. Only you have to have strayed up here alone, if you
are to pursue them with a net as they flutter away unsteadily
into the stillness. For in these deserted corners all sounds and
things still have their own silences, just as, at midday in the
mountains, there is a silence of hens, of the ax, of the cicadas.
But the chase is dangerous, and the net is finally torn when,
like a gigantic hornet, a grindstone impales it from behind
with its whizzing sting.

Notre Dame de la Garde. The hill from which she looks down
is the starry garment of the Mother of God, into which the
houses of the Cité Chabas snuggle. At night, the lamps in its
velvet lining form constellations that have not yet been named.
It has a zipper: the cabin at the foot of the steel band of the
rack railway is a jewel, from the colored bull's-eyes of which

the world shines back. A disused fortress is her holy footstool, and about her neck is an oval of waxen, glazed votive wreaths that look like relief profiles of her forebears. Little chains of streamers and sails are her earrings, and from the shady lips of the crypt issues jewelry of ruby-red and golden spheres on which swarms of pilgrims hang like flies.

Cathedral. On the least frequented, sunniest square stands the cathedral. This place is deserted, despite the proximity at its feet of La Joliette, the harbor, to the south, and a proletarian district to the north. As a reloading point for intangible, unfathomable goods, the bleak building stands between quay and warehouse. Nearly forty years were spent on it. But when all was complete, in 1893, place and time had conspired victoriously in this monument against its architects and sponsors, and the wealth of the clergy had given rise to a gigantic railway station that could never be opened to traffic. The façade gives an indication of the waiting rooms within, where passengers of the first to fourth classes (though before God they are all equal), wedged among their spiritual possessions as between cases, sit reading hymnbooks that, with their concordances and cross references, look very much like international timetables. Extracts from the railway traffic regulations in the form of pastoral letters hang on the walls, tariffs for the discount on special trips in Satan's luxury train are consulted, and cabinets where the long-distance traveler can discreetly wash are kept in readiness as confessionals. This is the Marseilles religion station. Sleeping cars to eternity depart from here at Mass times.

The light from greengroceries that is in the paintings of Monticelli comes from the inner streets of his city, the monotonous residential quarters of the long-standing inhabitants, who know something of the sadness of Marseilles. For childhood is the divining rod of melancholy, and to know the mourning of such radiant, glorious cities one must have been

a child in them. The gray houses of the Boulevard de Long-
champs, the barred windows of the Cours Puget, and the trees
of the Allée de Meilhan give nothing away to the traveler if
chance does not lead him to the cubiculum of the city, the
Passage de Lorette, the narrow yard where, in the sleepy
presence of a few women and men, the whole world shrinks
to a single Sunday afternoon. A real-estate company has carved
its name on the gateway. Does not this interior correspond
exactly to the white mystery ship moored in the harbor,
Nautique, which never puts to sea, but daily feeds foreigners
at white tables with dishes that are much too clean and as if
surgically rinsed?

Shellfish and oyster stalls. Unfathomable wetness that swills
from the upper tier, in a dirty, cleansing flood over dirty
planks and warty mountains of pink shellfish, bubbles between the thighs and bellies of glazed Buddhas, past yellow
domes of lemons, into the marshland of cresses and through
the woods of French pennants, finally to irrigate the palate
as the best sauce for the quivering creatures. *Oursins de l'Es-
taque, Portugaises, Maremmes, Clovisses, Moules marinières—*
all this is incessantly sieved, grouped, counted, cracked open,
thrown away, prepared, tasted. And the slow, stupid agent of
inland trade, paper, has no place in the unfettered element,
the breakers of foaming lips that forever surge against the
streaming steps. But over there, on the other quay, stretches
the mountain range of "souvenirs," the mineral hereafter of
sea shells. Seismic forces have thrown up this massif of paste
jewelry, shell limestone, and enamel, where inkpots, steamers,
anchors, mercury columns, and sirens commingle. The pressure of a thousand atmospheres under which this world of
imagery writhes, rears, piles up, is the same force that is tested
in the hard hands of seamen, after long voyages, on the thighs
and breasts of women, and the lust that, on the shell-covered
caskets, presses from the mineral world a red or blue velvet

heart to be pierced with needles and brooches, is the same that
sends tremors through these streets on paydays.

Walls. Admirable, the discipline to which they are subject in
this city. The better ones, in the center, wear livery and are
in the pay of the ruling class. They are covered with gaudy
patterns and have sold their whole length many hundreds of
times to the latest brand of apéritif, to department stores, to
the "Chocolat Menier," or Dolores del Rio. In the poorer
quarters they are politically mobilized and post their spacious
red letters as the forerunners of red guards in front of dock-
yards and arsenals.

The down-and-out who, after nightfall, sells his books on the
corner of rue de la République and the Vieux Port, awakens
bad instincts in the passers-by. They feel tempted to make use
of so much fresh misery. And they long to learn more about
such nameless misfortune than the mere image of catastrophe
that it presents to us. For what extremity must have brought
a man to tip such books as he has left on the asphalt before
him, and to hope that a passer-by will be seized at this late
hour by a desire to read? Or is it all quite different? And does
a poor soul here keep vigil, mutely beseeching us to lift the
treasure from the ruins? We hasten by. But we shall falter
again at every corner, for everywhere the Southern peddler
has so pulled his beggar's coat around him that fate looks at
us from it with a thousand eyes. How far we are from the sad
dignity of our poor, the war-disabled of competition, on whom
tags and tins of boot blacking hang like braid and medals.

Suburbs. The farther we emerge from the inner city, the more
political the atmosphere becomes. We reach the docks, the
inland harbors, the warehouses, the quarters of poverty, the
scattered refuges of wretchedness: the outskirts. Outskirts are
the state of emergency of a city, the terrain on which inces-

santly rages the great decisive battle between town and country. It is nowhere more bitter than between Marseilles and the Provençal landscape. It is the hand-to-hand fight of telegraph poles against Agaves, barbed wire against thorny palms, the miasmas of stinking corridors against the damp gloom under the plane trees in brooding squares, short-winded outside staircases against the mighty hills. The long rue de Lyon is the powder conduit that Marseilles has dug in the landscape in order, in Saint-Lazare, Saint-Antoine, Arenc, Septèmes, to blow it up, burying it in the shell splinters of every national and commercial language. Alimentation Moderne, rue de Jamaïque, Comptoir de la Limite, Savon Abat-Jour, Minoterie de la Campagne, Bar du Gaz, Bar Facultatif—and over all this the dust that here conglomerates out of sea salt, chalk, and mica, and whose bitterness persists longer in the mouths of those who have pitted themselves against the city than the splendor of sun and sea in the eyes of its admirers.

Hashish in Marseilles

Preliminary remark: One of the first signs that hashish is beginning to take effect "is a dull feeling of foreboding; something strange, ineluctable is approaching ... images and chains of images, long-submerged memories appear, whole scenes and situations are experienced; at first they arouse interest, now and then enjoyment, and finally, when there is no turning away from them, weariness and torment. By everything that happens, and by what he says and does, the subject is surprised and overwhelmed. His laughter, all his utterances happen to him like outward events. He also attains experiences that approach inspiration, illumination.... Space can expand, the ground tilt steeply, atmospheric sensations occur: vapor, an opaque heaviness of the air; colors grow brighter, more luminous; objects more beautiful, or else lumpy and threatening. ... All this does not occur in a continuous development; rather, it is typified by a continual alternation of dreaming and waking states, a constant and finally exhausting oscillation between totally different worlds of consciousness; in the middle of a sentence these transitions can take place.... All this the subject reports in a form that usually diverges very widely from the norm. Connections become difficult to perceive, owing to the frequently sudden rupture of all memory of past events, thought is not formed into words, the situation can become so compulsively hilarious that the hashish eater for minutes on end is capable of nothing except laughing.... The memory of the intoxication is surprisingly clear." "It is curious that hashish poisoning has not yet been experimentally studied. The most admirable description of the hashish trance is by Baudelaire (*Les paradis artificiels*)." From Joël and Fränkel, "Der Haschisch-Rausch," *Klinische Wochen-schrift*, 1926, vol. 5, p. 37.

Marseilles, July 29. At seven o'clock in the evening, after long hesitation, I took hashish. During the day I had been in Aix. With the absolute certainty, in this city of hundreds of thousands where no one knows me, of not being disturbed, I lie on the bed. And yet I am disturbed, by a little child crying. I think three-quarters of an hour have already passed. But it is only twenty minutes. . . . So I lie on the bed, reading and smoking. Opposite me always this view of the belly of Marseilles. The street I have so often seen is like a knife cut.

At last I left the hotel, the effects seeming nonexistent or so weak that the precaution of staying at home was unnecessary. My first port of call was the café on the corner of Cannebière and Cours Belsunce. Seen from the harbor, the one on the right, therefore not my usual café. What now? Only a certain benevolence, the expectation of being received kindly by people. The feeling of loneliness is very quickly lost. My walking stick begins to give me a special pleasure. One becomes so tender, fears that a shadow falling on the paper might hurt it. The nausea disappears. One reads the notices on the urinals. It would not surprise me if this or that person came up to me. But when no one does I am not disappointed, either. However, it is too noisy for me here.

Now the hashish eater's demands on time and space come into force. As is known, these are absolutely regal. Versailles, for one who has taken hashish, is not too large, or eternity too long. Against the background of these immense dimensions of inner experience, of absolute duration and immeasurable space, a wonderful, beatific humor dwells all the more fondly on the contingencies of the world of space and time. I feel this humor infinitely when I am told at the Restaurant Basso that the hot kitchen has just been closed, while I have just sat down to feast into eternity. Afterward, despite this, the feeling that all this is indeed bright, frequented, animated, and will remain so. I must note how I found my seat. What mattered to me was the view of the old port that one got from the upper floors. Walking past below, I had spied an empty table on the balcony of the second story. Yet in the end I only reached the first. Most of the window tables were occupied, so I went up to a very large one that had just been vacated. As I was sitting down, however, the disproportion of seating myself at so large a table caused me such shame that I walked across the entire floor to the opposite end to sit at a smaller table that became visible to me only as I reached it.

But the meal came later. First, the little bar on the harbor. I was again just on the point of retreating in confusion, for a concert, indeed a brass band, seemed to be playing there. I only just managed to explain to myself that it was nothing more than the blaring of car horns. On the way to the Vieux Port I already had this wonderful lightness and sureness of step that transformed the stony, unarticulated earth of the great square that I was crossing into the surface of a country road along which I strode at night like an energetic hiker. For at this time I was still avoiding the Cannebière, not yet quite sure of my regulatory functions. In that little harbor bar the hashish then began to exert its canonical magic with a primitive sharpness that I had scarcely felt until then. For it made me into a physiognomist, or at least a contemplator of physiognomies, and I underwent something unique in my experience: I positively fixed my gaze on the faces that I had around me, which were, in part, of remarkable coarseness or ugliness. Faces that I would normally have avoided for a twofold reason: I should neither have wished to attract their gaze nor endured their brutality. It was a very advanced post, this harbor tavern. (I believe it was the farthest accessible to me without danger, a circumstance I had gauged, in the trance, with the same accuracy with which, when utterly weary, one is able to fill a glass exactly to the brim without spilling a drop, as one can never do with sharp senses.) It was still sufficiently far from rue Bouterie, yet no bourgeois sat there; at the most, besides the true port proletariat, a few petit-bourgeois families from the neighborhood. I now suddenly understood how, to a painter—had it not happened to Rembrandt and many others?—ugliness could appear as the true reservoir of beauty, better than any treasure cask, a jagged mountain with all the inner gold of beauty gleaming from the wrinkles, glances, features. I especially remember a boundlessly animal and vulgar male face in which the "line of renunciation" struck me with sudden violence. It was above all men's faces that had begun to interest me. Now began the game, to be long maintained, of recognizing someone I knew in every face; often I knew the name, often not; the deception vanished as deceptions vanish in dreams: not in shame and compromised, but peacefully and amiably, like a being who has performed his service. Under these circumstances there was no question of loneliness. Was I my own company? Surely not so undisguisedly. I doubt whether that would have made me so happy. More likely this: I became my own most skillful, fond, shameless procurer, gratifying myself with the ambiguous assurance of one who knows from profound study the wishes of his employer. Then it began to take half an eternity until the waiter reappeared. Or, rather, I could not wait for him to appear. I went into the barroom and paid at the counter. Whether tips are usual in such taverns I do not know. But under other circumstances I should have given something in any case. Under hashish yesterday, however, I was on the stingy side; for fear of attracting attention by extravagance, I succeeded in making myself really conspicuous.

Similarly at Basso's. First I ordered a dozen oysters. The man wanted me to order the next course at the same time. I named some local dish. He came back with the news that none was left. I then pointed to a place in the menu in the vicinity of this dish, and was on the point of ordering each item, one after another, but then the name of the one above it caught my attention, and so on, until I finally reached the top of the list.

This was not just from greed, however, but from an extreme politeness toward the dishes that I did not wish to offend by a refusal. In short, I came to a stop at a *pâté de Lyon*. Lion paste, I thought with a witty smile, when it lay clean on a plate before me, and then, contemptuously: This tender rabbit or chicken meat—whatever it may be. To my lionish hunger it would not have seemed inappropriate to satisfy itself on a lion. Moreover, I had tacitly decided that as soon as I had finished at Basso's (it was about half past ten) I should go elsewhere and dine a second time.

But first, back to the walk to Basso's. I strolled along the quay and read one after another the names of the boats tied up there. As I did so an incomprehensible gaiety came over me, and I smiled in turn at all the Christian names of France. The love promised to these boats by their names seemed wonderfully beautiful and touching to me. Only one of them, *Aero II*, which reminded me of aerial warfare, I passed by without cordiality, exactly as, in the bar that I had just left, my gaze had been obliged to pass over certain excessively deformed countenances.

Upstairs at Basso's, when I looked down, the old games began again. The square in front of the harbor was my palette, on which imagination mixed the qualities of the place, trying them out now this way, now that, without concern for the result, like a painter daydreaming on his palette. I hesitated before taking wine. It was a half bottle of Cassis. A piece of ice was floating in the glass. Yet it went excellently with my drug. I had chosen my seat on account of the open window, through which I could look down on the dark square. And as I did so from time to time, I noticed that it had a tendency to change with everyone who stepped onto it, as if it formed a figure about him that, clearly, had nothing to do with the square as he saw it but, rather, with the view that the great portrait painters of the seventeenth century, in accordance with the character of the dignitary whom they placed before a colonnade or a window, threw into a relief by this colonnade, this window. Later I noted as I looked down, "From century to century things grow more estranged."

Here I must observe in general: the solitude of such trances has its dark side. To speak only of the physical aspect, there was a moment in the harbor tavern when a violent pressure in the diaphragm sought relief through humming. And there is no doubt that truly beautiful, illuminating visions were not awakened. On the other hand, solitude works in these states as a filter. What one writes down the following day is more than an enumeration of impressions; in the night the trance cuts itself off from everyday reality with fine, prismatic edges; it forms a kind of figure and is more easily memorable. I should like to say: it shrinks and takes on the form of a flower.

To begin to solve the riddle of the ecstasy of trance, one ought to meditate on Ariadne's thread. What joy in the mere act of unrolling a ball of thread. And this joy is very deeply related to the joy of trance, as to that of creation. We go forward; but in so doing we not only discover the twists and turns of the cave, but also enjoy this pleasure of discovery against the background of the other, rhythmical bliss of unwinding the thread. The certainty of unrolling an artfully wound skein—is that not the joy of all productivity, at least in prose? And under hashish we are enraptured prose-beings in the highest power.

A deeply submerged feeling of happiness that came over me afterward, on a square off the Cannebière where rue Paradis opens onto a park, is more difficult to recall than everything that went before. Fortunately I find on my newspaper the sentence "One should scoop sameness from reality with a spoon." Several weeks earlier I had noted another, by Johannes V. Jensen, which appeared to say something similar: "Richard was a young man with understanding for everything in the world that was of the same kind." This sentence had pleased me very much. It enabled me now to confront the political, rational sense it had had for me earlier with the individual, magical meaning of my experience the day before. Whereas Jensen's sentence amounted, as I had understood it, to saying that things are as we know them to be, thoroughly mechanized and rationalized, the particular being confined today solely to nuances, my new insight was entirely different. For I saw only nuances, yet these were the same. I immersed myself in contemplation of the sidewalk before me, which, through a kind of unguent with which I covered it, could have been, precisely as these very stones, also the sidewalk of Paris. One often speaks of stones instead of bread. These stones were the bread of my imagination, which was suddenly seized by a ravenous hunger to taste what is the same in all places and countries. And yet I thought with immense pride of sitting here in Marseilles in a hashish trance; of who else might be sharing my intoxication this evening, how few. Of how I was incapable of fearing future misfortune, future solitude, for hashish would always remain. The music from a nearby nightclub that I had been following played a part in this stage. G. rode past me in a cab. It happened suddenly, exactly as, earlier, from the shadows of the boat, U. had suddenly detached himself in the form of a harbor loafer and pimp. But there were not only known faces. Here, while I was in the state of deepest trance, two figures—citizens, vagrants, what do I know?—passed me as "Dante and Petrarch." "All men are brothers." So began a train of thought that I am no longer able to pursue. But its last link was certainly much less banal than its first and led on perhaps to images of animals.

"Barnabe," read the sign on a streetcar that stopped briefly at the square where I was sitting. And the sad confused story of Barnabas seemed to me no bad destination for a streetcar going into the outskirts of Marseilles. Something very beautiful was going on around the door of the dance hall. Now and then a Chinese in blue silk trousers and a glowing pink silk jacket stepped outside. He was the doorman. Girls displayed themselves in the doorway. My mood was free of all desire. It was amusing to see a young man with a girl in a white dress coming toward me and to be immediately obliged to think: "She got away from him in there in her shift, and now he is fetching her back. Well, well." I felt flattered by the thought of sitting here in a center of dissipation, and by "here" I did not mean the town but the little, not-very-eventful spot where I found myself. But events took place in such a way that the appearance of things touched me with a magic wand, and I sank into a dream of them. People and things behave at such hours like those little stage sets and people made of elder pith in the glazed tin-foil box, which, when the glass is rubbed, are electrified and fall at every movement into the most unusual relationships.

The music that meanwhile kept rising and falling, I called the rush switches of jazz. I have forgotten on what grounds I permitted myself to mark the beat with my foot. This is against my education, and it did not happen without inner disputation. There were times when the intensity of acoustic impressions blotted out all others. In the little bar, above all, everything was suddenly submerged in the noise of voices, not of streets. What was most peculiar about this din of voices was that it sounded entirely like dialect. The people of Marseilles suddenly did not speak good enough French for me. They were stuck at the level of dialect. The phenomenon of alienation that may be involved in this, which Kraus has formulated in the fine dictum "The more closely you look at a word the more distantly it looks back," appears to extend to the optical. At any rate I find among my notes the surprised comment "How things withstand the gaze."

The trance abated when I crossed the Cannebière and at last turned the corner to have a final ice cream at the little Café des Cours Belsunce. It was not far from the first café of the evening, in which, suddenly, the amorous joy dispensed by the contemplation of some fringes blown by the wind had convinced me that the hashish had begun its work. And when I recall this state I should like to believe that hashish persuades nature to permit us—for less egoistic purposes—that squandering of our own existence that we know in love. For if, when we love, our existence runs through nature's fingers like golden coins that she cannot hold and lets fall to purchase new birth thereby, she now throws us, without hoping or expecting anything, in ample handfuls to existence.

Paris, Capital of the Nineteenth Century

The waters are blue and the vegetation pink;
The evening sweet to behold;
People are out walking. Great ladies promenade;
    and behind them walk the small ladies.
    —Nguyen-Trong-Hiep: *Paris, Capital of France* (1897)

1. Fourier, or the Arcades

De ces palais les colonnes magiques
A l'amateur montrent de toutes parts
Dans les objets qu'étalent leurs portiques
Que l'industrie est rivale aux arts.
    —*Nouveaux tableaux de Paris* (1828)

Most of the Paris arcades are built in the decade and a half after 1822. The first condition for this new fashion is the boom in the textile trade. The *magasins de nouveauté*, the first establishments to keep large stocks of goods on their premises, begin to appear, precursors of the department stores. It is the time of which Balzac wrote, "The great poem of display chants its many-colored strophes from the Madeleine to the Porte-Saint-Denis." The arcades are a center of trade in luxury goods. In their fittings art is brought in to the service of commerce. Contemporaries never tire of admiring them. They long remain a center of attraction for foreigners. An *Illustrated Guide to Paris* said: "These arcades, a recent invention of industrial luxury, are glass-roofed, marble-walled passages cut through whole blocks of houses, whose owners have combined in this speculation. On either side of the passages, which draw their light from above, run the most elegant shops, so that an arcade of this kind is a city, indeed, a world in miniature." The arcades are the scene of the first gas lighting.

The second condition for the construction of the arcades is the advent of building in iron. The Empire saw in this technique an aid to a renewal of architecture in the ancient Greek manner. The architectural theorist Bötticher expresses a general conviction when he says, "with regard to the artistic form of the new system, the formal principle of the Hellenic style" should be introduced. *Empire* is the style of revolutionary heroism for which the state is an end in itself. Just as Napoleon failed to recognize the functional nature of the state as an instrument of domination by the bourgeois class, neither did the master builders of his time perceive the functional nature of iron, through which the constructive principle began its domination of architecture. These builders model their pillars on Pompeian columns, their factories on houses, as later the first railway stations are to resemble chalets. "Construction fills the role of the unconscious." Nevertheless the idea of the engineer, originating in the revolutionary wars, begins to assert itself, and battle is joined between constructor and decorator, Ecole Polytechnique and Ecole des Beaux-Arts.

In iron, an artificial building material makes its appearance for the first time in the history of architecture. It undergoes a development that accelerates in the course of the century. The decisive breakthrough comes when it emerges that the locomotive, with which experiments had been made since the end of the twenties, could only be used on iron rails. The rail becomes the first prefabricated iron component, the forerunner of the girder. Iron is avoided in residential buildings and used in arcades, exhibition halls, stations—buildings serving transitory purposes. Simultaneously, the architectonic scope for the application of glass expands. The social conditions for its intensified use as a building material do not arrive, however, until a hundred years later. Even in Scheerbart's "glass architecture" (1914) it appears in utopian contexts.

Chaque époque rêve la suivante.
—Michelet, *Avenir! Avenir!*

Corresponding in the collective consciousness to the forms of the new means of production, which at first were still dominated by the old (Marx), are images in which the new is intermingled with the old. These images are wishful fantasies, and in them the collective seeks both to preserve and to transfigure the inchoateness of the social product and the deficiencies in the social system of production. In addition, these wish-fulfilling images manifest an emphatic striving for dissociation with the outmoded—which means, however, with the most recent past. These tendencies direct the visual imagination, which has been activated by the new, back to the primeval past. In the dream in which, before the eyes of each epoch, that which is to follow appears in images, the latter appears wedded to elements from prehistory, that is, of a classless society. Intimations of this, deposited in the unconscious of the collective, mingle with the new to produce the utopia that has left its traces in thousands of configurations of life, from permanent buildings to fleeting fashions.

This state of affairs is discernible in Fourier's utopia. Its chief impetus comes from the advent of machines. But this is not directly expressed in his accounts of it; these have their origin in the morality of trade and the false morality propagated in its service. His phalanstery is supposed to lead men back to conditions in which virtue is superfluous. Its highly complicated organization is like a piece of machinery. The meshing of passions, the intricate interaction of the *passions mécanistes* with the *passion cabaliste,* are primitive analogies to machinery in the material of psychology. This human machinery produces the land of milk and honey, the primeval wish symbol that Fourier's utopia filled with new life.

In the arcades, Fourier saw the architectonic canon of the phalanstery. His reactionary modification of them is characteristic: whereas they originally serve commercial purposes, he makes them into dwelling places. The phalanstery becomes a city of arcades. Fourier installs in the austere, formal world of the Empire the colorful idyll of Biedermeier. Its radiance lasts, though paled, till Zola. He takes up Fourier's ideas in *Travail*, as he takes leave of the arcades in *Thérèse Raquin*. Marx defends Fourier to Carl Grün, emphasizing his "colossal vision of man." He also draws attention to Fourier's humor. And in fact Jean Paul in *Levana* is as closely related to Fourier the pedagogue as Scheerbart in his "glass architecture" is to Fourier the utopian.

2. *Daguerre, or the Panoramas*

Soleil, prends garde à toi!
—A. J. Wiertz, *Oeuvres littéraires*
(Paris 1870)

As architecture begins to outgrow art in the use of iron construction, so does painting in the panoramas. The climax of the preparation of panoramas coincides with the appearance of the arcades. There were tireless exertions of technical skill to make panoramas the scenes of a perfect imitation of nature. The attempt was made to reproduce the changing time of day in the landscape, the rising of the moon, the rushing of waterfalls. David advises his pupils to draw from nature in the panoramas. In striving to produce deceptively lifelike changes in their presentation of nature, the panoramas point ahead, beyond photography, to films and sound films.

Contemporary to the panoramas is a panoramic literature. *Le livre des cent-et-un, Les Français peints par eux-mêmes, Le diable à Paris, La grande ville* are part of it. In these books is being prepared the collective literary work for which, in the thirties, Girardin created an arena in the *feuilleton*. They consist of isolated sketches, the anecdotal form of which corresponds to the plastic foreground of the panorama, and their informational base to its painted background. This literature is also panoramic in a social sense. For the last time the worker appears, outside his class, as a trimming for an idyll.

The panoramas, which declare a revolution in the relation of art to technology, are at the same time an expression of a new feeling about life. The city dweller, whose political superiority over the country is expressed in many ways in the course of the century, attempts to introduce the countryside into the city. In the panoramas the city dilates to become landscape, as it does in a subtler way for the *flâneur*. Daguerre is a pupil of the panorama painter Prévost, whose establishment is situated in the Passage des Panoramas. Description of the panoramas by Prévost and Daguerre. In 1839 Daguerre's panorama burns down. In the same year he announces the invention of daguerreotype.

Arago introduces photography in an official speech. He indicates its place in the history of technology. He prophesies its scientific application. Artists, on the other hand, begin to debate its artistic value. Photography leads to the annihilation of the great profession of the portrait miniaturist. This happens not only for economic reasons. Artistically, early photographs were superior to portrait miniatures. The technical reason lies in the long exposure time, which demanded utmost concentration by the subject being portrayed. The social reason lies in the circumstance that the first photographers belonged to the avant-garde and drew their clientele for the most part from it. Nadar's advance over his professional colleagues is characterized by his undertaking to take photographs in the sewers of Paris. This is the first time that the lens is given the task of making discoveries. Its importance becomes greater the more questionable, in face of the new technical and social reality, the subjective element in painting and graphic information is felt to be.

The World Exhibition of 1855 presents for the first time a special display of photography. In the same year Wiertz publishes his major article on photography, in which he assigns it the task of philosophically enlightening painting. He understood this enlightenment, as his own paintings show, in a political sense. Wiertz can thus be described as the first to have demanded, if not foreseen, montage as a propagandistic application of photography. With the increasing scope of communications systems, the significance of painting in imparting information is reduced. It begins, in reaction against photography, to stress the color elements in pictures. When impressionism gives way to cubism, painting has created for itself a further domain into which photography cannot, for the time being, follow. Photography for its part has, since the middle of the century, enormously expanded the scope of the commodity trade by putting on the market in unlimited quantities figures, landscapes, events that have either not been salable at all or have been available only as pictures for single customers. To increase turnover, it renewed its objects through fashionable changes in photographic technique that determined the later history of photography.

3. *Grandville, or the World Exhibitions*

Oui, quand le monde entier, de Paris jusqu'en Chine,
O divin Saint-Simon, sera dans la doctrine,
L'âge d'or doit renaître avec tout son éclat,
Les fleuves rouleront du thé, du chocolat;
Les moutons tous rôtis bondiront dans la plaine,
Et les brochets au bleu nageront dans la Seine;
Les épinards viendront au monde fricassés,
Avec des croûtons frits tout au tour concassés.
Les arbres produiront des pommes en compotes
Et l'on moissonnera des cerricks et des bottes;
Il neigera du vin, il pleuvera des poulets,
Et du ciel les canards tomberont aux navets.

—Lauglé and Vanderbusch, *Louis et le Saint-Simonien*
(1832)

World exhibitions are the sites of pilgrimages to the commodity fetish. "Europe is on the move to look at merchandise," said Taine in 1855. The world exhibitions are preceded by national industrial exhibitions, the first of which takes place in 1798 on the Champ-de-Mars. It proceeds from the wish "to entertain the working classes, and becomes for them a festival of emancipation." The workers stand as customers in the foreground. The framework of the entertainment industry has not yet been formed. The popular festival supplies it. Chaptal's speech on industry opens this exhibition. The Saint-Simonists, who plan the industrialization of the earth, take up the idea of world exhibitions. Chevalier, the first authority in the new field, is a pupil of Enfantin and editor of the Saint-Simonist journal, *Globe*. The Saint-Simonists predicted the development of the world economy, but not of the class struggle. Beside their participation in industrial and commercial enterprises about the middle of the century stands their helplessness in questions concerning the proletariat. The world exhibitions glorify the exchange value of commodities. They create a framework in which commodities' intrinsic value is eclipsed. They open up a phantasmagoria that people enter to be amused. The entertainment industry facilitates this by elevating people to the level of commodities. They submit to being manipulated while enjoying their alienation from themselves and others. The enthronement of merchandise, with the aura of amusement surrounding it, is the secret theme of Grandville's art. This is reflected in the discord between its utopian and its cynical elements. Its subtleties in the presentation of inanimate objects correspond to what Marx called the "theological whims" of goods. This is clearly distilled in the term *spécialité*—a commodity description coming into use about this time in the luxury industry; under Grandville's pencil the whole of nature is transformed into *spécialités*. He presents them in the same spirit in which advertising—a word that is also coined at this time—begins to present its articles. He ends in madness.

Fashion: My dear Mr. Death!
—Leopardi, *Dialogue Between Fashion and Death.*

The world exhibitions build up the universe of commodities. Grandville's fantasies extend the character of a commodity to the universe. They modernize it. Saturn's ring becomes a cast-iron balcony on which the inhabitants of the planet take the air in the evening. The literary counterpart of this graphic utopia is presented by the book of the Fourierist natural scientist Toussenal. Fashion prescribes the ritual according to which the commodity fetish wishes to be worshiped; Grandville extends fashion's claims both to the objects of everyday use and to the cosmos. By pursuing it to its extremes he discloses its nature. This resides in its conflict with the organic. It couples the living body to the inorganic world. Against the living it asserts the rights of the corpse. Fetishism, which is subject to the sex appeal of the inorganic, is its vital nerve. The cult of commodities places it in its service.

On the occasion of the 1867 World Exhibition, Victor Hugo issues a manifesto: *To the Peoples of Europe.* Earlier, and more unambiguously, their interests had been represented by the French workers' delegations, the first of which had been sent to the London World Exhibition of 1851, and the second, consisting of seven hundred and fifty representatives, to that of 1862. The latter was of indirect importance for the foundation of the International Workingmen's Association by Marx. The phantasmagoria of capitalist culture reaches its most brilliant display in the World Exhibition of 1867. The Empire is at the height of its power. Paris reaffirms itself as the capital of luxury and fashion: Offenbach sets the rhythm of Parisian life. The operetta is the ironic utopia of the capital's lasting rule.

4. Louis-Philippe, or the Interior

Une tête, sur la table de nuit, repose
Comme un renoncule.
    —Baudelaire, *"Un martyre"*

Under Louis-Philippe the private citizen enters the stage of history. The extension of the democratic apparatus through a new franchise coincides with the parliamentary corruption organized by Guihot. Under its protection the ruling class makes history by pursuing its business interests. It promotes railway construction to improve its share holdings. It favors Louis-Philippe as a private citizen at the head of affairs. By the time of the July Revolution, the bourgeoisie has realized the aims of 1789 (Marx).

For the private person, living space becomes, for the first time, antithetical to the place of work. The former is constituted by the interior; the office is its complement. The private person who squares his accounts with reality in his office demands that the interior be maintained in his illusions. This need is all the more pressing since he has no intention of extending his commercial considerations into social ones. In shaping his private environment he represses both. From this spring the phantasmagorias of the interior. For the private individual the private environment represents the universe. In it he gathers remote places and the past. His drawing room is a box in the world theater.

Excursus on *art nouveau*. About the turn of the century, the interior is shaken by *art nouveau*. Admittedly the latter, through its ideology, seems to bring with it the consummation of the interior—the transfiguration of the solitary soul appears its goal. Individualism is its theory. In Vandervelde the house appears as the expression of personality. Ornament is to this house what the signature is to a painting. The real meaning of *art nouveau* is not expressed in this ideology. It represents art's last attempt to escape from its ivory tower, which is besieged by technology. *Art nouveau* mobilizes all the reserves of inwardness. They find their expression in mediumistic line-language, in the flower as the symbol of naked, vegetal nature confronting a technically armed environment. The new elements of iron building, girder forms, preoccupy *art nouveau*. In ornamentation it strives to win back these forms for art. Concrete offers it the prospect of new plastic possibilities in architecture. About this time the real center of gravity of living space is transferred to the office. The de-realized individual creates a place for himself in the private home. *Art nouveau* is summed up by *The Master Builder*—the attempt by the individual to do battle with technology on the basis of his inwardness leads to his downfall.

> *Je crois...à mon âme: la Chose.*
> —Léon Deubel, *Oeuvres* (Paris 1929)

The interior is the retreat of art. The collector is a true inmate of the interior. He makes the transfiguration of things his business. To him falls the Sisyphean task of obliterating the commodity-like character of things through his ownership of them. But he merely confers connoisseur value on them, instead of intrinsic value. The collector dreams that he is not only in a distant or past world but also, at the same time, in a better one, in which, although men are as unprovided with what they need as in the everyday world, things are free of the drudgery of being useful.

The interior is not only the universe but also the etui of the private person. To live means to leave traces. In the interior these are emphasized. An abundance of covers and protectors, liners and cases is devised, on which the traces of objects of everyday use are imprinted. The traces of the occupant also leave their impression on the interior. The detective story that follows these traces comes into being. His "philosophy of furniture," along with his detective novellas, shows Poe to be the

first physiognomist of the interior. The criminals of the first
detective novels are neither gentlemen nor apaches, but private
members of the bourgeoisie.

5. Baudelaire, or the Streets of Paris

Tout pour moi devient Allégorie.
—Baudelaire, *"Le cygne"*

Baudelaire's genius, which is fed on melancholy, is an allegori-
cal genius. In Baudelaire Paris becomes for the first time a
subject of lyric poetry. This poetry is not regional art; rather,
the gaze of the allegorist that falls on the city is estranged. It
is the gaze of the *flâneur,* whose mode of life still surrounds
the approaching desolation of city life with a propitiatory
luster. The *flâneur* is still on the threshold, of the city as of the
bourgeois class. Neither has yet engulfed him; in neither is he
at home. He seeks refuge in the crowd. Early contributions to
a physiognomics of the crowd are to be found in Engels and
Poe. The crowd is the veil through which the familiar city
lures the *flâneur* like a phantasmagoria. In it the city is now a
landscape, now a room. Both, then, constitute the department
store that puts even *flânerie* to use for commodity circulation.
The department store is the *flâneur's* last practical joke.

In the *flâneur* the intelligentsia pays a visit to the marketplace, ostensibly to look around, yet in reality to find a buyer.
In this intermediate phase, in which it still has patrons but is
already beginning to familiarize itself with the market, it appears as bohemianism. The uncertainty of its political function corresponds to the uncertainty of its economic position.
This is most strikingly expressed in the professional conspira-
tors, who are certainly a part of Bohemia. Their first field of
activity is the army; later it becomes the petit bourgeoisie,

occasionally the proletariat. Yet this stratum sees its opponents in the real leaders of the latter. The *Communist Manifesto* puts an end to their political existence. Baudelaire's poetry draws its strength from the rebellious emotionalism of this group. He throws his lot in with the asocial. His only sexual communion is realized with a whore.

Facilis descensus Averni
—Virgil, *Aeneid*

What is unique in Baudelaire's poetry is that the images of women and death are permeated by a third, that of Paris. The Paris of his poems is a submerged city, more submarine than subterranean. The chthonic elements of the city—its topographical formation, the old deserted bed of the Seine—doubtless left their impression on his work. Yet what is decisive in Baudelaire's "deathly idyll" of the city is a social, modern substratum. Modernity is a main accent in his poetry. He shatters the ideal as spleen (*Spleen et Idéal*). But it is precisely modernity that is always quoting primeval history. This happens here through the ambiguity attending the social relationships and products of this epoch. Ambiguity is the pictorial image of dialectics, the law of dialectics seen at a standstill. This standstill is utopia and the dialectic image therefore a dream image. Such an image is presented by the pure commodity: as fetish. Such an image are the arcades, which are both house and stars. Such an image is the prostitute, who is saleswoman and wares in one.

Le voyage pour découvrir ma géographie
—Note of a madman (Paris 1907)

The last poem of the *Flowers of Evil*, "The Journey": "Oh death, old captain, it is time, let us weigh anchor." The last journey of the *flâneur:* death. Its destination: the new. "To the depths of the unknown, there to find something new." Novelty is a quality independent of the intrinsic value of the commodity. It is the origin of the illusion inseverable from the images produced by the collective unconscious. It is the quintessence of false consciousness, whose indefatigable agent is fashion. The illusion of novelty is reflected, like one mirror in another, in the illusion of perpetual sameness. The product of this reflection is the phantasmagoria of "cultural history," in which the bourgeoisie savors its false consciousness to the last. The art that begins to doubt its task and ceases to be "inseparable from utility" (Baudelaire) must make novelty its highest value. The snob becomes its *arbiter novarum rerum*. He is to art what the dandy is to fashion. As in the seventeenth century the canon of dialectical imagery came to be allegory, in the nineteenth it is novelty. The *magasins de nouveauté* are joined by the newspapers. The press organizes the market in intellectual values, in which prices at first soar. Nonconformists rebel against the handing over of art to the market. They gather around the banner of *"l'art pour l'art."* This slogan springs from the conception of the total artwork, which attempts to isolate art from the development of technology. The solemnity with which it is celebrated is the corollary to the frivolity that glorifies the commodity. Both abstract from the social existence of man. Baudelaire succumbs to the infatuation of Wagner.

6. *Haussmann, or the Barricades*

J'ai le culte du Beau, du Bien, des grandes choses,
De la belle nature inspirant le grand art,
Qu'il enchante l'oreille ou charme le regard;
J'ai l'amour du printemps en fleurs: femmes et roses.
—Baron Haussmann, *Confession d'un lion devenu vieux*

> The blossomy realm of decoration,
> Landscape and architecture's charm
> And all effects of scenery repose
> Upon perspective's law alone.
> —Franz Böhle, *Theatrical Catechism*

Haussmann's urban ideal was of long perspectives of streets and thoroughfares. This corresponds to the inclination, noticeable again and again in the nineteenth century, to ennoble technical necessities by artistic aims. The institutions of the secular and clerical dominance of the bourgeoisie were to find their apotheosis in a framework of streets. Streets, before their completion, were draped in canvas and unveiled like monuments. Haussmann's efficiency is integrated with Napoleonic idealism. The latter favors finance capital. Paris experiences a flowering of speculation. Playing the stock exchange displaces the game of chance in the forms that had come down from feudal society. To the phantasmagorias of space to which the *flâneur* abandons himself, correspond the phantasmagorias of time indulged in by the gambler. Gambling converts time into a narcotic. Lafargue declares gaming an imitation in miniature of the mysteries of economic prosperity. The expropriations by Haussmann call into being a fraudulent speculation. The arbitration of the Court of Cassation, inspired by the bourgeois and Orleanist opposition, increases the financial risk of Haussmannization. Haussmann attempts to strengthen his dictatorship and to place Paris under an emergency regime. In 1864 he gives expression in a parliamentary speech to his hatred of the rootless population of big cities. The latter is constantly increased by his enterprises. The rise in rents drives the proletariat into the suburbs. The *quartiers* of Paris thus lose their individual physiognomies. The red belt is formed. Haussmann gave himself the name of "artist in demolition." He felt himself called to his work and stresses this in his memoirs. Meanwhile, he estranges Parisians from their city. They begin to be conscious of its inhuman character. Maxime du Camp's monumental work *Paris* has its origin in this consciousness. The *Jérémiades d'un Haussmannisé* give it the form of a biblical lament.

The true purpose of Haussmann's work was to secure the city against civil war. He wanted to make the erection of barricades in Paris impossible for all time. With such intent Louis-Philippe had already introduced wooden paving. Yet the barricades played a part in the February Revolution. Engels studies the technique of barricade fighting. Haussmann seeks to prevent barricades in two ways. The breadth of the streets is intended to make their erection impossible, and new thoroughfares are to open the shortest route between the barracks and the working-class districts. Contemporaries christen the enterprise "strategic embellishment."

> *Fais voir, en déjouant la ruse,*
> *O République, à ces pervers*
> *Ta grande face de Méduse*
> *Au milieu de rouges éclairs.*
> —Workers' song (about 1850).

The barricade is resurrected in the Commune. It is stronger and better secured than ever. It stretches across the great boulevards, often reaching the height of the first floor, and covers the trenches behind it. Just as the *Communist Manifesto* ends the epoch of the professional conspirator, the Commune puts an end to the phantasmagoria that dominates the freedom of the proletariat. It dispels the illusion that the task of the proletarian revolution is to complete the work of 1789 hand in hand with the bourgeoisie. This illusion prevailed from 1831 to 1871, from the Lyons uprising to the Commune. The bourgeoisie never shared this error. The struggle of the bourgeoisie against the social rights of the proletariat has already begun in the Great Revolution and coincides with the philanthropic movement that conceals it, attaining its fullest development under Napoleon III. Under him is written the monumental work of this political tendency: Le Play's *European Workers*. Besides the covert position of philanthropy, the bourgeoisie was always ready to take up the overt position of class struggle. As early as 1831 it recognizes, in the *Journal des Débats,* "Every industrialist lives in his factory like the plantation owners among their slaves." If, on the one hand, the lack of a guiding theory of revolution was the undoing of the old workers' uprisings, it was also, on the other, the condition for the immediate energy and enthusiasm with which they set about establishing a new society. This enthusiasm, which reached its climax in the Commune, for a time won over to the workers the best elements of the bourgeoisie, but in the end led them to succumb to their worst. Rimbaud and Courbet declare their support for the Commune. The Paris fire is the fitting conclusion to Haussmann's work of destruction.

> My good father had been in Paris.
> —Karl Gutzkow, *Letters from Paris* (1842)

Balzac was the first to speak of the ruins of the bourgeoisie. But only Surrealism exposed them to view. The development of the forces of production reduced the wish symbols of the previous century to rubble even before the monuments representing them had crumbled. In the nineteenth century this development emancipated constructive forms from art, as the sciences freed themselves from philosophy in the sixteenth. Architecture makes a start as constructional engineering. The reproduction of nature in photography follows. Fantasy creation prepares itself to become practical as commercial art. Literature is subjected to montage in the *feuilleton*. All these products are on the point of going to market as wares. But they hesitate on the brink. From this epoch stem the arcades and interiors, the exhibitions and panoramas. They are residues of a dream world. The realization of dream elements in waking is the textbook example of dialectical thinking. For this reason dialectical thinking is the organ of historical awakening. Each epoch not only dreams the next, but also, in dreaming, strives toward the moment of waking. It bears its end in itself and unfolds it—as Hegel already saw—with ruse. In the convulsions of the commodity economy we begin to recognize the monuments of the bourgeoisie as ruins even before they have crumbled.

Naples

WALTER BENJAMIN AND ASJA LACIS

Some years ago a priest was drawn on a cart through the streets of Naples for indecent offenses. He was followed by a crowd hurling maledictions. At a corner a wedding procession appeared. The priest stands up and makes the sign of a blessing, and the cart's pursuers fall on their knees. So absolutely, in ty, does Catholicism strive to reassert itself in every situ- Should it disappear from the face of the earth, its last ld would perhaps be not Rome, but Naples.

here can this people live out its rich barbarism, which source in the heart of the city itself, more securely than lap of the Church. It needs Catholicism, for even its s are then legalized by a legend, the feast day of a . Here Alfonso de Liguori was born, the saint who made ctice of the Catholic Church supple enough to accom- the trade of the swindler and the whore, in order to it with more or less rigorous penances in the con- l, for which he wrote a three-volume compendium. ion alone, not the police, is a match for the self-admin- n of the criminal world, the *camorra*.

does not occur to an injured party to call the police if xious to seek redress. Through civic or clerical mediators, if not personally, he approaches a *camorrista*. Through him he agrees on a ransom. From Naples to Castellamare, the length of the proletarian suburbs, run the headquarters of the mainland *camorra*. For these criminals avoid quarters in which they would be at the disposal of the police. They are dispersed over the city and the suburbs. That makes them dangerous.

The traveling citizen who gropes his way as far as Rome from one work of art to the next, as along a stockade, loses his nerve in Naples.

No more grotesque demonstration of this could be provided than in the convocation of an international congress of philosophers. It disintegrated without trace in the fiery haze of this city, while the seventh-centennial celebration of the university, part of whose tinny halo it was intended to be, unfolded amid the uproar of a popular festival. Complaining guests, who had been instantly relieved of their money and identification papers, appeared at the secretariat. But the banal tourist fares no better. Even Baedeker cannot propitiate him. Here the churches cannot be found, the starred sculpture always stands in the locked wing of the museum, and the word "mannerism" warns against the work of the native painters.

Nothing is enjoyable except the famous drinking water. Poverty and misery seem as contagious as they are pictured to be to children, and the foolish fear of being cheated is only a scanty rationalization for this feeling. If it is true, as Péladan said, that the nineteenth century inverted the medieval, the natural order of the vital needs of the poor, making shelter and clothing obligatory at the expense of food, such conventions have here been abolished. A beggar lies in the road propped against the sidewalk, waving his empty hat like a leave-taker at a station. Here poverty leads downward, as two thousand years ago it led down to the crypt: even today the way to the catacombs passes through a "garden of agony"; in it, even today, the disinherited are the leaders. At the hospital San Gennaro dei Poveri the entrance is through a white complex of buildings that one passes via two courtyards. On either side of the road stand the benches for the invalids, who follow those going out with glances that do not reveal whether they are clinging to their garments to be liberated or to satisfy unimaginable desires. In the second courtyard the doorways of the chambers have gratings; behind them cripples put their deformities on show, and the shock given to day-dreaming passers-by is their joy.

One of the old men leads and holds the lantern close to a fragment of early Christian fresco. Now he utters the centuries-old magic word "Pompeii." Everything that the foreigner desires, admires, and pays for is "Pompeii." "Pompeii" makes the plaster imitation of the temple ruins, the lava necklace, and the louse-ridden person of the guide irresistible. This fetish is all the more miraculous as only a small minority of those whom it sustains have ever seen it. It is understandable that the miracle-working Madonna enthroned there is receiving a brand-new, expensive church for pilgrims. In this building and not in that of the Vettii, Pompeii lives for the Neapolitans. And to it, again and again, swindling and wretchedness finally come home.

Fantastic reports by travelers have touched up the city. In reality it is gray: a gray-red or ocher, a gray-white. And entirely gray against sky and sea. It is this, not least, that disheartens the tourist. For anyone who is blind to forms sees little here. The city is craggy. Seen from a height not reached by the cries from below, from the Castell San Martino, it lies deserted in the dusk, grown into the rock. Only a strip of shore runs level; behind it buildings rise in tiers. Tenement blocks of six or seven stories, with staircases climbing their foundations, appear against the villas as skyscrapers. At the base of the cliff itself, where it touches the shore, caves have been hewn. As in the hermit pictures of the *Trecento,* a door is seen here and there in the rock. If it is open one can see into large cellars, which are at the same time sleeping places and storehouses. Farther on steps lead down to the sea, to fishermen's taverns installed in natural grottoes. Dim light and thin music come up from them in the evening.

As porous as this stone is the architecture. Building and action interpenetrate in the courtyards, arcades, and stair-

ways. In everything they preserve the scope to become a
theater of new, unforeseen constellations. The stamp of the
definitive is avoided. No situation appears intended forever,
no figure asserts its "thus and not otherwise." This is how
architecture, the most binding part of the communal rhythm,
comes into being here: civilized, private, and ordered only in
the great hotel and warehouse buildings on the quays; an-
archical, embroiled, villagelike in the center, into which
large networks of streets were hacked only forty years ago. And
only in these streets is the house, in the Nordic sense, the
cell of the city's architecture. In contrast, within the tenement
blocks, it seems held together at the corners, as if by iron
clamps, by the murals of the Madonna.

No one orients himself by house numbers. Shops, wells, and
churches are the reference points—and not always simple ones.
For the typical Neapolitan church does not ostentatiously
occupy a vast square, visible from afar, with transepts, gallery,
and dome. It is hidden, built in; high domes are often to be
seen only from a few places, and even then it is not easy to find
one's way to them, impossible to distinguish the mass of the
church from that of the neighboring secular buildings. The
stranger passes it by. The inconspicuous door, often only a
curtain, is the secret gate for the initiate. A single step takes
him from the jumble of dirty courtyards into the pure
solitude of a tall, whitewashed church interior. His private
existence is the baroque opening of a heightened public
sphere. For here his private self is not taken up by the four
walls, among wife and children, but by devotion or by despair.
Side alleys give glimpses of dirty stairs leading down to
taverns, where three or four men, at intervals, hidden behind
barrels as if behind church pillars, sit drinking.

In such corners one can scarcely discern where building is
still in progress and where dilapidation has already set in. For
nothing is concluded. Porosity results not only from the
indolence of the Southern artisan, but also, above all, from
the passion for improvisation, which demands that space and

opportunity be at any price preserved. Buildings are used as a popular stage. They are all divided into innumerable, simultaneously animated theaters. Balcony, courtyard, window, gateway, staircase, roof are at the same time stage and boxes. Even the most wretched pauper is sovereign in the dim, dual awareness of participating, in all his destitution, in one of the pictures of Neapolitan street life that will never return, and of enjoying in all his poverty the leisure to follow the great panorama. What is enacted on the staircases is a high school of stage management. The stairs, never entirely exposed, but still less enclosed in the gloomy box of the Nordic house, erupt fragmentarily from the buildings, make an angular turn, and disappear, only to burst out again.

In their materials, too, the street decorations are closely related to those of the theater. Paper plays the main part. Red, blue, and yellow fly catchers, altars of colored glossy paper on the walls, paper rosettes on the raw chunks of meat. Then the virtuosity of the variety show. Someone kneels on the asphalt, a little box beside him, and it is one of the busiest streets. With colored chalk he draws the figure of Christ on the stone, below it perhaps the head of the Madonna. Meanwhile a circle has formed around him, the artist gets up, and while he waits beside his work for fifteen minutes or half an hour, sparse, counted-out coins fall from the onlookers onto the limbs, head, and trunk of his portrait. Until he gathers them up, everyone disperses, and in a few moments the picture is erased by feet.

Not the least example of such virtuosity is the art of eating macaroni with the hands. This is demonstrated to foreigners for remuneration. Other things are paid for according to tariffs. Vendors give a fixed price for the cigarette butts that, after a café closes, are culled from the chinks in the floor. (Earlier they were sought by candlelight.) Alongside the leavings from restaurants, boiled cat skulls, and fish shells, they are sold at stalls in the harbor district. Music parades about: not mournful music for the courtyards, but brilliant sounds for the street. The broad cart, a kind of xylophone, is colorfully hung with song texts. Here they can be bought. One of the musicians turns the organ while the other, beside it, appears with his plate before anyone who stops dreamily to listen. So everything joyful is mobile: music, toys, ice cream circulate through the streets.

This music is both a residue of the last and a prelude to the next feast day. Irresistibly the festival penetrates each and every working day. Porosity is the inexhaustible law of the life of this city, reappearing everywhere. A grain of Sunday is hidden in each weekday, and how much weekday in this Sunday!

Nevertheless no city can fade, in the few hours of Sunday rest, more rapidly than Naples. It is crammed full of festal motifs nestling in the most inconspicuous places. When the blinds are taken down before a window, it is similar to flags being raised elsewhere. Brightly dressed boys fish in deep-blue streams and look up at rouged church steeples. High above the streets, washlines run, with garments suspended on them like rows of pennants. Faint suns shine from glass vats of iced drinks. Day and night the pavilions glow with the pale, aromatic juices that teach even the tongue what porosity can be.

If politics or the calendar offers the slightest pretext, however, this secret, scattered world condenses into a noisy feast. And regularly it is crowned with a fireworks display over the sea. From July to September, an unbroken band of fire runs, in the evenings, along the coast between Naples and Salerno. Now over Sorrento, now over Minori or Praiano, but always over Naples, stand fiery balls. Here fire is substance and shadow. It is subject to fashion and artifice. Each parish has to outdo the festival of its neighbor with new lighting effects.

In these festivals the oldest element of their Chinese origin, weather magic in the form of the rockets that spread like kites, proves far superior to terrestrial splendors: the earth-bound suns and the crucifix surrounded by the glow of Saint Elmo's fire. At the beach the stone pines of the Giardino Pubblico form a cloister. Riding under them on a festival night, you see a rain of fire in every treetop. But here, too, nothing is dreamy. Only explosions win an apotheosis popular favor. At Piedigrotta, the Neapolitans' main holiday, this childish joy in tumult puts on a wild face. During the night of September 7, bands of men, up to a hundred strong, roam through every street. They blow on gigantic paper cornets, the orifice disguised with grotesque masks. Violently if necessary, one is encircled, and from countless pipes the hollow sound clamors in the ears. Whole trades are based on the spectacle. Newspaper boys drag out the names of their wares, *Roma* and the *Corriere di Napoli,* as though they were sticks of gum. Their trumpeting is part of urban manufacture.

Trade, deeply rooted in Naples, borders on a game of chance and adheres closely to the holiday. The well-known list of the seven deadly sins located pride in Genoa, avarice in Florence (the old Germans were of a different opinion and called what is known as Greek love *Florenzen*), voluptuousness in Venice, anger in Bologna, greed in Milan, envy in Rome, and indolence in Naples. Lotto, alluring and consuming as nowhere else in Italy, remains the archetype of business life. Every Saturday at four o'clock, crowds form in front of the house where the numbers are drawn. Naples is one of the few cities with its own draw. With the pawnshop and lotto the state holds the proletariat in a vise: what it advances to them in one it takes back in the other. The more discreet and liberal intoxication of Hazard, in which the whole family takes part, replaces that of alcohol.

And business life is assimilated to it. A man stands in an unharnessed carriage on a street corner. People crowd around him. The lid of the coachman's box is open, and from it the vendor takes something, singing its praises all the while. It disappears before one has caught sight of it into a piece of pink or green paper. When it is thus wrapped, he holds it aloft, and in a trice it is sold for a few *soldi*. With the same mysterious gesture he disposes of one article after another. Are there lots in this paper? Cakes with a coin in every tenth one? What makes the people so covetous and the man as inscrutable as Mograby? He is selling toothpaste.

A priceless example of such business manners is the auction. When, at eight in the morning, the street vendor has begun unpacking his goods—umbrellas, shirt material, shawls—presenting each item singly to his public, mistrustfully, as if he had first to test it himself; when, growing heated, he asks fantastic prices, and, while serenely folding up the large cloth that he has spread out for five hundred lire, drops the price at every fold, and finally, when it lies diminished on his arm, is ready to part with it for fifty, he has been true to the most ancient fairground practices. There are delightful stories of the Neapolitan's playful love of trade. In a busy piazza a fat lady drops her fan. She looks around helplessly; she is too unshapely to pick it up herself. A cavalier appears and is prepared to perform his service for fifty lire. They negotiate, and the lady receives her fan for ten.

Blissful confusion in the storehouses! For here they are still one with the vendors' stalls: they are bazaars. The long gangway is favored. In a glass-roofed one there is a toyshop (in which perfume and liqueur glasses are also on sale) that would hold its own beside fairy-tale galleries. Like a gallery, too, is the main street of Naples, the Toledo. Its traffic is among the busiest on earth. On either side of this narrow alley all that has come together in the harbor city lies insolently, crudely, seductively displayed. Only in fairy tales are lanes so long that one must pass through without looking to left or right if one is not to fall prey to the devil. There is a department store, in other cities the rich, magnetic center of purchasing. Here it is devoid of charm, outdone by the tightly packed multiplicity. But with a tiny offshoot—rubber balls, soap, chocolates—it re-emerges somewhere else among the small traders' stalls.

Similarly dispersed, porous, and commingled is private life. What distinguishes Naples from other large cities is something it has in common with the African kraal; each private attitude or act is permeated by streams of communal life. To exist, for the Northern European the most private of affairs, is here, as in the kraal, a collective matter.

So the house is far less the refuge into which people retreat than the inexhaustible reservoir from which they flood out. Life bursts not only from doors, not only into front yards, where people on chairs do their work (for they have the faculty of making their bodies tables). Housekeeping utensils hang from balconies like potted plants. From the windows of the top floors come baskets on ropes for mail, fruit, and cabbage.

Just as the living room reappears on the street, with chairs, hearth, and altar, so, only much more loudly, the street migrates into the living room. Even the poorest one is as full of wax candles, biscuit saints, sheaves of photos on the wall, and iron bedsteads, as the street is of carts, people, and lights. Poverty has brought about a stretching of frontiers that mirrors the most radiant freedom of thought. There is no hour, often no place, for sleeping and eating.

The poorer the quarter, the more numerous the eating houses. From stoves in the open street, those who can do so fetch what they need. The same foods taste different at each stall; things are not done randomly but by proven recipes. In the way that, in the window of the smallest trattoria, fish and meat lie heaped up for inspection, there is a nuance that goes beyond the requirements of the connoisseur. In the fish market this seafaring people has created a marine sanctuary as grandiose as those of the Netherlands. Starfish, crayfish, cuttlefish from the gulf waters, which teem with creatures, cover the benches and are often devoured raw with a little lemon. Even the banal beasts of dry land become fantastic. In the fourth or fifth stories of these tenement blocks cows are kept. The animals never walk on the street, and their hoofs have become so long that they can no longer stand.

How could anyone sleep in such rooms? To be sure, there are beds, as many as the room will hold. But even if there are six or seven, there are often more than twice as many occupants. For this reason one sees children late at night—at twelve, even at two—still in the streets. At midday they then lie sleeping behind a shop counter or on a stairway. This sleep, which men and women also snatch in shady corners, is therefore not the protected Northern sleep. Here, too, there is interpenetration of day and night, noise and peace, outer light and inner darkness, street and home.

This extends even into toys. With the pale, watery colors of the Munich *Kindl*, the Madonna stands on the walls of the houses. The child that she holds away from her like a scepter is to be found, just as stiff, wrapped and without arms or legs, as a wooden doll in the poorest shops of Santa Lucia. With these toys the urchins can hit whatever they like. A scepter and a magic wand even in *their* fists; the Byzantine savior still asserts himself today. Bare wood at the back; only the front is painted. A blue garment, white spots, red hem, and red cheeks.

But the demon of profligacy has entered some of these dolls that lie beneath cheap notepaper, clothespins, and tin sheep. In the overpopulated quarters children are also quickly acquainted with sex. But if their increase becomes devastating, if the father of a family dies or the mother wastes away, close or distant relatives are not needed. A neighbor takes a child to her table for a shorter or longer period, and thus families interpenetrate in relationships that can resemble adoption. True laboratories of this great process of intermingling are the cafés. Life is unable to sit down and stagnate in them. They are sober, open rooms resembling the political People's Café, and the opposite of everything Viennese, of the confined, bourgeois, literary world. Neapolitan cafés are bluntly to the point. A prolonged stay is scarcely possible. A cup of excessively hot *caffé espresso*—in hot drinks this city is as unrivaled as in sherbets, spumoni, and ice cream—ushers the visitor out. The tables have a coppery shine, they are small and round, and a companion who is less than stalwart turns hesitantly on his heel in the doorway. Only a few people sit down briefly here. Three quick movements of the hand, and they have placed their order.

The language of gestures goes further here than anywhere else in Italy. The conversation is impenetrable to anyone from outside. Ears, nose, eyes, breast, and shoulders are signaling stations activated by the fingers. These configurations return in their fastidiously specialized eroticism. Helping gestures and impatient touches attract the stranger's attention through a regularity that excludes chance. Yes, here his cause would be hopelessly lost, but the Neapolitan benevolently sends him away, sends him a few kilometers farther on to Mori. "*Vedere Napoli e poi Mori*," he says, repeating an old pun. "See Naples and die," says the foreigner after him.

THREE

Surrealism

The Last Snapshot of
the European Intelligentsia

Intellectual currents can generate a sufficient head of water
for the critic to install his power station on them. The necessary gradient, in the case of Surrealism, is produced by the
difference in intellectual level between France and Germany.
What sprang up in 1919 in France in a small circle of literati
—we shall give the most important names at once: André
Breton, Louis Aragon, Philippe Soupault, Robert Desnos,
Paul Eluard—may have been a meager stream, fed on the
damp boredom of postwar Europe and the last trickle of
French decadence. The know-alls who even today have not
advanced beyond the "authentic origins" of the movement,
and even now have nothing to say about it except that yet
another clique of literati is here mystifying the honorable
public, are a little like a gathering of experts at a spring who,
after lengthy deliberation, arrive at the conviction that this
paltry stream will never drive turbines.

The German observer is not standing at the head of the
stream. That is his opportunity. He is in the valley. He can
gauge the energies of the movement. As a German he is long
acquainted with the crisis of the intelligentsia, or, more precisely, with that of the humanistic concept of freedom; and
he knows how frantic is the determination that has awakened
in the movement to go beyond the stage of eternal discussion
and, at any price, to reach a decision; he has had direct experience of its highly exposed position between an anarchistic
fronde and a revolutionary discipline, and so has no excuse

for taking the movement for the "artistic," "poetic" one it superficially appears. If it was such at the outset, it was, however, precisely at the outset that Breton declared his intention of breaking with a praxis that presents the public with the literary precipitate of a certain form of existence while withholding that existence itself. Stated more briefly and dialectically, this means that the sphere of poetry was here explored from within by a closely knit circle of people pushing the "poetic life" to the utmost limits of possibility. And they can be taken at their word when they assert that Rimbaud's *Saison en enfer* no longer had any secrets for them. For this book is indeed the first document of the movement (in recent times; earlier precursors will be discussed later). Can the point at issue be more definitively and incisively presented than by Rimbaud himself in his personal copy of the book? In the margin, beside the passage "on the silk of the seas and the arctic flowers," he later wrote, "There's no such thing."

In just how inconspicuous and peripheral a substance the dialectical kernel that later grew into Surrealism was originally embedded, was shown by Aragon in 1924—at a time when its development could not yet be foreseen—in his *Vague de rêves*. Today it can be foreseen. For there is no doubt that the heroic phase, whose catalogue of heroes Aragon left us in that work, is over. There is always, in such movements, a moment when the original tension of the secret society must either explode in a matter-of-fact, profane struggle for power and domination, or decay as a public demonstration and be transformed. Surrealism is in this phase of transformation at present. But at the time when it broke over its founders as an inspiring dream wave, it seemed the most integral, conclusive, absolute of movements. Everything with which it came into contact was integrated. Life only seemed worth living where the threshold between waking and sleeping was worn away in everyone as by the steps of multitudinous images flooding back and forth, language only seemed itself where sound and image, image and sound interpenetrated with automatic precision and such felicity that no chink was left for the penny-in-the-slot called "meaning." Image and language take precedence. Saint-Pol Roux, retiring to bed about daybreak, fixes a notice on his door: "Poet at work." Breton notes: "Quietly. I want to pass where no one yet has passed, quietly!—After you, dearest language." Language takes precedence.

Not only before meaning. Also before the self. In the world's structure dream loosens individuality like a bad tooth. This loosening of the self by intoxication is, at the same time, precisely the fruitful, living experience that allowed these people to step outside the domain of intoxication. This is not the place to give an exact definition of Surrealist experience. But anyone who has perceived that the writings of this circle are not literature but something else—demonstrations, watchwords, documents, bluffs, forgeries if you will, but at any rate not literature—will also know, for the same reason, that the writings are concerned literally with experiences, not with theories and still less with phantasms. And these experiences are by no means limited to dreams, hours of hashish eating, or opium smoking. It is a cardinal error to believe that, of "Surrealist experiences," we know only the religious ecstasies or the ecstasies of drugs. The opium of the people, Lenin called religion, and brought the two things closer together than the Surrealists could have liked. I shall refer later to the bitter, passionate revolt against Catholicism in which Rimbaud, Lautréamont, and Apollinaire brought Surrealism into the world. But the true, creative overcoming of religious illumination certainly does not lie in narcotics. It resides in a *profane illumination,* a materialistic, anthropological inspiration, to which hashish, opium, or whatever else can give an introductory lesson. (But a dangerous one; and the religious lesson is stricter.) This profane illumination did not always find the Surrealists equal to it, or to themselves, and the very writings that proclaim it most powerfully, Aragon's incomparable *Paysan de Paris* and Breton's *Nadja,* show very disturbing symptoms of deficiency. For example, there is in

Nadja an excellent passage on the "delightful days spent looting Paris under the sign of Sacco and Vanzetti"; Breton adds the assurance that in those days Boulevard Bonne-Nouvelle fulfilled the strategic promise of revolt that had always been implicit in its name. But Madame Sacco also appears, not the wife of Fuller's victim but a *voyante,* a fortuneteller who lives at 3 rue des Usines and tells Paul Eluard that he can expect no good from Nadja. Now I concede that the breakneck career of Surrealism over rooftops, lightning conductors, gutters, verandas, weathercocks, stucco work—all ornaments are grist to the cat burglar's mill—may have taken it also into the humid backroom of spiritualism. But I am not pleased to hear it cautiously tapping on the windowpanes to inquire about its future. Who would not wish to see these adoptive children of revolution most rigorously severed from all the goings-on in the conventicles of down-at-heel dowagers, retired majors, and *émigré* profiteers?

In other respects Breton's book illustrates well a number of the basic characteristics of this "profane illumination." He calls *Nadja* "a book with a banging door." (In Moscow I lived in a hotel in which almost all the rooms were occupied by Tibetan lamas who had come to Moscow for a congress of Buddhist churches. I was struck by the number of doors in the corridors that were always left ajar. What had at first seemed accidental began to be disturbing. I found out that in these rooms lived members of a sect who had sworn never to occupy closed rooms. The shock I had then must be felt by the reader of *Nadja.*) To live in a glass house is a revolutionary virtue par excellence. It is also an intoxication, a moral exhibitionism, that we badly need. Discretion concerning one's own existence, once an aristocratic virtue, has become more and more an affair of petit-bourgeois parvenus. *Nadja* has achieved the true, creative synthesis between the art novel and the *roman-à-clef.*

Moreover, one need only take love seriously to recognize in it, too—as *Nadja* also indicates—a "profane illumination."

"At just that time" (i.e., when he knew Nadja), the author tells us, "I took a great interest in the epoch of Louis VII, because it was the time of the 'courts of love,' and I tried to picture with great intensity how people saw life then." We have from a recent author quite exact information on Provençal love poetry, which comes surprisingly close to the Surrealist conception of love. "All the poets of the 'new style,' " Erich Auerbach points out in his excellent *Dante: Poet of the Secular World,* "possess a mystical beloved, they all have approximately the same very curious experience of love; to them all Amor bestows or withholds gifts that resemble an illumination more than sensual pleasure; all are subject to a kind of secret bond that determines their inner and perhaps also their outer lives." The dialectics of intoxication are indeed curious. Is not perhaps all ecstasy in one world humiliating sobriety in that complementary to it? What is it that courtly *Minne* seeks—and it, not love, binds Breton to the telepathic girl—if not to make chastity, too, a transport? Into a world that borders not only on tombs of the Sacred Heart or altars to the Virgin, but also on the morning before a battle or after a victory.

The lady, in esoteric love, matters least. So, too, for Breton. He is closer to the things that Nadja is close to than to her. What are these things? Nothing could reveal more about Surrealism than their canon. Where shall I begin? He can boast an extraordinary discovery. He was the first to perceive the revolutionary energies that appear in the "outmoded," in the first iron constructions, the first factory buildings, the earliest photos, the objects that have begun to be extinct, grand pianos, the dresses of five years ago, fashionable restaurants when the vogue has begun to ebb from them. The relation of these things to revolution—no one can have a more exact concept of it than these authors. No one before these visionaries and augurs perceived how destitution—not only social but architectonic, the poverty of interiors, enslaved and enslaving objects—can be suddenly transformed into revolutionary nihilism. Leaving aside Aragon's *Passage de l'Opéra,* Breton and Nadja are the lovers who convert everything that we have experienced on mournful railway journeys (railways are beginning to age), on Godforsaken Sunday afternoons in the proletarian quarters of the great cities, in the first glance through the rain-blurred window of a new apartment, into revolutionary experience, if not action. They bring the immense forces of "atmosphere" concealed in these things to the point of explosion. What form do you suppose a life would take that was determined at a decisive moment precisely by the street song last on everyone's lips?

The trick by which this world of things is mastered—it is more proper to speak of a trick than a method—consists in the substitution of a political for a historical view of the past. "Open, graves, you, the dead of the picture galleries, corpses behind screens, in palaces, castles, and monasteries, here stands the fabulous keeper of keys holding a bunch of the keys to all times, who knows where to press the most artful lock and invites you to step into the midst of the world of today, to mingle with the bearers of burdens, the mechanics whom money ennobles, to make yourself at home in their automobiles, which are beautiful as armor from the age of chivalry, to take your places in the international sleeping cars, and to weld yourself to all the people who today are still proud of their privileges. But civilization will give them short shrift." This speech was attributed to Apollinaire by his friend Henri Hertz. Apollinaire originated this technique. In his volume of novellas, *L'hérésiarque,* he used it with Machiavellian calculation to blow Catholicism (to which he inwardly clung) to smithereens.

At the center of this world of things stands the most dreamed-of of their objects, the city of Paris itself. But only revolt completely exposes its Surrealist face (deserted streets in which whistles and shots dictate the outcome). And no face is surrealistic in the same degree as the true face of a city. No picture by de Chirico or Max Ernst can match the sharp elevations of the city's inner strongholds, which one must overrun and occupy in order to master their fate and, in their fate, in the fate of their masses, one's own. Nadja is an exponent of these masses and of what inspires them to revolution: "The great living, sonorous unconsciousness that inspires my only convincing acts, in the sense that I always want to prove that it commands forever everything that is mine." Here, therefore, we find the catalogue of these fortifications, from Place Maubert, where as nowhere else dirt has retained all its symbolic power, to the "Théâtre Moderne," which I am inconsolable not to have known. But in Breton's description of the bar on the upper floor—"it is quite dark, with arbors like impenetrable tunnels—a drawing room on the bottom of a lake"—there is something that brings back to my memory that most uncomprehended room in the old Princess Café. It was the back room on the first floor, with couples in the blue light. We called it the "anatomy school"; it was the last restaurant designed for love. In such passages in Breton, photography intervenes in a very strange way. It makes the streets, gates, squares of the city into illustrations of a trashy novel, draws off the banal obviousness of this ancient architecture to inject it with the most pristine intensity toward the events described, to which, as in old chambermaids' books, word-for-word quotations with page numbers refer. And all the parts of Paris that appear here are places where what is between these people turns like a revolving door.

The Surrealists' Paris, too, is a "little universe." That is to say, in the larger one, the cosmos, things look no different. There, too, are crossroads where ghostly signals flash from the traffic, and inconceivable analogies and connections between events are the order of the day. It is the region from which the lyric poetry of Surrealism reports. And this must be noted if only to counter the obligatory misunderstanding of *l'art pour l'art*. For art's sake was scarcely ever to be taken literally; it was almost always a flag under which sailed a cargo that could not be declared because it still lacked a name. This is the moment to embark on a work that would illuminate as has no other the crisis of the arts that we are witnessing: a history of esoteric poetry. Nor is it by any means fortuitous that no such work yet exists. For written as it demands to be written—that is, not as a collection to which particular "specialists" all contribute "what is most worth knowing" from their fields, but as the deeply grounded composition of an individual who, from inner compulsion, portrays less a historical evolution than a constantly renewed, primal upsurge of esoteric poetry—written in such a way it would be one of those scholarly confessions that can be counted in every century. The last page would have to show an X-ray picture of Surrealism. Breton indicates in his *Introduction au discours sur le peu de réalité* how the philosophical realism of the Middle Ages was the basis of poetic experience. This realism, however—that is, the belief in a real, separate existence of concepts whether outside or inside things—has always very quickly crossed over from the logical realm of ideas to the magical realm of words. And it is as magical experiments with words, not as artistic dabbling, that we must understand the passionate phonetic and graphical transformational games that have run through the whole literature of the avant-garde for the past fifteen years, whether it is called Futurism, Dadaism, or Surrealism. How slogans, magic formulas, and concepts are here intermingled is shown by the following words of Apollinaire's from his last manifesto, *L'esprit nouveau et les poètes*. He says, in 1918: "For the speed and simplicity with which we have all become used to referring by a single word to such complex entities as a crowd, a nation, the universe, there is no modern equivalent in literature. But today's writers fill this gap; their synthetic works create new realities the plastic manifestations of which are just as complex as those referred to by the words standing for collectives." If, however, Apollinaire and Breton advance even more energetically in the same direction and complete the linkage of Surrealism to the outside world with the declaration, "The conquests of science rest far more on a surrealistic than on a logical thinking"—if, in other words, they make mystification, the culmination of which Breton sees in poetry (which is defensible), the foundation of scientific and technical development, too—then such integration is too impetuous. It is very instructive to compare the movement's overprecipitous embrace of the uncomprehended miracle of machines—"the old fables have for the most part been realized, now it is the turn of poets to create new ones that the inventors on their side can then again make real" (Apollinaire)—to compare these overheated fantasies with the well-ventilated utopias of a Scheerbart.

"The thought of all human activity makes me laugh." This utterance of Aragon's shows very clearly the path Surrealism had to follow from its origins to its politicization. In his excellent essay *"La révolution et les intellectuels,"* Pierre Naville, who originally belonged to this group, rightly called this development dialectical. In the transformation of a highly contemplative attitude into revolutionary opposition, the hostility of the bourgeoisie toward every manifestation of radical intellectual freedom played a leading part. This hostility pushed Surrealism to the left. Political events, above all the war in Morocco, accelerated this development. With the manifesto "Intellectuals Against the Moroccan War," which appeared in *L'Humanité,* a fundamentally different platform was gained from that which was characterized by, for example, the famous scandal at the Saint-Pol Roux banquet. At that time, shortly after the war, when the Surrealists, who deemed the celebration for a poet they worshiped compromised by the presence of nationalistic elements, burst out with the cry "Long live Germany," they remained within the boundaries of scandal, toward which, as is known, the bourgeoisie is as thick-skinned as it is sensitive to all action. There is remarkable agreement between the ways in which, under such political auspices, Apollinaire and Aragon saw the future of the poet. The chapters "Persecution" and "Murder" in Apollinaire's *Poète assas-*

siné contain the famous description of a pogrom against poets. Publishing houses are stormed, books of poems thrown on the fire, poets lynched. And the same scenes are taking place at the same time all over the world. In Aragon, "Imagination," in anticipation of such horrors, calls its company to a last crusade.

To understand such prophecies, and to assess strategically the line arrived at by Surrealism, one must investigate the mode of thought widespread among the so-called well-meaning left-wing bourgeois intelligentsia. It manifests itself clearly enough in the present Russian orientation of these circles. We are not of course referring here to Béraud, who pioneered the lie about Russia, or to Fabre-Luce, who trots behind him like a devoted donkey, loaded with every kind of bourgeois ill will. But how problematic is even the typical mediating book by Duhamel. How difficult to bear is the strained uprightness, the forced animation and sincerity of the Protestant method, dictated by embarrassment and linguistic ignorance, of placing things in some kind of symbolic illumination. How revealing his résumé: "the true, deeper revolution, which could in some sense transform the substance of the Slavonic soul itself, has not yet taken place." It is typical of these left-wing French intellectuals—exactly as it is of their Russian counterparts, too—that their positive function derives entirely from a feeling of obligation, not to the Revolution, but to traditional culture. Their collective achievement, as far as it is positive, approximates conservation. But politically and economically they must always be considered a potential source of sabotage.

Characteristic of this whole left-wing bourgeois position is its irremediable coupling of idealistic morality with political practice. Only in contrast to the helpless compromises of "sentiment" are certain central features of Surrealism, indeed of the Surrealist tradition, to be understood. Little has happened so far to promote this understanding. The seduction was too great to regard the Satanism of a Rimbaud and a Lautréamont as a pendant to art for art's sake in an inventory of snobbery. If, however, one resolves to open up this romantic dummy, one finds something usable inside. One finds the cult of evil as a political device, however romantic, to disinfect and isolate against all moralizing dilettantism. Convinced of this, and coming across the scenario of a horror play by Breton that centers about a violation of children, one might perhaps go back a few decades. Between 1865 and 1875 a number of great anarchists, without knowing of one another, worked on their infernal machines. And the astonishing thing is that independently of one another they set its clock at exactly the same hour, and forty years later in Western Europe the writings of Dostoyevsky, Rimbaud, and Lautréamont exploded at the same time. One might, to be more exact, select from Dostoyevsky's entire work the one episode that was actually not published until about 1915, "Stavrogin's Confession" from *The Possessed*. This chapter, which touches very closely on the third canto of the *Chants de Maldoror*, contains a justification of evil in which certain motifs of Surrealism are more powerfully expressed than by any of its present spokesmen. For Stavrogin is a Surrealist *avant la lettre*. No one else understood, as he did, how naïve is the view of the Philistines that goodness, for all the manly virtue of those who practice it, is God-inspired; whereas evil stems entirely from our spontaneity, and in it we are independent and self-sufficient beings. No one else saw inspiration, as he did, in even the most ignoble actions, and precisely in them. He considered vileness itself as something preformed, both in the course of the world and also in ourselves, to which we are disposed if not called, as the bourgeois idealist sees virtue. Dostoyevsky's God created not only heaven and earth and man and beast, but also baseness, vengeance, cruelty. And here, too, he gave the devil no opportunity to meddle in his handiwork. That is why all these vices have a pristine vitality in his work; they are perhaps not "splendid," but eternally new, "as on the first day," separated by an infinity from the clichés through which sin is perceived by the Philistine.

The pitch of tension that enabled the poets under discussion to achieve at a distance their astonishing effects is documented quite scurrilously in the letter Isidore Ducasse addressed to his publisher on October 23, 1869, in an attempt to make his poetry look acceptable. He places himself in the line of descent from Mickiewicz, Milton, Southey, Alfred de Musset, Baudelaire, and says: "Of course, I somewhat swelled the note to bring something new into this literature that, after all, only sings of despair in order to depress the reader and thus make him long all the more intensely for goodness as a remedy. So that in the end one really sings only of goodness, only the method is more philosophical and less naïve than that of the old school, of which only Victor Hugo and a few others are still alive." But if Lautréamont's erratic book has any lineage at all, or, rather, can be assigned one, it is that of insurrection. Soupault's attempt, in his edition of the complete works in 1927, to write a political curriculum vitae for Isidore Ducasse was therefore a quite understandable and not unperceptive venture. Unfortunately, there is no documentation for it, and that adduced by Soupault rests on a confusion. On the other hand, and happily, a similar attempt in the case of Rimbaud was successful, and it is the achievement of Marcel Coulon to have defended the poet's true image against the Catholic usurpation by Claudel and Berrichon. Rimbaud is indeed a Catholic, but he is one, by his own account, in the most wretched part of himself, which he does not tire of denouncing and consigning to his own and everyone's hatred, his own and everyone's contempt: the part that forces him to confess that he does not understand revolt. But that is the concession of a communard dissatisfied with his own contribution who, by the time he turned his back on poetry, had long since—in his earliest work—taken leave of religion. "Hatred, to you I have entrusted my treasure," he writes in the *Saison en enfer.* This is another dictum around which a poetics of Surrealism might grow like a climbing plant, to sink its roots deeper than the theory of "surprised" creation originated by Apollinaire, to the depth of the insights of Poe.

Since Bakunin, Europe has lacked a radical concept of freedom. The Surrealists have one. They are the first to liquidate the sclerotic liberal-moral-humanistic ideal of freedom, because they are convinced that "freedom, which on this earth can only be bought with a thousand of the hardest sacrifices, must be enjoyed unrestrictedly in its fullness without any kind of pragmatic calculation, as long as it lasts." And this proves to them that "mankind's struggle for liberation in its simplest revolutionary form (which, however, is liberation in every respect), remains the only cause worth serving." But are they successful in welding this experience of freedom to the other revolutionary experience that we have to acknowledge because it has been ours, the constructive, dictatorial side of revolution? In short, have they bound revolt to revolution? How are we to imagine an existence oriented solely toward Boulevard Bonne-Nouvelle, in rooms by Le Corbusier and Oud?

To win the energies of intoxication for the revolution—this is the project about which Surrealism circles in all its books and enterprises. This it may call its most particular task. For them it is not enough that, as we know, an ecstatic component lives in every revolutionary act. This component is identical with the anarchic. But to place the accent exclusively on it would be to subordinate the methodical and disciplinary preparation for revolution entirely to a praxis oscillating between fitness exercises and celebration in advance. Added to this is an inadequate, undialectical conception of the nature of intoxication. The aesthetic of the painter, the poet, *en état de surprise,* of art as the reaction of one surprised, is enmeshed in a number of pernicious romantic prejudices. Any serious exploration of occult, surrealistic, phantasmagoric gifts and phenomena presupposes a dialectical intertwinement to which a romantic turn of mind is impervious. For histrionic or fanatical stress on the mysterious side of the mysterious takes us no further; we penetrate the mystery only to the degree that we recognize it in the everyday world, by virtue of a dialectical optic that perceives the everyday as impenetrable, the impenetrable as everyday. The most passionate investigation of telepathic phenomena, for example, will not teach us half as much about reading (which is an eminently telepathic process), as the profane illumination of reading about telepathic phenomena. And the most passionate investigation of the hashish trance will not teach us half as much about thinking (which is eminently narcotic), as the profane illumination of thinking about the hashish trance. The reader, the thinker, the loiterer, the *flâneur*, are types of illuminati just as much as the opium eater, the dreamer, the ecstatic. And more profane. Not to mention that most terrible drug—ourselves—which we take in solitude.

"To win the energies of intoxication for the revolution"— in other words, poetic politics? "We have tried that beverage. Anything, rather than that!" Well, it will interest you all the more how much an excursion into poetry clarifies things. For what is the program of the bourgeois parties? A bad poem on springtime, filled to bursting with metaphors. The socialist sees that "finer future of our children and grandchildren" in a condition in which all act "as if they were angels," and everyone has as much "as if he were rich," and everyone lives "as if he were free." Of angels, wealth, freedom, not a trace. These are mere images. And the stock imagery of these poets of the social-democratic associations? Their *gradus ad parnassum?* Optimism. A very different air is breathed in the Naville essay that makes the "organization of pessimism" the call of the hour. In the name of his literary friends he delivers an ultimatum in face of which this unprincipled, dilettantish optimism must unfailingly show its true colors: where are the conditions for revolution? In the changing of attitudes or of external circumstances? That is the cardinal question that determines the relation of politics to morality and cannot be glossed over. Surrealism has come ever closer to the Communist answer. And that means pessimism all along the line. Absolutely. Mistrust in the fate of literature, mistrust in the fate of freedom, mistrust in the fate of European humanity, but three times mistrust in all reconciliation: between classes, between nations, between individuals. And unlimited trust only in I. G. Farben and the peaceful perfection of the air force. But what now, what next?

Here due weight must be given to the insight that in the *Traité du style*, Aragon's last book, required a distinction between metaphor and image, a happy insight into questions of style that needs extending. Extension: nowhere do these two—metaphor and image—collide so drastically and so irreconcilably as in politics. For to organize pessimism means nothing other than to expel moral metaphor from politics and to discover in political action a sphere reserved one hundred percent for images. This image sphere, however, can no longer be measured out by contemplation. If it is the double task of the revolutionary intelligentsia to overthrow the intellectual predominance of the bourgeoisie and to make contact with the proletarian masses, the intelligentsia has failed almost entirely in the second part of this task because it can no longer be performed contemplatively. And yet this has hindered hardly anybody from approaching it again and again as if it could, and calling for proletarian poets, thinkers, and artists. To counter this, Trotsky had to point out—as early as *Literature and Revolution*—that such artists would only emerge from a victorious revolution. In reality it is far less a matter of making the artist of bourgeois origin into a master of "proletarian art" than of deploying him, even at the expense of his artistic activity, at important points in this sphere of imagery. Indeed, might not perhaps the interruption of his "artistic career" be an essential part of his new function?

The jokes he tells are the better for it. And he tells them better. For in the joke, too, in invective, in misunderstanding, in all cases where an action puts forth its own image and exists, absorbing and consuming it, where nearness looks with its own eyes, the long-sought image sphere is opened, the world of universal and integral actualities, where the "best room" is missing—the sphere, in a word, in which political materialism and physical nature share the inner man, the psyche, the individual, or whatever else we wish to throw to them, with dialectical justice, so that no limb remains unrent. Nevertheless—indeed, precisely after such dialectical annihilation—this will still be a sphere of images and, more concretely, of bodies. For it must in the end be admitted: metaphysical materialism, of the brand of Vogt and Bukharin, as is attested by the experience of the Surrealists, and earlier of Hebel, Georg Büchner, Nietzsche, and Rimbaud, cannot lead without rupture to anthropological materialism. There is a residue. The collective is a body, too. And the *physis* that is being organized for it in technology can, through all its political and factual reality, only be produced in that image sphere to which profane illumination initiates us. Only when in technology body and image so interpenetrate that all revolutionary tension becomes bodily collective innervation, and all the bodily innervations of the collective become revolutionary discharge, has reality transcended itself to the extent demanded by the *Communist Manifesto*. For the moment, only the Surrealists have understood its present commands. They exchange, to a man, the play of human features for the face of an alarm clock that in each minute rings for sixty seconds.

Brecht's
Threepenny Novel

Eight Years

Eight years separate *Threepenny Opera* from *Threepenny Novel*. The new work has developed from the old. But this did not happen in the quaint manner in which the maturing of a work of art is usually imagined. For these were politically decisive years. The author made their lesson his own, called their misdeeds by their name, lit a light for their victims. He has written a major satirical novel.

To write it he went back almost to the beginning. Little remains of the foundation, the plot of the opera. Only the main characters are the same. For it was they who began before our eyes to grow into these years, and to make such bloodstained room for their growing. When *Threepenny Opera* was performed for the first time in Germany, the gangster was still a strange face here. In the meantime he has made himself at home, and barbarism has been installed. For only at a late stage does barbarism in the exploiters take on the same drastic form that already characterizes the poverty of the exploited at the beginning of capitalism. Brecht is concerned with both; he therefore draws the epochs together and assigns his gangster type to quarters in a London that has the rhythm and appearance of the age of Dickens. Private life is subject to the earlier conditions, the class struggle to those of today. These Londoners have no telephones, but their police already have tanks. It has been said that present-day London shows that it is good for capitalism to preserve a certain backwardness. This cir-

cumstance has proved its worth for Brecht. The badly venti-
lated offices, humid public baths, foggy streets, he populates
with types who in manner are often patriarchal, but in their
methods always modern. Such displacements are part of the
optics of satire. Brecht underlines them through the liberties
he has taken with the topography of London. The behavior
of his characters, drawn from reality, is, the satirist may tell
himself, far more impossible than a Brobdingnag or London
that he has built in his head.

Old Acquaintances

So these characters stepped once more before their creator.
There is Peachum, who always keeps his hat on because there
is no roof that he does not expect to crash on his head. He
has neglected his instrument shop and, with his transport
ships, taken a step nearer military commerce, in the course of
which his army of beggars is put to use at critical moments as
an "excited crowd." The ships are to serve as troop carriers
during the Boer War. As they are rotten, they go down with
the troops not far from the Thames estuary. Peachum insists
on attending the funeral for the drowned soldiers; along with
many others, among whom is a certain Fewkoombey, he hears
a sermon by the bishop on the biblical admonition to make
one's talent grow. At this time he had already secured himself
against any dubious consequences of his arms-supply business
by eliminating his partner, though he does not commit the
murder himself. His daughter, too, "Peach," has brushes with
crime—but only such as befit a lady, an abortion and adultery.
We meet the doctor who is constrained to perform the operation, and from him hear a speech that is a counterpart to that
of the bishop.

The hero, Macheath, was still very close to his apprentice-
ship in *Threepenny Opera*. The novel recapitulates this only

briefly; with regard to "whole groups of years" it observes the silence "that makes many pages of the biographies of our big-business men so void of content," and Brecht leaves open the question whether, at the outset of the transformation that leads from the lumber dealer Beckett to the wholesale merchant Macheath, there was the murderer Stanford Sills, called "The Knife." It is clear only that the businessman remains loyal to certain earlier friends who have not found their way into legality. This is its own reward, for these friends obtain by robbery the goods that Macheath's combine markets cheaply and without competitors.

Macheath's combine consists of the B shops, whose tenants —independent agents—are contracted only to buy his goods and to pay rent for the shops. In a number of newspaper interviews he has spoken of his "decisive discovery of the human instinct of independence." Admittedly these independent agents are badly off, and one of them finishes in the Thames when Macheath, for business reasons, temporarily interrupts his supply of goods. Murder is suspected; a criminal affair arises. But this criminal affair merges into the satirical theme. The society seeking the murderer of the woman who has committed suicide will never be able to recognize him in Macheath, who has only exercised his contractual rights. "The murder of the small-business woman Mary Sawyer" not only is central to the plot but also contains its moral. The impoverished shopkeepers, the soldiers crammed into leaky ships, the burglars whose employer has the police president in his pay—this gray mass, which in the novel takes the place of the chorus in the opera, provides the rulers with their victims. On it they commit their crimes. To it belongs Mary Sawyer, who is forced to drown herself, and from its midst comes Fewkoombey, who to his astonishment is hanged for her murder.

A New Face

The soldier Fewkoombey, who in the prologue is given lodgings on Peachum's suggestion, and to whom in the epilogue "the talent of the poor" is revealed in a dream, is a new face, or, rather, scarcely a face but "transparent and faceless," like the millions who fill barracks and basement apartments. Hard against the frame, he is a lifesize figure pointing into the picture. He points to the bourgeois criminal society in the middle ground. In this society he has the first word, because without him it would make no profit; therefore Fewkoombey is in the prologue. And he is in the epilogue as a judge, because otherwise this society would have the last word. Between the two lies the short span of a half year that he dawdles through, but during which certain affairs of the ruling class have developed so far and so favorably that they end with his execution, which is interrupted by no "king's messenger on horseback."

Shortly before this he has, as we have mentioned, a dream. It is a dream of a trial revolving around a "special crime." "Because no one can keep a dreamer from triumphing, our friend became president of the greatest court of all time, of the only truly necessary, comprehensive, and just court. . . . After long reflection, itself lasting months, the Supreme Judge decided to begin with a man who, according to the statement of a bishop at a funeral for drowned soldiers, had invented a parable that had been used for two thousand years from every kind of pulpit and represented in the view of the Supreme Judge a special crime." The judge proves his point of view by specifying the consequences of the parable and cross-examining the long series of witnesses who have to report on *their* talents.

" 'Has your talent increased?' the Supreme Judge asked sternly. Frightened, they answered, 'No.' 'Did he'—referring to the accused—'see that it did not increase?' To this they did not know at first how to reply. After a period of deliberation, however, one of them stepped forward, a small boy. . . . 'He must have seen it; for we froze when it was cold, and were hungry before and after our meals. See for yourself whether it shows or not.' He put two fingers into his mouth and whistled and ... out ... stepped a female figure exactly resembling the small trader Mary Sawyer." When the accused, in view of such compromising evidence, is conceded a defense counsel, Fewkoombey says, "But he must suit you"; and when Mr. Peachum presents himself in this capacity, the guilt of his client is specified. He must be charged with aiding and abetting, because, says the Supreme Judge, he put into the hands of his people this parable that is also a talent. He then condemns him to death. But the gallows receive only the dreamer, who has understood in a waking minute how far back go the traces of the crime to which he and his kind fall victim.

The Party of Macheath

In handbooks on criminality, lawbreakers are described as asocial elements. This may be accurate for the majority. For some, however, it is refuted by recent history. By making many into criminals they made them social models. So it is with Macheath. He is of the new school, while his father-in-law, his equal and long his enemy, is still of the old. Peachum does not know how to put himself across. He hides his greed behind concern for his family, his impotence behind asceticism, his blackmail behind care for the poor. Best of all, he likes to disappear into his office. This cannot be said of Macheath. He is a born leader. His words have a statesmanlike timbre, his deeds a businesslike stamp. The tasks he has to perform are manifold. For a leader they were never harder than they are today. It is not enough to exercise force in preserving property relationships. It is not enough to coerce the dispossessed themselves into exercising it. These practicalities must be dealt with. But just as a ballet dancer is expected not only to be able to dance but also to be pretty, fascism requires not only that there be a savior for capital, but also that he be a noble human being. That is the reason why a type like Macheath is in these times invaluable.

He knows how to parade what the stunted petit bourgeois imagines a personality to be. Ruled by hundreds of authorities, tossed on the waves of price increases, the victim of crises, this habitué of statistics seeks an individual to whom he can hold on. No one will give him an answer, someone must. For this is the dialectic of the matter: if someone is willing to take responsibility, the petit bourgeois thank him with the promise not to take him to account. They decline to make demands, "because that would show Mr. Macheath that we have lost our trust in him." His nature, that of a leader, is the reverse side of their contentment. The latter tirelessly gratifies Macheath. He misses no opportunity to show himself. And he is a different man before bank directors, before the tenants of the B shops, before the court, and before the members of his gang. He proves "that you can say anything if only you have an unshakable will"; for example, the following:

"In my opinion, and it is the opinion of a serious, hardworking businessman, we do not have the right people at the head of the state. They all belong to some party or other, and parties are egoistical. Their point of view is one-sided. We need men who stand above the parties, as we businessmen do. We sell our goods to rich and poor alike. We sell everyone, without regard for persons, a hundredweight of potatoes, install his electrical wiring, paint his house. The government of the state is a moral task. We have to reach a point where the employers are good employers, the employees good employees, in brief: where the rich are good rich and the poor good poor. I am convinced that the day of such a regime will come. It will find me among its supporters."

Coarse Thinking

Brecht had Macheath's program and numerous other reflections printed in italics, so that they stand out from the narrative text. In this way he has produced a collection of speeches
and maxims, confessions and pleas that may be called unique.
It alone would assure the work's permanence. What these
passages say no one has yet uttered, and yet everyone talks
like this. These passages interrupt the text; they are—comparable in this to illustrations—an invitation to the reader
now and again to dispense with illusion. Nothing is more appropriate to a satirical novel. Some of these passages lastingly
illuminate the assumptions to which Brecht owes his persua-
sive power. For example: "The main thing is to learn coarse
thinking, that is, the thinking of the great."

There are many who believe the dialectician an amateur of
subtleties. So it is uncommonly useful that Brecht puts his
finger on the "coarse thinking" that dialectics produces as its
antithesis, includes within itself, and needs. Coarse thoughts
have a special place in dialectical thinking because their sole
function is to direct theory toward practice. They are directives *toward* practice, not *for* it: action can, of course, be as
subtle as thought. But a thought must be coarse to find its
way into action.

The forms of coarse thinking change slowly, for they are
created by the masses. Even from defunct forms we can still
learn. One of these is the proverb, and the proverb is a school
of coarse thinking. "Does Mr. Macheath have Mary Sawyer on
his conscience?" people ask. Brecht rubs their noses in the
answer and gives this section the heading "Wherever a foal is
drowned there must be water." He might have entitled another, "Wherever wood is planed there must be shavings." It
is the section in which Peachum, "the first authority in the
field of destitution," reviews the foundations of the begging
industry.

"I well know," he says to himself, "why people do not check

the infirmities of beggars more carefully before giving. They are convinced there must be wounds where they have aimed blows! Shall none be ruined where they have done business? If they care for their families, must not families end up under the bridges? Everyone is convinced in advance that in face of his own mode of life, mortally wounded and unspeakably helpless people must everywhere creep about. Why take the trouble to check. For the few pence they are prepared to give!"

Criminal Society

Peachum has grown since *Threepenny Opera*. Before his in-fallible gaze the conditions of his successful speculations lie exposed to view like the errors of those that failed. No veil, not the slightest illusion hides from him the laws of exploita-tion. Thereby this old-fashioned, unrealistic little man proves himself a highly modern thinker. He need not fear comparison with Spengler, who showed how useless the humanitarian and philanthropic ideologies from the early days of the bourgeoisie have become for present-day entrepreneurs. But the feats of technology benefit in the first place the ruling classes. That is true of advanced forms of thinking as much as of modern forms of locomotion. The gentlemen in *Threepenny Novel* have no cars, but they are all dialectical thinkers. Peachum, for example, reflects that murder is punishable. "But not to murder," he thinks, "is also and more dreadfully punishable ... to sink into the slums, as I and my whole family threatened to do, is nothing less than imprisonment. The slums are prison for life!"

The crime novel, which, in its early days, in the hands of Dostoyevsky, did much for psychology, has at the height of its development put itself at the disposal of social criticism. If Brecht's book makes more exhaustive use of the genre than did Dostoyevsky, one of the reasons is that—as in reality—the

criminal has his livelihood in society, and society—as in reality
—has its share in his theft. Dostoyevsky was concerned with
psychology; he made visible the criminal element hidden in
each person. Brecht is concerned with politics; he makes
visible the element of crime hidden in all business.

Bourgeois legality and crime—these are, by the rules of the
crime novel, opposites. Brecht's procedure consists in retaining
the highly developed technique of the crime novel but dis-
carding its rules. In *this* crime novel the actual relation between bourgeois legality and crime is presented. The latter
is shown to be a special case of exploitation sanctioned by the
former. Occasionally natural transitions between the two occur. The thoughtful Peachum observes "how complex deals
often turn into very simple actions, customary from time immemorial! . . . It began with contracts and government stamps
and by the end murder was needed! How strongly I, of all
people, am opposed to murder! . . . And to think that we were
only doing business with each other!"

It is natural that this borderline case of the crime novel has
no room for the detective. The role of preserver of the legal
order allotted to him by the rules is here taken over by competition. What takes place between Macheath and Peachum is
a struggle between two gangs, and the happy end a gentlemen's agreement that gives legal sanction to the distribution
of the spoils.

Satire and Marx

Brecht strips the conditions in which we live, removing the
drapings of legal concepts. Naked as it will be when it reaches
posterity, their human content emerges. Unfortunately it looks
dehumanized, but that is not the satirist's fault. His task is to
undress his fellow citizen. If he then gives him a new outfit, as
Cervantes does in the dog Berganza, Swift in the horse figure

of the Houyhnhnms, Hoffmann in a tomcat, his real concern is nevertheless only with the posture in which his subject stands naked between his costumes. The satirist confines himself to the nakedness that confronts him in the mirror. Beyond this his duty does not go.

So Brecht contents himself with a small rearrangement of the costumes of his contemporaries. It just suffices, incidentally, to establish continuity with the nineteenth century, which produced not only imperialism but also the Marxism that has such useful questions for it. "When the German Kaiser telegraphed President Krüger, which stock prices were rising there and which falling?" "Of course, only Communists ask that." But Marx, who was the first to undertake to bring back the relations between people from their debasement and obfuscation in capitalist economics into the light of criticism, became in so doing a teacher of satire who was not far from being a master of it. Brecht was his pupil. Satire, which was always a materialistic art, has in him now become a dialectical one, too. Marx stands in the background of his novel—roughly as Confucius and Zoroaster stand behind the mandarins and shahs who, in the satires of the Enlightenment, survey the Frenchmen around them. It is Marx who here determines the distance that every great writer, but particularly the great satirist, maintains between himself and his object. It was always this distance that posterity made its own when it declared a writer a classic. We may assume that it will find ample accommodation in *Threepenny Novel*.

Conversations
with Brecht

Svendborg Notes

July 4, 1934. A long conversation in Brecht's sickroom at Svendborg yesterday revolved around my essay "The Author as Producer." The theory it develops—that a decisive criterion for judging the revolutionary function of literary works lies in the degree of technical progress in literature that leads to a revised function of art forms and thus also of the intellectual means of production—Brecht would only accept with regard to a single type, the upper-middle-class writer, among whom he counts himself. "Such a writer," he says, "does indeed enjoy solidarity with the interests of the proletariat at one point: where the development of his own means of production is concerned. But in feeling solidarity at this one point, he is at this point, as producer, proletarianized, and utterly so. This complete proletarianization at one point, however, brings about solidarity with the proletariat on the entire front." My criticism of proletarian writers of Becher's type Brecht found too abstract. He tried to improve it with an analysis of the Becher poem printed in one of the latest numbers of one of the official proletarian literary journals under the title "I Say in All Frankness..." Brecht compared it, on the one hand, with his didactic poem on the art of acting written for Carola Neher, and, on the other, with *"Bateau ivre."* "I taught Carola Neher a number of things," he said; "she learned not only how to act, but also how to wash, for example. For she used to wash in order not to be dirty. There was no question of that. I taught her how to wash her face. She then brought this to such perfection that I wanted to film her doing it. But this came to nothing because at that time I was unwilling to film, and she unwilling to be filmed by anyone else. This didactic poem was a model. Every pupil was intended to put himself in the place of the 'I.' When Becher says 'I,' he be- lieves himself—as president of the Union of Proletarian- Revolutionary Writers in Germany—to be exemplary. Only no one wants to follow the example. One gathers simply that he is pleased with himself." Brecht said on this occasion that he had long intended to write a series of such model poems for different professions—engineer, writer. On the other hand, Brecht compares Becher's poem to Rimbaud's. In the latter, he thought, Marx and Lenin, too—had they read it—would have detected the great historical movement of which it is an expression. They would have recognized very clearly that it does not describe the perambulations of an eccentric stroller, but the vagabond flight of a person who can no longer endure the limits of his class, which—with the Crimean War, the Mexican adventure—was beginning to open up exotic parts of the world to its mercantile interests. To assimilate the ges- ture of the unfettered vagabond, putting his affairs in the hands of chance and turning his back on society, was patently impossible for the stereotype of the proletarian fighter.

July 6. Brecht, in the course of yesterday's conversation: "I often think of a tribunal before which I am being questioned. 'What was that? Do you really mean that seriously?' I would then have to admit: Not quite seriously. After all I think too much about artistic matters, about what would go well on the stage, to be quite serious; but when I have answered this important question in the negative, I will add a still more important affirmation: that my conduct is *legitimate*." This formulation, it is true, came later in the conversation. Brecht had begun with doubts not of the legitimacy but of the effec- tiveness of his procedure. With a sentence that arose from

some remarks I had made on Gerhart Hauptmann: "I sometimes wonder whether they are not, after all, the only writers
who really achieve anything: the *writers of substance,* I mean."
By this Brecht means writers who are entirely serious. And to
explain this idea he starts from the fiction that Confucius had
written a tragedy or Lenin a novel. One would think this in-
admissible, he declares, conduct unworthy of them. "Let us
suppose that you read an excellent political novel and afterward find out it is by Lenin; your opinion of both would be
changed, and to the disadvantage of both. Nor would Confucius be allowed to write a play by Euripides; it would be
thought undignified. Yet his parables are not." In short, all
this points to a distinction between two literary types: the
visionary, who is serious, on the one hand, and the reflective
man, who is not quite serious, on the other. Here I raise the
question of Kafka. To which of the two groups does he belong? I know, the question cannot be decided. And this very
thing is for Brecht a sign that Kafka, whom he considers a
great writer, like Kleist, Grabbe, or Büchner, is a failure. His
starting point is really the parable, which is responsible to
reason and therefore, as far as its wording is concerned, cannot
be entirely serious. But this parable is then subject to artistic
elaboration. It grows into a novel. And, strictly speaking, it
carried the germ of one from the start. It was never quite
transparent. Moreover, Brecht is convinced that Kafka would
not have found his own form without Dostoyevsky's Grand
Inquisitor and the other parabolic passage in *The Brothers
Karamazov,* where the corpse of the saintly Starets begins to
stink. In Kafka, therefore, parable is in conflict with vision.
But as a visionary, Brecht says, Kafka saw what was to come
without seeing what is. He stresses—as he had done earlier in
Le Lavandou, but, to me, more clearly—the prophetic side of
his work. Kafka, he says, had only one problem, that of organization. What seized him was fear of the ant-colony state:
how people become estranged from themselves by the forms
of their communal life. And certain forms of this estrangement

he foresaw—for example, the procedure of the G.P.U. He did not, however, find a solution, and did not wake from his nightmare. Of Kafka's precision, Brecht says it is that of someone vague, a dreamer.

July 12. Yesterday, after a game of chess, Brecht said: "If Korsch comes we shall have to work out a new game with him. A game in which the positions do not always remain the same; where the function of the pieces changes if they have stood for a while on the same square: then they become either more effective or weaker. Like this, the game does not develop; it stays the same too long."

July 23. Yesterday a visit from Karin Michaelis, who is just back from her Russian journey and full of enthusiasm. Brecht recalls his guide, Tretiakov, who showed him Moscow, proud of everything his guest saw, no matter what. "That is no bad thing," says Brecht; "it shows that it belongs to him. No one is proud of other people's property." After a while he adds: "Well, in the end I did get a bit tired. I could not admire everything, nor did I want to. It's like this: they are his soldiers, his trucks. But, unfortunately, not mine."

July 24. On a beam supporting the ceiling of Brecht's study are painted the words "Truth is concrete." On a window sill stands a little wooden donkey that can nod its head. Brecht has hung a little notice around its neck saying, "I, too, must understand it."

August 5. Three weeks ago I gave B. my essay on Kafka. He certainly read it, but never spoke about it of his own accord, and both times I brought the conversation around to it, he replied evasively. Finally I took back the manuscript without a word. Yesterday evening he suddenly came back to this essay. The transition to it, somewhat abrupt and breakneck, was effected by the comment that I, too, could not be entirely absolved from the reproach of a diarist's style of writing, in the manner of Nietzsche. My Kafka essay, for example—he was concerned with Kafka merely from the phenomenal point of view—took the work as something that had grown by itself—the man, too—severed all its connections, even that with its author. It was always the question of *essence* that finally interested me. Whereas such a matter ought to be approached by asking the question of Kafka: what does he do? how does he behave? And by looking in the first place more at the general than at the particular. It then emerges that he lived in Prague in a bad milieu of journalists and self-important literati; in this world literature was the main, if not the only, reality. With this attitude Kafka's strengths and weaknesses are connected; his artistic value, but also his manifold futility. He is a Jewboy—as one might also coin the term Aryanboy—a skinny, unlikable creature, a bubble on the iridescent morass of Prague culture, nothing more. Nevertheless, he also had certain very interesting sides. These could be brought out; one would have to imagine a conversation between Lao-tse and his disciple Kafka. Lao-tse says: "Well now, disciple Kafka, the organizations, the leaseholds and other economic forms in which you live make you uneasy?" "Yes." "You can't cope with them any more?" "No." "A stock certificate worries you?" "Yes." "And now you are looking for a leader to hold on to, disciple Kafka." That is of course despicable, says Brecht. I reject Kafka. And he goes on to talk about a parable of a Chinese philosopher on "the pains of usefulness." In the forest there are various kinds of tree trunks. From the thickest, beams for ships are cut; from less thick but still respectable trunks, box lids and coffin sides are made; the very thin ones are used for rods; but nothing comes of the stunted ones—they escape the pains of usefulness. "In what Kafka wrote you have to look around as in such a forest. You will then find a number of very useful things. The images are good. But the rest is obscurantism. It is sheer mischief. You have to ignore it. Depth takes you no further. Depth is a dimension of its own, just depth—which is why nothing comes to light in it." I explain to B. in conclusion that plumbing the depths is my way of going to the antipodes. In my essay on Kraus I did indeed come out there. I know that the one on Kafka was not so successful: I could not rebut the charge that it consisted of diarylike notes. Discussion within the frontier zone designated by Kraus, and in another way by Kafka, did indeed interest me. I had not yet, I said, explored this area in Kafka's case. That it contained a good deal of rubbish and detritus, much real obscurantism, I fully realized. Nevertheless, other aspects were more decisive, and I had touched on a number of them in my essay. B.'s critical approach must, after all, prove itself in the interpretation of the particular. I open "The Next Village." At once I was able to observe the conflict produced in B. by this suggestion. Eisler's remark that this story was "worthless" he rejected emphatically. On the other hand, he was equally unable to explain its value. "It would need close study," he thought. Then the conversation broke off; it was ten o'clock, and the radio news was on the air from Vienna.

August 31. The day before yesterday we had a long and heated debate on my Kafka. Its basis: the charge that it advanced Jewish fascism. It increased and propagated the obscurity surrounding this author instead of dispersing it. Whereas it was of crucial importance to clarify Kafka, that is, to formulate practicable proposals that can be derived from his stories. That proposals were derivable from them could be supposed, if only from the serene calm of their viewpoint. However, these suggestions would have to be sought in the direction of the great general abuses afflicting present-day humanity. Brecht tries to show their imprint in Kafka's work. He confines himself chiefly to *The Trial.* There above all, he thinks, we find the fear of the unending and irresistible growth of cities. He claims to know from personal experience the crushing weight of this phenomenon on human beings. The inexplicable mediations, dependencies, entanglements besetting men as a result of their present form of existence, find expression in these cities. They find expression in another way in the desire for a "Leader," who for the petit bourgeois represents the man whom—in a world where blame can be passed from one person to the next so that everyone escapes it—he can hold accountable for all his misfortunes. Brecht calls *The Trial* a prophetic book. "What can become of the Cheka you can see from the Gestapo." Kafka's perspective: that of the man who has gone to the dogs. Odradek is characteristic of this: Brecht interprets the janitor as representing the cares of the father of a family. Things must go wrong for the petit bourgeois. His situation is Kafka's. But whereas the type of petit bourgeois current today— that is, the fascist—decides in face of this situation to exert his iron, indomitable will, Kafka hardly resists; he is wise. Where the fascist imposes heroism, he poses questions. He asks for guarantees of his situation. But the latter is so constituted that the guarantees would have to exceed all reasonable measure. It is a Kafkaesque irony that the man who seemed convinced of nothing more than of the invalidity of all guarantees was an insurance official. Moreover, his unrestricted pessimism is free of any tragic sense of fate. For not only has his expectation of misfortune a solely empirical foundation—albeit a perfect one; he also places the criterion of final success with incorrigible naïveté in the most trivial and banal of enterprises: the visit of a commercial traveler or an application to an authority. The conversation concentrated at times on the story "The Next Village." Brecht declares it a counterpart to the story of Achilles and the tortoise. Someone who composes the ride from its smallest particles—leaving aside all incidents—will never reach the next village. Life itself is too short for such a ride. But the error lies in the "someone." For just as the ride is deceptive, so, too, is the rider. And just as the unity of life is now done away with, so, too, is its brevity. No matter how brief it may be. This makes no difference, because a different person from him who started the ride arrives at the village. For my part, I give the following interpretation: the true meas-

ure of life is remembrance. Retrospectively, it traverses life
with the speed of lightning. As quickly as one turns back a few
pages, it has gone back from the next village to the point
where the rider decided to set off. He whose life has turned
into writing, like old people's, likes to read this writing only
backward. Only so does he meet himself, and only so—in flight
from the present—can his life be understood.

September 27, Dragør.   In a conversation one evening a few
days ago, Brecht explained the curious indecision that at present prevents his making definite plans. The first reason for this
indecision is—as he emphasizes himself—the advantages dis-
tinguishing his personal situation from that of most emigrants.
If in this he scarcely acknowledges emigration in general as the
basis for undertakings and plans, any such conception of it in
his particular case is all the more irrevocably abolished. His
plans have a wider compass. This presents him with a choice.
On the one hand, prose projects are waiting. The smaller one
on Ui—a satire on Hitler in the style of the historiographers
of the Renaissance—and the big project of the Tui-novel. The
Tui-novel is intended to give an encyclopedic survey of the
follies of the Tellectual-Ins (intellectuals); it will, it seems, take
place at least in part in China. A small model for this work is
ready. But besides these prose plans he is claimed by projects
that go back to very old studies and reflections. And while it
was just possible to include the reflections that originated in
connection with epic theater in the notes and introductions to
the *Versuche,* ideas that arose from the same interests but were
later combined with the study of Leninism, on the one hand,
and with the scientific tendencies of the empiricists, on the
other, have outgrown so restricted a framework. For years they
have been grouped, now under this, now under that heading,
so that in turn non-Aristotelian logic, behavior theory, the new
encyclopedia, the critique of ideas, moved to the center of
Brecht's endeavors. These different activities are converging
at present in the idea of a philosophical, didactic poem.

Brecht's scruples originate in the question whether—in view
of all his previous work, but especially its satirical part and
above all *Threepenny Novel*—he would find acceptance with
the public for this work. In this doubt two different trains of
thought come together. On the one hand, there are the misgivings to which—the more intense Brecht's concern with the
problems and methods of the proletarian class struggle became
—the satirical and even more the ironic standpoint must as
such be exposed. These misgivings—of a primarily practical
nature—would, however, be misunderstood if they were identified with other, more fundamental considerations. This deeper
layer of scruples concerns the artistic and playful element in
literature, but above all those moments that sometimes, in part,
make themselves refractory to reason. These heroic efforts of
Brecht's to legitimize art in relation to reason have thrown
him back time and again on the parable, in which artistic
mastery is proved by the final abolition in it of all elements of
art. And it is just this concern with parable that is now prominent in more radical form in the considerations surrounding
the didactic poem. In the course of the conversation itself I
tried to explain to Brecht that such a didactic poem would
have to justify itself less to the bourgeois public than to the
proletarian, which would presumably take its criteria less from
Brecht's earlier, partly bourgeois-orientated work than from
the dogmatic and theoretical content of the didactic poetry
itself. "If this didactic poem is able to mobilize for itself the
authority of Marxism"—I told him—"the fact of your earlier
work will hardly shake it."

October 4. Yesterday Brecht left for London. Whether he is
now and then particularly tempted by me, or whether he has
recently become generally more prone to it than earlier, what
he himself called the baiting stance of his thought is now far
more noticeable in conversation than earlier. Indeed, I am
struck by a particular term that stems from this attitude. He
is especially fond of using the concept of "nobodies" with such

intent. In Dragør I read *Crime and Punishment* by Dostoyevsky. First of all, he blamed this for being the chief cause of my
illness. And to back up his argument he told me how when he
was in his youth a protracted illness, the germ of which he had
probably carried for a long time, had broken out when, one
afternoon, already too weak to protest, he had listened to a
schoolfellow playing Chopin on the piano. Brecht attributes to
Chopin and Dostoyevsky an especially detrimental influence
on health. But he took up every other possible position against
my reading as well, and as he was himself at the same time
reading *Schweik,* he did not miss the opportunity to compare
the value of the two authors. At all events, Dostoyevsky could
not hold a candle to Hasek, but was, rather, consigned unceremoniously to the "nobodies," and he was doubtless close to
extending to his work the term that he holds ready of late for
all writings that lack, or to which he denies, an enlightening
character. He calls them "clods."

June 28, 1938. I found myself in a labyrinth of staircases.
This labyrinth was not everywhere roofed. I climbed up; other
stairways led downward. On one landing I found myself standing on a summit. A wide prospect opened across the country. I
saw others standing on other peaks. One of these people was
suddenly gripped by vertigo and plunged down. The giddiness
spread; other people now fell from other summits into the
depths. When I, too, was seized by this feeling, I woke up.

On June 22 I arrived at Brecht's.

Brecht points to a nonchalant elegance in the posture of
Virgil and Dante, describing it as the background against which
Virgil's grand gesture stands out. He called them both *prome-
neurs.* He stresses the classical status of the *Inferno:* "You can
read it in the country."

Brecht speaks of his inveterate hatred of clergymen, inherited from his grandmother. He insinuates that those who have
adopted the theoretical doctrines of Marx in a form that is
doctored to suit themselves will always form a clerical cama-

rilla. Marxism lends itself far too easily to "interpretation." It is a hundred years old and has been shown ... (At this point we are interrupted.) " 'The state must be abolished.' Who says that? The state." (Here he can only mean the Soviet Union.) Brecht comes and stands in an artful, crushed posture in front of the armchair in which I am sitting—he is imitating 'the state'—and says, with a sidelong squint at imaginary clients; " 'I know, I *ought* to be abolished.' "

A conversation on the modern Soviet novel. We have given up following it. We then turn to poetry and to the translations of Soviet lyric poetry from the most diverse languages with which *Das Wort* is inundated. Brecht remarks that the authors over there are having a difficult time. "It is taken as deliberate if the name Stalin does not appear in a poem."

June 29.   Brecht speaks of the epic theater; he mentions the children's theater in which errors of presentation, functioning as alienation effects, give the performance epic features. With small companies something similar can happen. I recall the Geneva performance of *Le Cid,* at which the sight of the king's crooked crown gave me the first idea for the book on tragedy I wrote nine years later. Here Brecht, on his side, quotes the moment in which the idea of epic theater is rooted. It was a rehearsal for the Munich performance of *Edward II.* The battle that occurs in the play has to hold the stage for three-quarters of an hour. Brecht could not cope with the soldiers. (Nor could Asja [Lacis], his assistant director.) He finally turned to Valentin, a close friend of his at that time, who was attending the rehearsal, with the despairing question "Well, what *is* the matter with the soldiers?" Valentin: "They're pale —they're afraid." This was the decisive remark. Brecht added, "They're tired." The soldiers' faces were given a thick coat of chalk. And on that day the style was discovered.

Shortly afterward, the old theme of "logical positivism" came up. I was fairly intransigent, and the conversation threatened to take a disagreeable turn. This was prevented by Brecht's admitting for the first time the superficiality of his formula-tions. He did so with the fine dictum "A deep need must be approached superficially." Later, when we went over to his house—for the conversation had taken place in my room: "It is a good thing to be overtaken in an extreme position by a reactionary epoch. That way you reach a middle position." This, he said, was what had happened to him; he had become benevolent.

In the evening: I should like to give someone a small present for Asja; gloves. Brecht thinks it would be difficult. The view could be taken that Jahnn* was rewarding her for espionage services with two gloves. "The worst thing is that entire direc-tions† are always kicked out. But their arrangements will prob-ably stay unchanged."

July 1. Very skeptical answers are elicited whenever I touch on conditions in Russia. When I inquired recently whether Ottwald was still in prison, the answer was, "If he's still alive, he's in prison." Yesterday Steffin said she doubted whether Tretiakov were still alive.

July 4. Yesterday evening. Brecht (in a conversation on Baudelaire): I'm not against the asocial—I'm against the non-social.

July 21. The publications of writers like Lukács and Kurella cause Brecht much concern. He thinks, however, that they should not be opposed in the theoretical sphere. I switch the question to the political sphere. Here, too, he does not mince his words. "The socialist economy does not need war and therefore has no stomach for it. The 'peace-loving' disposition of the 'Russian people' means no more than that. There can be no socialist economy in one country. Arms production has

---

* The name, probably of the intended intermediary, is not clearly legible; perhaps Hans Henny Jahnn?—ED.
† Uncertain reading.—ED.

necessarily been a severe setback for the Russian proletariat; in some areas it has pushed them back to stages of historical development they had long since left behind. The monarchist stage, among others. In Russia a personal regime is in power. That, of course, can be denied only by blockheads." This short conversation was soon interrupted. Furthermore, Brecht stressed in this connection that with the dissolution of the First International, Marx and Engels lost contact with the workers' movement and henceforth sent only private advice, not intended for publication, to individual leaders. Nor was it by chance—though regrettable—that Engels finally turned to natural science.

Béla Kun was, he said, his greatest admirer in Russia. Brecht and Heine were the only German lyric poets he favored. (Brecht occasionally alluded to a certain man in the Central Committee who supported him.)

July 25. Yesterday morning Brecht came over to show me his Stalin poem, entitled "The Farmer to His Oxen." At first I could not see the point; and when, after a moment, the thought of Stalin crossed my mind, I did not dare hold on to it. This effect corresponded roughly to Brecht's intention. He explained it in the ensuing conversation, stressing, among other things, the positive moment in the poem. It did indeed pay tribute to Stalin—who in his view had immense merits. But he was not yet dead. Moreover he, Brecht, was not entitled to pay any other, more enthusiastic tribute; he was in exile waiting for the Red Army. He was following Russian developments, and equally the writings of Trotsky. They prove that grounds for suspicion exist; justified suspicion that called for a skeptical view of Russian affairs. Such skepticism was in the spirit of the classical writers. Should the suspicions one day be confirmed, one would have to oppose the regime—and that means *publicly*. But "alas, or thank God, whichever you prefer," this suspicion was not yet a certainty. To derive a policy like Trotsky's from it would be irresponsible. "On the other hand, the fact that certain criminal cliques are at work in Russia itself is beyond doubt. It can be seen periodically from their misdeeds." Finally, Brecht emphasized that we were injured inwardly by this regression. "We have paid for our position; we are covered with scars. It is natural that we are also particularly sensitive."

Toward evening Brecht found me in the garden reading *Das Kapital*. Brecht: "I am very pleased to see you studying Marx now—at a time when he is less and less in evidence, above all among our people." I replied that I preferred to read much-discussed books when they were out of fashion. We went on to talk about Russian policy toward literature. "With these people," I said, referring to Lukács, Gabor, Kurella, "you just cannot build a state." Brecht: "Or *only* a state, but not a community. They are quite simply enemies of production. Production makes them uneasy. It can't be trusted. It is the unpredictable. You never know where it will end. And they themselves do not want to produce. They want to play the *apparatchik* and supervise others. Each of their criticisms contains a threat." We found ourselves, I do not know how, discussing Goethe's novels; Brecht only knows *Elective Affinities*. In it, he said, he had admired the elegance of the young man. When I told him that Goethe wrote the book at sixty, he was very surprised. The book was entirely without Philistinism. That was an immense achievement. He could applaud this, since German drama, even in the most important works, bore Philistine traces. I remarked that as a result *Elective Affinities* had had a miserable reception. Brecht: "I'm glad to hear it. The Germans are a dreadful people. It is not true that you cannot draw conclusions about the Germans from Hitler. In me, too, everything is bad that is German. What makes Germans unbearable is their narrow-minded self-sufficiency. Nothing like the free imperial cities, such as the detestable town of Augsburg, ever existed elsewhere. Lyons was never a free city; the independent cities of the Renaissance were city-states—

Lukács is an adoptive German. He has almost completely run out of wind."

In the *Best Tales of the Robber Woynok* by Seghers, Brecht praised the signs it gave that she had freed herself from her commission. "Seghers cannot write for a commission, just as I, without one, would have no idea how to start." He also approved the central role given in these stories to a stubborn outsider.

July 26.   Brecht yesterday evening: "There is no longer any doubt—the struggle against ideology has become a new ideology."

July 29.   Brecht reads me a number of polemical disputes with Lukács, studies for an essay that he is to publish in *Das Wort*. They are disguised but vehement attacks. Brecht asks my advice concerning their publication. Since he tells me at the same time that Lukács now has an important position "over there," I say that I cannot advise him. "These are questions of power. Someone over there ought to say something. After all, you have friends there." Brecht: "Actually I have no friends there. The Muscovites don't have any, either—like the dead."

August 3.   On the evening of July 29, in the garden, a discussion arose on the question whether a part of the cycle "Children's Songs" should be included in the new volume of poems. I was not in favor, because I thought the contrast between the political and the private poem expressed the experience of exile particularly clearly; this effect should not be weakened by a disparate collection. I hinted that in his proposal Brecht's destructive character, which calls into question what has scarcely been achieved, was once again involved. Brecht: "I know people will say of me, 'He was a manic.' If this age goes down to posterity, understanding for my mania will go down with it. The age will provide the background for manic tendencies. But what I should really like is for people one day to say, 'He was a *moderate* manic.' " Recognition of his moderation should not be neglected in the volume of poems; that life, despite Hitler, goes on, that there will aways be children. Brecht thinks of an age without history, of which his poem to sculptors gives a portrait, and about which he told me a few days later that he thought its arrival more likely than victory over fascism. But then, still as an argument for the inclusion of the "Children's Songs" in the *Poems from Exile,* something else asserted itself, which Brecht expressed as he stood before me in the grass, with a passion he seldom shows. "In the fight against them nothing must be omitted. Their intentions are not trivial. They are planning for the next thirty thousand years. Monstrous. Monstrous crimes. They stop at nothing. They hit out at everything. Every cell flinches under their blows. That is why not one of us can be forgotten. They deform the baby in the mother's womb. We must under no circumstances leave out the children." While he spoke I felt a force acting on me that was equal to that of fascism; I mean a power that has its source no less deep in history than fascism. It was a very curious feeling, new to me. It was matched by the direction Brecht's thought now took. "They are planning devastation of icy proportions. That is why they cannot come to an agreement with the Church, which is also a march into millennia. They have proletarianized me as well. They have not only taken away my house, my fishpond, and my car; they have also stolen my theater and my public. From my standpoint, I cannot admit that Shakespeare was fundamentally a greater talent. But he, too, would have been unable to write from stock. He had his models in front of him. The people he portrayed were actually there. He managed with great difficulty to snatch up a few characteristics of their behavior; many equally important ones he left out."

Beginning of August. "In Russia a dictatorship is in power *over* the proletariat. We must avoid disowning it for as long

as this dictatorship still does practical work for the proletariat
—that is, as long as it contributes to a balance between proletariat and peasantry with a preponderant regard for proletarian interests." Some days later Brecht spoke of a "workers'
monarchy," and I compared this organism to the grotesque
jokes of nature that, in the form of a horned fish or some
other monster, are extracted from the ocean.

August 25. A Brechtian maxim: do not build on the good old
days, but on the bad new ones.

The Author as Producer[*]

> The task is to win over the in-
> tellectuals to the working class
> by making them aware of the
> identity of their spiritual enter-
> prises and of their conditions as
> producers.
>
> —Ramón Fernandez

You will remember how Plato, in his model state, deals with poets. He banishes them from it in the public interest. He had a high conception of the power of poetry, but he believed it harmful, superfluous—in a *perfect* community, of course. The question of the poet's right to exist has not often, since then, been posed with the same emphasis; but today it poses itself. Probably it is only seldom posed in this *form,* but it is more or less familiar to you all as the question of the autonomy of the poet, of his freedom to write whatever he pleases. You are not disposed to grant him this autonomy. You believe that the present social situation compels him to decide in whose service he is to place his activity. The bourgeois writer of entertainment literature does not acknowledge this choice. You must prove to him that, without admitting it, he is working in the service of certain class interests. A more advanced type of writer does recognize this choice. His decision, made on the basis of a class struggle, is to side with the proletariat. That puts an end to his autonomy. His activity is now decided by what is useful to the proletariat in the class struggle. Such writing is commonly called *tendentious.*

There you have the catchword around which has long cir-

[*] Address at the Institute for the Study of Fascism in Paris on April 27, 1934.—ED.

cled a debate familiar to you. Its familiarity tells you how unfruitful it has been, for it has not advanced beyond the monotonous reiteration of arguments for and against: *on the one hand,* the correct political line is demanded of the poet; *on the other,* it is justifiable to expect his work to have quality. Such a formulation is of course unsatisfactory as long as the connection between the two factors, political line and quality, has not been *perceived.* Of course, the connection can be asserted dogmatically. You can declare: a work that shows the correct political tendency need show no other quality. You can also declare: a work that exhibits the correct tendency must of necessity have every other quality.

This second formulation is not uninteresting, and, moreover, it is correct. I make it my own. But in doing so I abstain from asserting it dogmatically. It must be *proved.* And it is in order to attempt to prove it that I now claim your attention. This is, you will perhaps object, a very specialized, out-of-the-way theme. And how do I intend to promote the study of fascism with such a proof? That is indeed my intention. For I hope to be able to show you that the concept of political tendency, in the summary form in which it usually occurs in the debate just mentioned, is a perfectly useless instrument of political literary criticism. I should like to show you that the tendency of a literary work can only be politically correct if it is also literarily correct. That is to say, the politically correct tendency includes a literary tendency. And, I would add straightaway, this literary tendency, which is implicitly or explicitly contained in every *correct* political tendency of a work includes its literary quality *because* it includes its literary *tendency.*

This assertion—I hope I can promise you—will soon become clearer. For the moment I should like to interject that I might have chosen a different starting point for my reflections. I started from the unfruitful debate on the relationship between tendency and quality in literature. I could have started from an even older and no less unfruitful debate: what is the relationship between form and content, particularly in political poetry? This kind of question has a bad name; rightly so. It is the textbook example of the attempt to explain literary connections with undialectical clichés. Very well. But what, then, is the dialectical approach to the same question?

The dialectical approach to this question—and here I come to my central point—has absolutely no use for such rigid, isolated things as work, novel, book. It has to insert them into the living social context. You rightly declare that this has been done time and again among our friends. Certainly. Only they have often done it by launching at once into large, and therefore necessarily often vague, questions. Social conditions are, as we know, determined by conditions of production. And when a work was criticized from a materialist point of view, it was customary to ask how this work stood vis-à-vis the social relations of production of its time. This is an important question, but also a very difficult one. Its answer is not always unambiguous. And I should like now to propose to you a more immediate question, a question that is somewhat more modest, somewhat less far-reaching, but that has, it seems to me, more chance of receiving an answer. Instead of asking, "What is the attitude of a work to the relations of production of its time? Does it accept them, is it reactionary—or does it aim at overthrowing them, is it revolutionary?"—instead of this question, or at any rate before it, I should like to propose another. Rather than ask, "What is the *attitude* of a work to the relations of production of its time?" I should like to ask, "What is its *position* in them?" This question directly concerns the function the work has within the literary relations of production of its time. It is concerned, in other words, directly with the literary *technique* of works.

In bringing up technique, I have named the concept that makes literary products directly accessible to a social, and therefore a materialist analysis. At the same time, the concept of technique provides the dialectical starting point from which the unfruitful antithesis of form and content can be surpassed. And furthermore, this concept of technique contains an indication of the correct determination of the relation between tendency and quality, the question raised at the outset. If, therefore, I stated earlier that the correct political tendency of a work includes its literary quality, because it includes its literary tendency, I can now formulate this more precisely by saying that this literary tendency can consist either in progress or in regression in literary technique.

You will certainly approve if I now pass on, with only an appearance of arbitrariness, to very concrete literary conditions. Russian conditions. I should like to direct your attention to Sergei Tretiakov and to the type, defined and embodied by him, of the "operating" writer. This operating writer provides the most tangible example of the functional interdependency that always, and under all conditions, exists between the correct political tendency and progressive literary technique. I admit, he is only one example; I hold others in reserve. Tretiakov distinguishes the operating from the informing writer. His mission is not to report but to struggle; not to play the spectator but to intervene actively. He defines this mission in the account he gives of his own activity. When, in 1928, at the time of the total collectivization of agriculture, the slogan "Writers to the *Kolkhoz!*" was proclaimed, Tretiakov went to the "Communist Lighthouse" commune and there, during two lengthy stays, set about the following tasks: calling mass meetings; collecting funds to pay for tractors; persuading independent peasants to enter the *kolkhoz* [collective farm]; inspecting the reading rooms; creating wall newspapers and editing the *kolkhoz* newspaper; reporting for Moscow newspapers; introducing radio and mobile movie houses, etc. It is not surprising that the book *Commanders of the Field,* which Tretiakov wrote following these stays, is said to have had considerable influence on the further development of collective agriculture.

You may have a high regard for Tretiakov and yet still be of the opinion that his example does not prove a great deal in this context. The tasks he performed, you will perhaps object, are those of a journalist or a propagandist; all this has little to do with literature. However, I did intentionally quote the example of Tretiakov in order to point out to you how comprehensive is the horizon within which we have to rethink our conceptions of literary forms or genres, in view of the technical factors affecting our present situation, if we are to identify the forms of expression that channel the literary energies of the present. There were not always novels in the past, and there will not always have to be; not always tragedies, not always great epics; not always were the forms of commentary, translation, indeed, even so-called plagiarism, playthings in the margins of literature; they had a place not only in the philosophical but also in the literary writings of Arabia and China. Rhetoric has not always been a minor form, but set its stamp in antiquity on large provinces of literature. All this to accustom you to the thought that we are in the midst of a mighty recasting of literary forms, a melting down in which many of the opposites in which we have been used to think may lose their force. Let me give an example of the unfruitfulness of such opposites, and of the process of their dialectical transcendence. And we shall remain with Tretiakov. For this example is the newspaper.

"In our writing," a left-wing author writes,* "opposites that in happier periods fertilized one another have become insoluble antinomies. Thus science and belles-lettres, criticism and production, education and politics, fall apart in disorder. The theater of this literary confusion is the newspaper, its content 'subject-matter,' which denies itself any other form of organization than that imposed on it by the readers' impatience. And this impatience is not just that of the politician expecting information, or of the speculator on the lookout for a tip; behind it smolders that of the man on the sidelines who believes he has the right to see his own interests expressed. The fact that nothing binds the reader more tightly to his paper than this impatient longing for daily nourishment has long been exploited by the publishers, who are constantly opening

* Benjamin himself; see *Schriften*, Frankfurt/M., 1955, vol. I, p. 384.—ED.

new columns to his questions, opinions, protests. Hand in hand, therefore, with the indiscriminate assimilation of facts, goes the equally indiscriminate assimilation of readers who are instantly elevated to collaborators. In this, however, a dialectic moment is concealed: the decline of writing in the bourgeois press proves to be the formula for its revival in that of Soviet Russia. For as writing gains in breadth what it loses in depth, the conventional distinction between author and public, which is upheld by the bourgeois press, begins in the Soviet press to disappear. For the reader is at all times ready to become a writer, that is, a describer, but also a prescriber. As an expert— even if not on a subject but only on the post he occupies—he gains access to authorship. Work itself has its turn to speak. And the account it gives of itself is a part of the competence needed to perform it. Literary qualification is founded no longer on specialized but, rather, on polytechnic education, and is thus public property. It is, in a word, the literarization of the conditions of living that masters the otherwise insoluble antinomies, and it is in the theater of the unbridled debasement of the word—the newspaper—that its salvation is being prepared."

I hope to have shown by means of this quotation that the description of the author as a producer must extend as far as the press. For through the press, at any rate through the Soviet Russian press, one recognizes that the mighty process of recasting that I spoke of earlier not only affects the conventional distinction between genres, between writer and poet, between scholar and popularizer, but also revises even the distinction between author and reader. Of this process the press is the decisive example, and therefore any consideration of the author as producer must include it.

It cannot, however, stop at this point. For the newspaper in Western Europe does not constitute a serviceable instrument of production in the hands of the writer. It still belongs to capital. Since, on the one hand, the newspaper, technically speaking, represents the most important literary position, but, on the other, this position is controlled by the opposition, it is no wonder that the writer's understanding of his dependent position, his technical possibilities, and his political task has to grapple with the most enormous difficulties. It has been one of the decisive processes of the last ten years in Germany that a considerable proportion of its productive minds, under the pressure of economic conditions, have passed through a revolutionary development in their attitudes, without being able simultaneously to rethink their own work, their relation to the means of production, their technique, in a really revolutionary way. I am speaking, as you see, of the so-called left-wing intellectuals, and will limit myself to the bourgeois left. In Germany the leading politico-literary movements of the last decade have emanated from this left-wing intelligentsia. I shall mention two of them, Activism and New Matter-of-factness, to show with these examples that a political tendency, however revolutionary it may seem, has a counterrevolutionary function as the writer feels his solidarity with the proletariat only in his attitudes, not as a producer.

The catchword in which the demands of Activism are summed up is "logocracy"; in plain language, rule of the mind. This is apt to be translated as rule of the intellectuals. In fact, the concept of the intellectual, with its attendant spiritual values, has established itself in the camp of the left-wing intelligentsia, and dominates its political manifestoes from Heinrich Mann to Döblin. It can readily be seen that this concept has been coined without any regard for the position of the intellectuals in the process of production. Hiller, the theoretician of Activism, himself means intellectuals to be understood not as "members of certain professions" but as "representatives of a certain characterological type." This characterological type naturally stands as such between the classes. It encompasses any number of private individuals without offering the slightest basis for organizing them. When Hiller formulates his denunciation of the party leaders, he concedes them a good deal; they may be "in important matters better informed ..., have more popular

appeal . . . , fight more courageously" than he, but of one thing
he is sure: that they "think more defectively." Probably, but
where does this lead him, since politically it is not private
thinking but, as Brecht once expressed it, the art of thinking
in other people's heads that is decisive. Activism attempted to
replace materialistic dialectics by the—in class terms unquanti-
fiable—notion of common sense.* Its intellectuals represent at
best a social group. In other words, the very principle on
which this collective is formed is reactionary; no wonder that
its effect could never be revolutionary.

However, this pernicious principle of collectivization continues to operate. This could be seen three years ago, when
Döblin's *Wissen und Verändern* [*Know and Change*] came out.
As is known, this pamphlet was written in reply to a young
man—Döblin calls him Herr Hocke—who had put to the
famous author the question "What is to be done?" Döblin
invites him to join the cause of socialism, but with reservations.
Socialism, according to Döblin, is "freedom, a spontaneous
union of men, the rejection of all compulsion, indignation at
injustice and coercion, humanity, tolerance, a peaceful disposition." However this may be, on the basis of this socialism
he sets his face against the theory and practice of the radical
workers' movement. "Nothing," Döblin declares, "can come
out of anything that was not already in it—and from a
murderously exacerbated class war justice can come, but not
socialism." Döblin formulates the recommendation that, for
these and other reasons, he gives Herr Hocke: "You, my dear
sir, cannot put into effect your agreement in principle with
the struggle (of the proletariat) by joining the proletarian
front. You must be content with an agitated and bitter
approval of this struggle, but you also know that if you do
more, an immensely important post will remain unmanned . . . :

* In place of this sentence there was in the manuscript originally a different one that was deleted: "Or, to speak with Trotsky: 'If the enlightened
pacifists attempt to abolish war by means of rationalistic argument, they
simply make fools of themselves, but if the armed masses begin to use the
arguments of reason against war, that means the end of war.'"—ED.

the original communistic position of human individual freedom, of the spontaneous solidarity and union of men. . . . It
is this position, my dear sir, that alone falls to you." Here it
is quite palpable where the conception of the "intellectual,"
as a type defined by his opinions, attitudes, or dispositions,
but not by his position in the process of production, leads.
He must, as Döblin puts it, find his place *beside* the proletariat. But what kind of place is that? That of a benefactor,
of an ideological patron—an impossible place. And so we
return to the thesis stated at the outset: the place of the in-
intellectual in the class struggle can be identified, or, better,
chosen, only on the basis of his position in the process of
production.

For the transformation of the forms and instruments of
production in the way desired by a progressive intelligentsia
—that is, one interested in freeing the means of production
and serving the class struggle—Brecht coined the term *Umfunktionierung* [functional transformation]. He was the first
to make of intellectuals the far-reaching demand not to supply
the apparatus of production without, to the utmost extent
possible, changing it in accordance with socialism. "The
publication of the *Versuche*," the author writes in introducing
the series of writings bearing this title, "occurred at a time
when certain works ought no longer to be individual experiences (have the character of works) but should, rather,
concern the use (transformation) of certain institutes and
institutions." It is not spiritual renewal, as fascists proclaim,
that is desirable: technical innovations are suggested. I shall
come back to these innovations. I should like to content myself here with a reference to the decisive difference between
the mere supplying of a productive apparatus and its transformation. And I should like to preface my discussion of the
"New Matter-of-factness" with the proposition that to supply
a productive apparatus without—to the utmost extent possible
—changing it would still be a highly censurable course even
if the material with which it is supplied seemed to be of a

revolutionary nature. For we are faced with the fact—of which the past decade in Germany has furnished an abundance of examples—that the bourgeois apparatus of production and publication can assimilate astonishing quantities of revolutionary themes, indeed, can propagate them without calling its own existence, and the existence of the class that owns it, seriously into question. This remains true at least as long as it is supplied by hack writers, even if they be revolutionary hacks. I define the hack writer as the man who abstains in principle from alienating the productive apparatus from the ruling class by improving it in ways serving the interests of socialism. And I further maintain that a considerable proportion of so-called left-wing literature possessed no other social function than to wring from the political situation a continuous stream of novel effects for the entertainment of the public. This brings me to the New Matter-of-factness. Its stock in trade was reportage. Let us ask ourselves to whom this technique was useful.

For the sake of clarity I shall place its photographic form in the foreground, but what is true of this can also be applied to the literary form. Both owe the extraordinary increase in their popularity to the technology of publication: the radio and the illustrated press. Let us think back to Dadaism. The revolutionary strength of Dadaism consisted in testing art for its authenticity. Still lifes put together from tickets, spools of cotton, cigarette butts, that were linked with painted elements. The whole thing was put in a frame. And thereby the public was shown: look, your picture frame ruptures time; the tiniest authentic fragment of daily life says more than painting. Just as the bloody fingerprint of a murderer on the page of a book says more than the text. Much of this revolutionary content has gone on into photomontage. You need only think of the work of John Heartfield, whose technique made the book cover into a political instrument. But now follow the path of photography further. What do you see? It becomes ever more *nuancé,* ever more modern, and the result is that it can no longer depict a tenement block or a refuse heap without transfiguring it. It goes without saying that photography is unable to say anything about a power station or a cable factory other than this: what a beautiful world! *A Beautiful World*—that is the title of the well-known picture anthology by Renger-Patsch, in which we see New Matter-of-fact photography at its peak. For it has succeeded in transforming even abject poverty, by recording it in a fashionably perfected manner, into an object of enjoyment. For if it is an economic function of photography to restore to mass consumption, by fashionable adaptation, subjects that had earlier withdrawn themselves from it—springtime, famous people, foreign countries—it is one of its political functions to renew from within—that is, fashionably—the world as it is.

Here we have a flagrant example of what it means to supply a productive apparatus without changing it. To change it would have meant to overthrow another of the barriers, to transcend another of the antitheses, that fetter the production of intellectuals, in this case the barrier between writing and image. What we require of the photographer is the ability to give his picture the caption that wrenches it from modish commerce and gives it a revolutionary useful value. But we shall make this demand most emphatically when we—the writers—take up photography. Here, too, therefore, technical progress is for the author as producer the foundation of his political progress. In other words, only by transcending the specialization in the process of production that, in the bourgeois view, constitutes its order can one make this production politically useful; and the barriers imposed by specialization must be breached jointly by the productive forces that they were set up to divide. The author as producer discovers—in discovering his solidarity with the proletariat—simultaneously his solidarity with certain other producers who earlier seemed scarcely to concern him. I have spoken of the photographer; I shall very briefly insert a word of Eisler's on the musician: "In the development of music, too, both in production and in reproduction, we must learn to perceive an ever-increasing process of rationalization.... The phonograph record, the sound film, jukeboxes can purvey top-quality music ... canned as a commodity. The consequence of this process of rationalization is that musical reproduction is consigned to ever-diminishing, but also ever more highly qualified groups of specialists. The crisis of the commercial concert is the crisis of an antiquated form of production made obsolete by new technical inventions." The task therefore consisted of an *Umfunktionierung* of the form of the concert that had to fulfill two conditions: to eliminate the antithesis firstly between performers and listeners and secondly between technique and content. On this Eisler makes the following illuminating observation: "One must beware of overestimating orchestral music and considering it the only high art. Music without words gained its great importance and its full extent only under capitalism." This means that the task of changing the concert is impossible without the collaboration of the word. It alone can effect the transformation, as Eisler formulates it, of a concert into a political meeting. But that such a transformation does indeed represent a peak of musical and literary technique, Brecht and Eisler prove with the didactic play *The Measures Taken.*

If you look back from this vantage point on the recasting of literary forms that I spoke of earlier, you can see how photography and music, and whatever else occurs to you, are entering the growing, molten mass from which the new forms are cast. You find it confirmed that only the literarization of all the conditions of life provides a correct understanding of the extent of this melting-down process, just as the state of the class struggle determines the temperature at which—more or less perfectly—it is accomplished.

I spoke of the procedure of a certain modish photography whereby poverty is made an object of consumption. In turning to New Matter-of-factness as a literary movement, I must take a step further and say that it has made the *struggle against poverty* an object of consumption. The political importance of the movement was indeed exhausted in many cases by the conversion of revolutionary impulses, insofar as they occurred among bourgeoisie, into objects of amusement that found their way without difficulty into the big-city cabaret business. The transformation of the political struggle from a compulsion to decide into an object of contemplative enjoyment, from a means of production into a consumer article, is the defining characteristic of this literature. A perceptive critic has explained this, using the example of Erich Kästner, as follows: "With the workers' movement this left-wing radical intelligentsia has nothing in common. It is, rather, as a phenomenon of bourgeois decomposition, a counterpart of the feudalistic disguise that the Second Empire admired in the reserve officer. the radical-life publicists of the stamp of Kästner, Mehring, or Tucholsky are the proletarian camouflage of decayed bourgeois strata. Their function is to produce, from the political standpoint, not parties but cliques; from the literary standpoint, not schools but fashions; from the economic standpoint, not producers but agents. Agents or hacks who make a great display of their poverty, and a banquet out of yawning emptiness. One could not be more totally accommodated in an uncozy situation."

This school, I said, made a great display of its poverty. It thereby shirked the most urgent task of the present-day writer: to recognize how poor he is and how poor he has to be in order to begin again from the beginning. For that is what is involved. The Soviet state will not, it is true, banish the poet like Plato, but it will—and this is why I recalled the Platonic state at the outset—assign him tasks that do not permit him to display in new masterpieces the long-since-counterfeit wealth of creative personality. To expect a renewal in terms of such personalities and such works is a privilege of fascism, which gives rise to such scatterbrained formulations as that with which Günter Gründel in his *Mission of the Young Generation* rounds off the section on literature: "We cannot better conclude this... survey and prognosis than with the observation that the *Wilhelm Meister* and the *Green Henry* of our generation have not yet been written." Nothing will be further from the author who has reflected deeply on the conditions of present-day production than to expect, or desire, such works. His work will never be merely work on products but always, at the same time, on the means of production. In other words, his products must have, over and above their character as works, an organizing function, and in no way must their organizational usefulness be confined to their value as propaganda. Their political tendency alone is not enough. The excellent Lichtenberg has said, "A man's opinions are not what matters, but the kind of man these opinions make of him." Now it is true that opinions matter greatly, but the best are of no use if they make nothing useful out of those who have them. The best political tendency is wrong if it does not demonstrate the attitude with which it is to be followed. And this attitude the writer can only demonstrate in his particular activity: that is, in writing. A political tendency is the necessary, never the sufficient condition of the organizing function of a work. This further requires a directing, instructing stance on the part of the writer. And today this is to be demanded more than ever before. *An author who teaches writers nothing, teaches no one.* What matters, therefore, is the exemplary character of production, which is able first to induce other producers to produce, and second to put an improved apparatus at their disposal. And this apparatus is better the more consumers it is able to turn into producers—that is, readers or spectators into collaborators. We already possess such an example, to which, however, I can only allude here. It is Brecht's epic theater.

Tragedies and operas are constantly being written that apparently have a well-tried theatrical apparatus at their disposal, but in reality they do nothing but supply a derelict one. "The lack of clarity about their situation that prevails among musicians, writers, and critics," says Brecht, "has immense consequences that are far too little considered. For, thinking that they are in possession of an apparatus that in reality possesses them, they defend an apparatus over which they no longer have any control and that is no longer, as they still believe, a means for the producers, but has become a means against the producers." This theater, with its complicated machinery, its gigantic supporting staff, its sophisticated effects, has become a "means against the producers" not least in seeking to enlist them in the hopeless competitive struggle in which film and radio have enmeshed it. This theater—whether in its educating or its entertaining role; the two are complementary—is that of a sated class for which everything it touches becomes a stimulant. Its position is lost. Not so that of a theater that, instead of competing with newer instruments of publication, seeks to use and learn from them, in short, to enter into debate with them. This debate the epic theater has made it own affair. It is, measured by the present state of development of film and radio, the contemporary form.

In the interest of this debate Brecht fell back on the most primitive elements of the theater. He contented himself, by and large, with a podium. He dispensed with wide-ranging plots. He thus succeeded in changing the functional connection between stage and public, text and performance, director and actor. Epic theater, he declared, had to portray situations, rather than develop plots. It obtains such situations, as we shall see presently, by interrupting the plot. I remind you here of the songs, which have their chief function in interrupting the action. Here—in the principle of interruption—epic theater, as you see, takes up a procedure that has become familiar to you in recent years from film and radio, press and photography. I am speaking of the procedure of montage: the superimposed element disrupts the context in which it is inserted. But that this procedure has here a special right, perhaps even a perfect right, allow me briefly to indicate. The interruption of action, on account of which Brecht described his theater as *epic*, constantly counteracts an illusion in the audience. For such illusion is a hindrance to a theater that proposes to make use of elements of reality in experimental rearrangements. But it is at the end, not the beginning, of the experiment that the situation appears—a situation that, in this or that form, is always ours. It is not brought home to the spectator but distanced from him. He recognizes it as the real situation, not with satisfaction, as in the theater of naturalism, but with astonishment. Epic theater, therefore, does not reproduce situations; rather, it discovers them. This discovery is accomplished by means of the interruption of sequences. Only interruption here has not the character of a stimulant but an organizing function. It arrests the action in its course, and thereby compels the listener to adopt an attitude vis-à-vis the process, the actor vis-à-vis his role. I should like to show you through an example how Brecht's discovery and use of the *gestus* is nothing but the restoration of the method of montage decisive in radio and film, from an often merely modish procedure to a human event. Imagine a family scene: the wife is just about to grab a bronze sculpture to throw it at her daughter; the father is opening the window to call for help. At this moment a stranger enters. The process is interrupted; what appears in its place is the situation on which the stranger's eyes now fall: agitated faces, open window, disordered furniture. There are eyes, however, before which the more usual scenes of present-day existence do not look very different: the eyes of the epic dramatist.

To the total dramatic artwork he opposes the dramatic laboratory. He makes use in a new way of the great, ancient opportunity of the theater—to expose what is present. At the center of his experiment is man. Present-day man; a reduced man, therefore, chilled in a chilly environment. Since, however, this is the only one we have, it is in our interest to know him. He is subjected to tests, examinations. What emerges is this: events are alterable not at their climaxes, not by virtue and resolution, but only in their strictly habitual course, by reason and practice. To construct from the smallest elements of behavior what in Aristotelian dramaturgy is called "action" is the purpose of epic theater. Its means are therefore more modest than those of traditional theater; likewise its aims. It is less concerned with filling the public with feelings, even seditious ones, than with alienating it in an enduring manner, through thinking, from the conditions in which it lives. It may be noted, by the way, that there is no better start for thinking than laughter. And, in particular, convulsion of the diaphragm usually provides better opportunities for thought than convulsion of the soul. Epic theater is lavish only in occasions for laughter.

It has perhaps struck you that the train of thought that is about to be concluded presents to the writer only one demand, the demand *to think,* to reflect on his position in the process of production. We may depend on it: this reflection leads, sooner or later, for the writers who *matter*—that is, for the best technicians in their subject—to observations that provide the most factual foundation for solidarity with the proletariat. I should like to conclude by adducing a topical illustration in the form of a small extract from a journal published here, *Commune. Commune* circulated a questionnaire: "For whom do you write?" I quote from the reply of Réne Maublanc and from the comment added by Aragon. "Unquestionably," says Maublanc, "I write almost exclusively for a bourgeois public. Firstly, because I am obliged to"—here Maublanc is alluding to his professional duties as a grammar-school teacher—"secondly, because I have bourgeois origins and a bourgeois education and come from a bourgeois milieu, and so am naturally inclined to address myself to the class to which I belong, which I know and understand best. This does not mean, however, that I write in order to please or support it. I am convinced, on the one hand, that the proletarian revolution is necessary and desirable and, on the other, that it will be the more rapid, easy, successful, and the less bloody, the weaker the opposition of the bourgeoisie.... The proletariat today needs allies from the camp of the bourgeoisie, exactly as in the eighteenth century the bourgeoisie needed allies from the feudal camp. I wish to be among those allies."

On this Aragon comments: "Our comrade here touches on a state of affairs that affects a large number of present-day writers. Not all have the courage to look it in the face.... Those who see their own situation as clearly as René Maublanc are few. But precisely from them more must be required. ... It is not enough to weaken the bourgeoisie from within, it is necessary to fight them *with* the proletariat.... René Maublanc and many of our friends among the writers who are still hesitating, are faced with the example of the Soviet Russian writers who came from the Russian bourgeoisie and nevertheless became pioneers of the building of socialism."

Thus Aragon. But how did they become pioneers? Certainly not without very bitter struggles, extremely difficult debates. The considerations I have put before you are an attempt to draw some conclusions from these struggles. They are based on the concept to which the debate on the attitude of the Russian intellectuals owes its decisive clarification: the concept of the specialist. The solidarity of the specialist with the proletariat—herein lies the beginning of this clarification— can only be a mediated one. The Activists and the representatives of New Matter-of-factness could gesticulate as they pleased: they could not do away with the fact that even the proletarianization of an intellectual hardly ever makes a proletarian. Why? Because the bourgeois class gave him, in the form of education, a means of production that, owing to educational privilege, makes him feel solidarity with it, and still more it with him. Aragon was thereby entirely correct when, in another connection, he declared, "The revolutionary intellectual appears first and foremost as the betrayer of his class of origin." This betrayal consists, in the case of the writer, in conduct that transforms him from a supplier of the productive apparatus into an engineer who sees it as his task to adapt this apparatus to the purposes of the proletarian revolution. This is a mediating activity, yet it frees the intellectual from that purely destructive task to which Maublanc and many of his comrades believe it necessary to confine him. Does he succeed in promoting the socialization of the intellectual means of production? Does he see how he himself can organize the intellectual workers in the production process? Does he have proposals for the *Umfunktionierung* of the novel, the drama, the poem? The more completely he can orient his activity toward this task, the more correct will be the political tendency, and necessarily also the higher the technical quality, of his work. And at the same time, the more exactly he is thus informed on his position in the process of production, the less it will occur to him to lay claim to "spiritual" qualities. The spirit that holds forth in the name of fascism *must* disappear. The spirit that, in opposing it, trusts in its own miraculous powers *will* disappear. For the revolutionary struggle is not between capitalism and spirit, but between capitalism and the proletariat.

Karl Kraus

Dedicated to Gustav Glück

---

1. Cosmic Man

How noisy everything grows.
—*Words in Verse II*

In old engravings there is a messenger who rushes toward us
crying aloud, his hair on end, brandishing a sheet of paper
in his hands, a sheet full of war and pestilence, of cries of
murder and pain, of danger from fire and flood, spreading
everywhere the "latest news." News in this sense, in the sense
that the word has in Shakespeare, is disseminated by *Die
Fackel* [*The Torch*].* Full of betrayal, earthquakes, poison,
and fire from the *mundus intelligibilis*. The hatred with
which it pursues the tribe of journalists that swarms into
infinity is not only a moral but a vital one, such as is hurled
by an ancestor upon a race of degenerate and dwarfish rascals
that has sprung from his seed. The very term "public opinion"
outrages him. Opinions are a private matter. The public has
an interest only in judgments. Either it is a judging public,
or it is none. But it is precisely the purpose of the public
opinion generated by the press to make the public incapable
of judging, to insinuate into it the attitude of someone
irresponsible, uninformed. Indeed, what is even the most
precise information in the daily newspapers in comparison to
the hair-raising meticulousness observed by *Die Fackel* in the
presentation of legal, linguistic, and political facts? *Die
Fackel* need not trouble itself about public opinion, for the

* See Introduction, pp. xxxv–xxxvi.—ED.

blood-steeped novelties of this "newspaper" demand a passing of judgment. And on nothing more impetuously, urgently, than on the press itself.

A hatred such as that which Kraus has heaped on journalists can never be founded simply on what they do—however obnoxious this may be; this hatred must have its reason in their very nature, whether it be antithetical or akin to his own. In fact, it is both. His most recent portrait characterizes the journalist in the first sentence as "a person who has little interest either in himself and his own existence, or in the mere existence of things, but who feels things only in their relationships, above all where these meet in events—and only in this moment become united, substantial, and alive." What we have in this sentence is nothing other than the negative of an image of Kraus. Indeed, who could have shown a more burning interest in himself and his own existence than the writer who is never finished with this subject; who a more attentive concern for the mere existence of things, their origin; whom does that coincidence of the event with the date, the witness, or the camera cast into deeper despair than him? In the end he brought together all his energies in the struggle against the empty phrase, which is the linguistic expression of the despotism with which, in journalism, topicality sets up its dominion over things.

This side of his struggle against the press is illuminated most vividly by the life's work of his comrade-in-arms, Adolf Loos. Loos found his providential adversaries in the arts-and-crafts mongers and architects who, in the ambit of the "Vienna Workshops," were striving to give birth to a new art industry. He sent out his rallying cry in numerous essays, particularly, in its enduring formulation, in the article "Ornamentation and Crime," which appeared in 1908 in the *Frankfurter Zeitung*. The lightning flash ignited by this essay described a curiously zigzag course. "On reading the words with which Goethe censures the way the Philistine, and thus many an art connoisseur, run their fingers over engravings and reliefs, the revelation came to him that what may be touched cannot be a work of art, and that a work of art must be out of reach." It was therefore Loos's first concern to separate the work of art from the article of use, as it was that of Kraus to keep apart information and the work of art. The hack journalist is in his heart at one with the ornamentalist. Kraus did not tire of denouncing Heine as an ornamentalist, as one who blurred the boundary between journalism and literature, as the creator of the *feuilleton* in poetry and prose; indeed, he later placed even Nietzsche beside Heine as the betrayer of the aphorism to the impression. "It is my opinion," he says of the latter, "that to the mixture of elements . . . in the decomposing European style of the last half century, he added psychology, and that the new level of language that he created is the level of essayism, as Heine's was that of feuilletonism." Both forms appear as symptoms of the chronic sickness of which all attitudes and standpoints merely mark the temperature curve: inauthenticity. It is from the unmasking of the inauthentic that this battle against the press arose. "Who was it that brought into the world this great excuse: I can do what I am not?"

The empty phrase. It, however, is an abortion of technology. "The newspaper industry, like a factory, demands separate areas for working and selling. At certain times of day—twice, three times in the bigger newspapers—a particular quantity of work has to have been procured and prepared for the machine. And not from just any material: everything that has happened in the meantime, anywhere, in any region of life, politics, economics, art, etc., must by now have been reached and journalistically processed." Or, as Kraus so splendidly sums it up: "He ought to throw light on the way in which technology, while unable to coin new platitudes, leaves the spirit of mankind in the state of being unable to do without the old ones. In this duality of a changed life dragging on in unchanged forms, the world's ills grow and prosper." In these words Kraus deftly tied the knot binding technology to the empty phrase. True, its untying would have to follow a different pattern, journalism being clearly seen as the expression of the changed function of language in the world of high capitalism. The empty phrase of the kind so relentlessly pursued by Kraus is the label that makes a thought marketable, the way flowery language, as ornament, gives it value for the connoisseur. But for this very reason the liberation of language has become identical with that of the empty phrase—its transformation from reproduction to productive instrument. *Die Fackel* itself contains models of this, even if not the theory: its formulas are of the kind that tie up, never that untie. The combination of biblical magniloquence with stiff-necked fixation on the indecencies of Viennese life—that is its way of approaching phenomena. It is not content to call on the world as witness to the misdemeanors of a cashier; it must summon the dead from their graves. Rightly so. For the shabby, obtrusive abundance of these Viennese coffeehouses, press, and society scandals is only a minor manifestation of a foreknowledge that then, more swiftly than any could perceive, suddenly arrived at its true and original subject; two months after the outbreak of war, he called this subject by its name in the speech "In This Great Age," with which all the demons that had populated this possessed man passed into the herd of the swine who were his contemporaries.

"In these great times, which I knew when they were small, which will again be small if they still have time, and which, because in the field of organic growth such transformations are not possible, we prefer to address as fat times and truly also as hard times; in these times, when precisely what is happening could not be imagined, and when what must *happen* can no longer be *imagined,* and if it could it would not happen; in these grave times that have laughed themselves to death at the possibility of growing serious and, overtaken by their own tragedy, long for distraction and then, catching themselves in the act, seek words; in these loud times, booming with the fearful symphony of deeds that engender reports, and of reports that bear the blame for deeds; in these unspeakable times, you can expect no word of my own from me. None except this, which just preserves silence from misinterpretation. Too deeply am I awed by the unalterable, is language subordinate to misfortune. In the empires bereft of imagination, where man is dying of spiritual starvation while not feeling spiritual hunger, where pens are dipped in blood and swords in ink, that which is not thought must be done, but that which is only thought is inexpressible. Expect from me no word of my own. Nor should I be capable of saying anything new; for in the room where someone writes the noise is so great, and whether it comes from animals, from children, or merely from mortars shall not be decided now. He who addresses deeds violates both word and deed and is twice despicable. This profession is not extinct. Those who now have nothing to say because it is the turn of deeds to speak, talk on. Let him who has something to say step forward and be silent!"

Everything Kraus wrote is like that: a silence turned inside out, a silence that catches the storm of events in its black folds, billows, its livid lining turned outward. Notwithstanding their abundance, each of the instances of this silence seems to have broken upon it with the suddenness of a gust of wind. Immediately, a precise apparatus of control is brought into play: through a meshing of oral and written forms the polemical possibilities of every situation are totally exhausted. With what precautions this is surrounded can be seen from the barbed wire of editorial pronouncements that encircles each edition of *Die Fackel,* as from the razor-sharp definitions and provisos in the programs and lectures accompanying his readings from his own work. The trinity of silence, knowledge, and alertness constitutes the figure of Kraus the polemicist. His silence is a dam before which the reflecting basin of his knowledge is constantly deepened. His alertness permits no one to ask it questions, forever unwilling to conform to principles proffered to it. Its first principle is, rather, to dismantle the situation, to discover the true question the situation poses, and to present this in place of any other to his opponents. If in Johann Peter Hebel we find, developed to the utmost, the constructive, creative side of tact, in Kraus we see its most destructive and critical face. But for both, tact is moral alertness—Stössl calls it "conviction refined into dialectics"—and the expression of an unknown convention more important than the acknowledged one. Kraus lived in a world in which the most shameful act was still the *faux pas;* he distinguishes between degrees of the monstrous, and does so precisely because his criterion is never that of bourgeois respectability, which once above the threshold of trivial misdemeanor becomes so quickly short of breath that it can form no conception of villainy on a world-historical scale.

Kraus knew this criterion from the first, and moreover there is no other criterion for true tact. It is a theological criterion. For tact is not—as narrow minds imagine it—the gift of allotting to each, on consideration of all relationships, what is socially befitting. On the contrary, tact is the capacity to treat social relationships, though not departing from them, as natural, even as paradisiac relationships, and so not only to approach the king as if he had been born with the crown on his brow, but the lackey like an Adam in livery. Hebel possessed this *noblesse* in his priestly bearing, Kraus in armor. His concept of creation contains the theological inheritance of speculations that last possessed contemporary validity for the whole of Europe in the seventeenth century. At the theological core of this concept, however, a transformation has taken place that has caused it, quite without constraint, to coincide with the cosmopolitan credo of Austrian worldliness, which made creation into a church in which nothing remained to recall the rite except an occasional whiff of incense in the mists. Stifter gave this creed its most authentic stamp, and his echo is heard wherever Kraus concerns himself with animals, plants, children.

"The stirring of the air," Stifter writes, "the rippling of

water, the growing of corn, the tossing of the sea, the verdure
of the earth, the shining of the sky, the twinkling of the stars
I hold great: the thunderstorm approaching in splendor, the
lightning flash that cleaves houses, the storm driving the surf,
the mountains spewing fire, the earthquake laying waste to
countries, I do not hold greater than the former phenomena;
indeed, I believe them smaller, because they are only effects
of far higher laws. . . . When man was in his infancy, his spiritual eye not yet touched by science, he was seized by what
was close at hand and obtrusive, and was moved to fear and
admiration; but when his mind was opened, when his gaze
began to be directed at the connections between things, particular phenomena sank from sight and the law rose even
higher, miracles ceased, and wonder increased. . . . Just as in
nature the general laws act silently and incessantly, and conspicuous events are only single manifestations of these laws, so
the moral law acts silently, animating the soul through the
infinite intercourse of human beings, and the miracles of the
moment when deeds are performed are only small signs of
this general power." Tacitly, in these famous sentences, the
holy has given place to the modest yet questionable concept
of law. But this nature of Stifter's and his moral universe are
transparent enough to escape any confusion with Kant, and to
be still recognizable in their core as creation. This insolently
secularized thunder and lightning, storms, surf, and earthquakes—cosmic man has won them back for creation by making them its world-historical answer to the criminal existence
of men. Only the span between Creation and the Last Judgment here finds no redemptive fulfillment, let alone a historical resolution. For as the landscape of Austria fills unbroken
the captivating expanse of Stifter's prose, so for him, Kraus,
the terrible years of his life are not history, but nature, a river
condemned to meander through a landscape of hell. It is a
landscape in which every day fifty thousand tree trunks are
felled for sixty newspapers. Kraus imparted this information
under the title "The End." For that mankind is losing the

fight against the creaturely world is to him just as certain as
that technology, once deployed against creation, will not stop
short of its master, either. His defeatism is of a supranational,
that is, planetary kind, and history for him is merely the
wilderness dividing his race from creation, whose last act is
world conflagration. As a deserter to the camp of animal creation—so he measures out this wilderness. "And only the animal that is conquered by humanity is the hero of life": never
was Adalbert Stifter's patriarchal credo given so lugubrious
and heraldic a formulation.

It is in the name of animal creation that Kraus again and
again bends toward the animal and toward "the heart of all
hearts, that of the dog," for him creation's true mirror of virtue, in which fidelity, purity, gratitude smile from times lost
and remote. How lamentable that people usurp its place!
These are his followers. More numerously and eagerly than
about their master they throng with unlovely sniffings about
the mortally wounded opponent. Certainly the dog is not for
nothing the emblematic beast of this author: the dog, the ideal
example of the follower, who is nothing except devoted creaturely life. And the more personal and unfounded this devotion, the better. Kraus is right to put it to the hardest test. But
if anything makes plain what is infinitely questionable in these
creatures, it is that they are recruited solely from those whom
Kraus himself first called intellectually to life, whom he conceived and convinced in one and the same act. His word can
be decisive only for those whom it did not beget.

It is entirely logical when the impoverished, reduced human
being of our days, the contemporary, can only seek sanctuary
in the temple of living things in that most withered form, as
a private individual. How much renunciation and how much
irony lie in the curious struggle for the "nerves," the last
root fibers of the Viennese to which Kraus could still find
Mother Earth adhering. "Kraus," writes Robert Scheu, "had
discovered a great subject that had never before set in motion
the pen of a publicist: the rights of the nerves. He found

that they were just as worthy an object of impassioned defense as were property, house and home, party, and constitution. He became the advocate of the nerves and took up the fight against the petty, everyday imitations, but the subject grew under his hands, became the problem of private life. To defend this against police, press, morality, and concepts, finally against neighbors in every form, constantly to find new enemies, became his profession." Here, if anywhere, is manifest the strange interplay between reactionary theory and revolutionary practice that is met everywhere in Kraus. Indeed, to secure private life against morality and concepts in a society that perpetrates the political radioscopy of sexuality and family, of economic and physical existence, in a society that is in the process of building houses with glass walls, and patios extending far into the drawing rooms that are no longer drawing rooms—such a watchword would be the most reactionary of all were not the private life that Kraus had made it his business to defend precisely that which, unlike the bourgeois form, is in strict accordance with this social upheaval; in other words, the private life that is dismantling itself, openly shaping itself, that of the poor, from whose ranks came Peter Altenberg, the agitator, and Adolf Loos. In this fight—and only in it—his followers also have their use, since it is they who most sublimely ignore the anonymity with which the satirist has tried to surround his private existence, and nothing holds them in check except Kraus's decision to step in person before his threshold and pay homage to the ruins in which he is a "private individual."

As decisively as he makes his own existence a public issue when the fight demands it, he has always just as ruthlessly opposed the distinction between personal and objective criticism with the aid of which polemics are discredited, and which is a chief instrument of corruption in our literary and political affairs. That Kraus attacks people less for what they are than for what they do, more for what they say than for what they write, and least of all for their books, is the precondition of his polemical authority, which is able to lift the intellectual universe of an author—all the more surely the more worthless it is, in confidence of a truly prestabilized, reconciling harmony—whole and intact from a single fragment of sentence, a single word, a single intonation. But the coincidence of personal and objective elements not only in his opponents but above all in himself is best demonstrated by the fact that he never puts forward an opinion. For opinion is false objectivity that can be separated from the person and incorporated in the circulation of commodities. Kraus never offered an argument that had not engaged his whole person. Thus he embodies the secret of authority: never to disappoint. Authority has no other end than this: it dies or it disappoints. It is not in the least undermined by what others must avoid: its own despotism, injustice, inconsistency. On the contrary, it would be disappointing to observe how it arrived at its pronouncements—by fairness, for example, or even self-consistency. "For the man," Kraus once said, "being right is not an erotic matter, and he gladly prefers others' being right to his being wrong." To prove his manhood in this way is denied to Kraus; his existence demands that at most the self-righteousness of others is opposed to his wrongness, and how right he then is to cling to this. "Many will be right one day. But it will be a rightness resulting from my wrongness today." That is the language of true authority. Insight into its operations can discover only one thing: that it is binding, mercilessly binding toward itself in the same degree as toward others; that it does not tire of trembling before itself, though never before others; that it never does enough to satisfy itself, to fulfill its responsibility toward itself, and that this sense of responsibility never allows him to accept arguments derived from his private constitution or even from the limits of human capacity, but always only from the matter at hand, however unjust, from a private point of view, it may be.

The characteristic of such unlimited authority has for all time been the union of legislative and executive power. But it was never a more intimate union than in the theory of language. This is therefore the most decisive expression of Kraus's authority. Incognito like Haroun al Raschid, he passes by night among the sentence constructions of the journals, and, from behind the petrified façades of phrases, he peers into the interior, discovers in the orgies of "black magic" the violation, the martyrdom of words: "Is the press a messenger? No: the event. Is it speech? No: life. It not only claims that the true events are its news of events, but it also brings about a sinister identification that constantly creates the illusion that deeds are reported before they are carried out, and frequently also the possibility of a situation, which in any case exists, that while war correspondents are not allowed to witness events, soldiers become reporters. I therefore welcome the charge that all my life I have overestimated the press. It is not a servant—how could a servant demand and receive so much—it is the event. Once again the instrument has run away with us. We have placed the person who is supposed to report outbreaks of fire, and who ought doubtless to play the most subordinate role in the state, in power over the world, over fire and over the house, over fact and over our fantasy." Authority and word against corruption and magic—these are the catchwords distributed in this struggle. It is not idle to prognosticate its outcome. No one, Kraus least of all, can leave the utopia of an "objective" newspaper, the chimera of an "impartial transmission of news," to its own devices. The newspaper is an instrument of power. It can derive its value only from the character of the power it serves; not only in what it represents, but also in what it does, it is the expression of this power. If, however, high capitalism defiles not only the ends but also the means of journalism, then a new blossoming of paradisiac, cosmic humanity can no more be expected of a power that defeats it than a second blooming of the language of Goethe or Claudius. From that now prevailing it will distinguish itself first of all by putting out of circulation ideals that debase the former. This is enough to give a measure of how little Kraus would have to win or lose in such a struggle, of how unerringly *Die Fackel* would illuminate it. To the ever-repeated sensations with which the daily press serves its public he opposes the eternally fresh "news" of the history of creation: the eternally renewed, the uninterrupted lament.

2. Demon

Have I slept? I am just falling asleep.
—*Words in Verse IV*

It is deeply rooted in Kraus's nature, and it is the stigma of every debate concerning him, that all apologetic arguments miss their mark. The great work of Leopold Liegler springs from an apologetic posture. To certify Kraus as an "ethical personality" is his first objective. That cannot be done. The dark background from which his image detaches itself is not formed by his contemporaries, but is the primeval world or the world of the demon. The light of the first day falls on him —thus he emerges from this darkness. But not in all parts; others remain that are more deeply immersed in it than one suspects. An eye that cannot adjust to this darkness will never perceive the outline of this figure. On it will be wasted all the gestures that Kraus tirelessly makes in his unconquerable need to be perceived. For, as in the fairy tale, the demon in Kraus has made vanity the expression of his being. The demon's solitude, too, is felt by him who gesticulates wildly on the hidden hill: "Thank God nobody knows my name is Rumpelstiltskin." Just as this dancing demon is never still, in Kraus eccentric reflection is in continuous uproar. "The patient of his gifts," Viertel called him. In fact, his capacities are maladies, and over and above the real ones, his vanity makes him a hypochondriac.

If he does not see his reflection in himself, he sees it in the adversary at his feet. His polemics have been from the first the most intimate intermingling of a technique of unmasking that works with the most advanced means, and a self-expressive art operating with the most archaic. In this zone, too, however, ambiguity, the demon, is manifest: self-expression and unmasking merge in it as self-unmasking. Kraus has said, "Anti-Semitism is the mentality... that means seriously a tenth part of the jibes that the stock-exchange wit holds ready for his own blood"; he thereby indicates the nature of the relationship of his own opponents to himself. There is no reproach to him, no vilification of his person, that could not find its most legitimate formulation in his own writings, in those passages where self-reflection is raised to self-admiration. He will pay any price to get himself talked about, and is always justified by the success of these speculations. If style is the power to move freely in the length and breadth of linguistic thinking without falling into banality, it is attained chiefly by the cardiac strength of great thoughts, which drives the blood of language through the capillaries of syntax into the remotest limbs. While such thoughts are quite unmistakable in Kraus, the powerful heart of his style is nevertheless the image he bears of himself in his own breast and exposes in the most merciless manner. Yes, he is vain. As such he has been described by Karin Michaelis, crossing a room with swift, restless bounds to reach the lecture podium. And if he then offers a sacrifice to his vanity, he would not be the demon that he is were it not finally himself, his life and his suffering, that he exposes with all its wounds, all its nakedness. In this way his style comes into being, and with it the typical reader of *Die Fackel,* for whom in a subordinate clause, in a particle, indeed in a comma, fibers and nerves quiver; from the obscurest and driest fact a piece of his mutilated flesh hangs. Idiosyncrasy as the highest critical organ—that is the hidden logic of this self-reflection and the hellish state known only to a writer for whom every act of gratification becomes at the same time a station of his martyrdom, a state that was experienced, apart from Kraus, by no one as deeply as by Kierkegaard.

"I am," Kraus has said, "perhaps the first instance of a writer who simultaneously writes and acts his writing," and thus he shows his vanity its most legitimate place: in mime. His mimetic genius, imitating while it glosses, pulling faces in the midst of polemics, is festively unleashed in the readings of dramas whose authors do not for nothing occupy a peculiarly intermediate position: Shakespeare and Nestroy, dramatists and actors; Offenbach, composer and conductor. It is as if the demon in the man sought the tumultuous atmosphere of these dramas, shot through with all the lightning flashes of improvisation, because it alone offered him the thousand opportunities to break out, teasing, tormenting, threatening. In them his own voice tries out the abundance of *personae* inhabiting the performer—*persona:* that through which sound passes—and about his fingertips dart the gestures of the figures populating his voice. But in his polemics, too, mimesis plays a decisive role. He imitates his subjects in order to insert the crowbar of his hate into the finest joints of their posture. This quibbler, probing between syllables, digs out the grubs of humbug. The grubs of venality and garrulity, ignominy and bonhomie, childishness and covetousness, gluttony and dishonesty. Indeed, the exposure of inauthenticity— more difficult than that of wickedness—is here performed behavioristically. The quotations in *Die Fackel* are more than documentary proof: they are masks stripped off mimetically by the quoter. Admittedly, what emerges in just this connection is how closely the cruelty of the satirist is linked to the ambiguous modesty of the interpreter, which in his public readings is heightened beyond comprehension. To creep—so is termed, not without cause, the lowest kind of flattery; and Kraus creeps into those he impersonates, in order to annihilate them. Has courtesy here become the camouflage of hate, hate the camouflage of courtesy? However that may be, both have attained perfection, the Chinese pitch. "Torment," of which there is so much talk in Kraus in such opaque allusions, here has its seat. His protests against letters, printed matter, documents are nothing but the defensive reaction of a man who is himself implicated. But what implicates him so deeply is more than the deeds and misdeeds; it is the language of his fellow men. His passion for imitating them is at the same time the expression of and the struggle against this implication, and also the cause and the result of that ever-watchful guilty conscience in which the demon has his habitat.

The economy of his errors and weaknesses—a fantastic edifice, rather than the totality of his gifts—is so delicately and precisely organized that all outward confirmation only disrupts it. Well it may, if this man is to be certified as the "pattern of a harmoniously and perfectly formed human type," if he is to appear—in a term as absurd stylistically as semantically—as a philanthropist, so that anyone listening to his "hardness" with "the ears of the soul" would find the reason for it in compassion. No! This incorruptible, piercing, resolute assurance does not spring from the noble poetic or humane disposition that his followers are so fond of attributing to him. How utterly banal, and at the same time how fundamentally wrong, is their derivation of his hatred from love, when it is obvious how much more elemental are the forces here at work: a humanity that is only an alternation of malice and sophistry, sophistry and malice, a nature that is the highest school of aversion to mankind and a pity that is alive only when mingled with vengeance. "Oh, had I only been left the choice / to carve the dog or the butcher, / I should have chosen." Nothing is more perverse than to try to fashion him after the image of what he loves. Rightly, Kraus the "timeless world-disturber" has been confronted with the "eternal world-improver" on whom benign glances not infrequently fall.

"When the age laid hands upon itself, he was the hands," Brecht said. Few insights can stand beside this, and certainly not the comment of his friend Adolf Loos. "Kraus," he declares, "stands on the frontier of a new age." Alas, by no means. For he stands on the threshold of the Last Judgment. As in the most opulent examples of baroque altar painting, saints hard-pressed against the frame extend defensive hands toward the breathtakingly foreshortened extremities of the angels, the blessed, and the damned floating before them, so the whole of world history presses in on Kraus in the extremities of a single item of local news, a single phrase, a single advertisement. This is the inheritance that has come down to him from the sermon of Abraham a Santa Clara. Thence the overwhelming immediacy, the ready wit of the wholly uncontemplative moment, and the inversion that allows his will only theoretical, his knowledge only practical expression. Kraus is no historic genius. He does not stand on the frontier of a new age. If he ever turns his back on creation, if he breaks off in lamentation, it is only to file a complaint at the Last Judgment.

Nothing is understood about this man until it has been perceived that, of necessity and without exception, everything —language and fact—falls for him within the sphere of justice. All his fire-eating, sword-swallowing philology in the newspapers pursues justice just as much as language. It is to misunderstand his theory of language to see it as other than a contribution to the linguistic rules of court, the word of someone else in his mouth as other than a *corpus delicti*, and his own as other than a judging word. Kraus knows no system. Each thought has its own cell. But each cell can in an instant, and apparently almost without cause, become a chamber, a legal chamber over which language presides. It has been said of Kraus that he has to "suppress the Jewishness in himself," even that he "travels the road from Jewishness to freedom"; nothing better refutes this than the fact that, for him, too, justice and language remain founded in each other. To worship the image of divine justice in language—even in the German language—that is the genuinely Jewish somersault by which he tries to break the spell of the demon. For this is the last official act of this zealot: to place legal system itself under accusation. And not in a petit-bourgeois revolt against the enslavement of the "free individual" by "dead formulas." Still less in the posture of those radicals who storm paragraphs without ever for a moment having taken thought of justice. Kraus accuses the law in its substance, not in its effect. His charge is the betrayal of justice by law. More exactly, of the word by the concept, which derives its existence from the word: the premeditated murder of imagination, which dies of the absence of a single letter and for which, in his "Elegy on the Death of a Sound," he has sung the most moving lament. For over jurisdiction, right-saying, stands orthography, right-spelling, and woe to the former if the latter should be wanting. Here, too, therefore, he confronts the press; indeed, in this charmed circle he holds his fondest rendezvous with the lemures. He has seen through law as have few others. If he nevertheless invokes it, he does so precisely because his own demon is drawn so powerfully by the abyss it represents. By the abyss that, not without reason, he finds most gaping where mind and sexuality meet—in the trial for sexual offenses—and has sounded in these famous words: "A sexual trial is the deliberate development from an individual to a general immorality, against which dark background the proven guilt of the accused stands out luminously."

Mind and sexuality move in this sphere with a solidarity whose law is ambiguity. The possession of demonic sexuality is that of the ego that, surrounded by sweet feminine mirages "such as the bitter earth does not harbor," enjoys itself. And no different is the loveless and self-gratifying trope of possessed mind: the joke. Neither reaches its object, the ego women no more than the joke words. Decomposition has taken the place of procreation, stridency that of secrecy. Now, however, they shimmer in the most winsome nuances: in the repartee lust comes into its own, and in onanism, the joke. Kraus portrayed himself as hopelessly subjugated to the demon; in the pandemonium of the age he reserved for himself the most melancholy place in the icy wilderness lit by reflected flames. There he stands on the "Last Day of Mankind"—the "grumbler" who has described the preceding days. "I have taken the tragedy, which is divided into the scenes of decaying humanity, on myself, so that it might be heard by the spirit who takes pity on the victims, even though he may have renounced for all time his connection with a human ear. May he receive the keynote of this age, the echo of my bloodstained madness, through which I share the guilt for these noises. May he accept it as redemption!"

"I share the guilt...." Because this has the ring of the manifestoes of an intelligentsia seeking to call to mind the memory of an epoch that seemed to be turning away from it, there is something to be said about this guilt feeling in which private and historical consciousness so vividly meet. This guilt will always lead to Expressionism, from which his mature work was nourished by roots that cracked open their soil. The slogans are well known—with what scorn did not Kraus himself register them: *"geballt," "gestuft," "gesteilt"* [clenched, stepped, steeped], stage sets, sentences, paintings were composed. Unmistakable—and the Expressionists themselves proclaim it—is the influence of early medieval miniatures on the world of their imagination. But anyone who examines their figures—for example, in the Vienna Genesis—is struck by something very mysterious, not only in their wide-open eyes, not only in the unfathomable folds of their garments, but also in their whole expression. As if falling sickness had overtaken them thus, in their running that is always precipitous, they lean toward one another. "Inclination" may be seen, before all else, as the deep human affect tremulously pervading the world of these miniatures, as it does the manifestoes of that generation of poets. But only one, as it were inwardly curved, aspect is revealed by the front of these figures. The same phenomenon appears quite different to someone who looks at their backs. These backs are piled—in the saints of the adorations, in the servants of the Gethsemane scene, in the wit-

nesses of the entrance into Jerusalem—into terraces of human
necks, of human shoulders that, really clenched in steep steps,
lead less toward heaven than downward, to and even under
the earth. It is impossible to find for their emotional impact
an expression that ignores the fact that they could be climbed
like heaped rocks or rough-hewn steps. Whatever powers may
have fought out their spiritual battles on these shoulders, one
of them, from our experience of the condition of the defeated
masses immediately after the end of the war, we are able to
call by its name. What finally remained of Expressionism, in
which an originally human impulse was converted almost
without residue into a fashion, was the experience and the
name of that nameless power toward which the backs of people bent: guilt. "That an obedient mass is led into danger not
by an unknown will but by an unknown guilt, makes them
pitiable," Kraus wrote as early as 1912. As a "grumbler" he
participates in their lot in order to denounce them, and de-
nounces them in order to participate. To meet them through
sacrifice he one day threw himself into the arms of the Catholic Church.

In those biting minuets that Kraus whistled to the *chassé-
croisé* of Justitia and Venus, the leitmotif—that the Philistine
knows nothing of love—is articulated with a sharpness and
persistence that have a counterpart only in the corresponding
attitude of *décadence,* in the proclamation of art for art's sake.
For it was precisely art for art's sake, which for the decadent
movement applies to love as well, that linked expertise as
closely as possible to craftsmanship, to technique, and allowed
poetry to shine at its brightest only against the foil of hack
writing, as it made love stand out against perversion. "Penury
can turn every man into a journalist, but not every woman
into a prostitute." In this formulation Kraus betrayed the
false bottom of his polemic against journalism. It is much
less the philanthropist, the enlightened friend of man and
nature, who unleashed this implacable struggle, than the
literary expert, artiste, indeed the dandy who has his forebear

in Baudelaire. Only Baudelaire hated as Kraus did the satiety of healthy common sense, and the compromise that intellectuals made with it in order to find shelter in journalism. Journalism is betrayal of the literary life, of mind, of the demon. Idle chatter is its true substance, and every *feuilleton* poses anew the insoluble question of the relationship between the forces of stupidity and malice, whose expression is gossip. It is, fundamentally, the complete agreement of two forms of existence—life under the aegis of mere mind or of mere sexuality—in which is founded that solidarity of the man of letters with the whore to which Baudelaire's existence is once again the most inviolable testimony. So Kraus can call by their name the laws of his own craft, entwined with those of sexuality, as he did in the *Wall of China*. The man "has wrestled a thousand times with the other, who perhaps does not live, but whose victory over him is certain. Not because he has superior qualities but because he is the other, the late-comer, who brings the woman the joy of variety and will triumph as the last in the sequence. But they rub it from her brow like a bad dream, and want to be the first." Now if language—this we read between the lines—is a woman, how far is the author removed, by an unerring instinct, from those who hasten to be the first with her, how multifariously he forms his thought, which incites her with intuition, rather than slake her with knowledge, how he lets hatred, contempt, malice ensnare one another, how he slows his step and seeks the detour of followership, in order finally to end her joy in variety with the last thrust that Jack holds in readiness for Lulu.

The life of letters is existence under the aegis of mere mind, as prostitution is existence under the aegis of mere sexuality. The demon, however, who leads the whore to the street exiles the man of letters to the courtroom. This is therefore for Kraus the forum that it has always been for the great journalist—for a Carrel, a Paul-Louis Courier, a Lassalle. Evasion of the genuine and demonic function of mere mind, to be a disturber of the peace; abstention from attacking the whore from behind—Kraus sees this double omission as defining the journalist. Robert Scheu rightly perceived that for Kraus prostitution was a natural form, not a social deformation, of female sexuality. Yet it is only the entanglement of sexual with commercial intercourse that constitutes the character of prostitution. It is a natural phenomenon as much in terms of its natural economic aspect, as a manifestation of commodity exchange, as in terms of its natural sexuality. "Contempt for prostitution? / Harlots worse than thieves? / Learn this: not only is love paid, / but payment, too, wins love!" This ambiguity—this double nature as twofold naturalness—makes prostitution demonic. But Kraus "enlists with the power of nature." That the sociological area never becomes transparent to him—no more in his attack on the press than in his defense of prostitution—is connected to this attachment to nature. That to him the fit state of man appears not as the destiny and fulfillment of nature liberated through revolutionary change, but as an element of nature per se, of an archaic nature without history, in its pristine, primeval state, throws uncertain, disquieting reflections even on his idea of freedom and of humanity. It is not removed from the realm of guilt that he has traversed from pole to pole: from mind to sexuality.

In face of this reality, however, to which Kraus exposed himself more harrowingly than any other, the "pure mind" that his followers worship in the master's activity is revealed as a worthless chimera. For this reason, none of the motives for his development is more important than the continuous curbing and checking of mind. *By Night,* he entitles the logbook of this control. For night is the mechanism by which mere mind is converted into mere sexuality, mere sexuality into mere mind, and where these two abstractions hostile to life find rest in recognizing each other. "I work day and night. So I have a lot of free time. To ask a picture in the room how it likes work, to ask the clock whether it is tired and the night how it has slept." These questions are sacrificial gifts that he throws to the demon while working. His night, however, is not maternal, or a moonlit, romantic night: it is the hour between sleeping and waking, the night watch, the centerpiece of his threefold solitude: that of the coffeehouse where he is alone with his enemy, of the nocturnal room where he is alone with his demon, of the lecture hall where he is alone with his work.

3. Monster

Already the snow falls.
—*Words in Verse III*

Satire is the only legitimate form of regional art. This, however, was not what people meant by calling Kraus a Viennese satirist. Rather, they were attempting to shunt him for as long as possible into this siding where his work could be assimilated in the great store of literary consumer goods. The presentation of Kraus as a satirist can thus yield the deepest insight both into what he is and into his most melancholy caricature. For this reason, he was at pains from the first to distinguish the genuine satirist from the scribblers who make a trade of mockery and in their invectives have little more in mind than giving the public something to laugh about. In contrast, the great type of the satirist never had firmer ground under his feet than amid a generation about to board tanks and put on gas masks, a mankind that has run out of tears but not of laughter. In him civilization prepares to survive, if it must, and communicates with him in the true mystery of satire, which consists in the devouring of the adversary. The satirist is the figure in whom the cannibal was received into civilization. His recollection of his origin is not without filial piety, so that the proposal to eat people has become an essential constituent of his inspiration, from Swift's pertinent project concerning the use of the children of the less wealthy classes, to Léon Bloy's suggestion that landlords of insolvent lodgers be conceded a right to the sale of their flesh. In such directives the great satirists have taken the measure of the humanity of their fellow men. "Humanity, culture, and freedom are precious things that cannot be bought dearly enough with blood, understanding, and human dignity"—thus Kraus concludes the dispute between the cannibal and human rights. It should be compared to Marx's treatment of the "Jewish question," in order to judge how totally this playful reaction of 1909— the reaction against the classical ideal of humanity—was likely to become a confession of materialist humanism at the first opportunity. Admittedly, one would need to understand *Die Fackel* from the first number on literally word for word to predict that this aesthetically oriented journalism, without sacrificing or gaining a single motif, was destined to become the political prose of 1930. For that it had to thank its partner, the press, which disposed of humanity in the way to which Kraus alludes in these words: "Human rights are the fragile toy that grownups like to trample on and so will not give up." Thus drawing the frontier between the private and public spheres, which in 1789 was supposed to inaugurate freedom, became a mockery. "Through the newspaper," says Kierkegaard, "the distinction between public and private affairs is abolished in private-public prattle...."

To open a dialectical debate between the public and private zones that commingle demonically in prattle, to lead materialist humanity to victory, that is "the Purpose of the operetta" that Kraus discovered and in Offenbach* raised to its most expressive level. Just as prattle seals the enslavement of language with stupidity, so operetta transfigures stupidity through music. To fail to recognize the beauty of feminine stupidity was for Kraus always the blackest Philistinism. Before its radiance the chimeras of progress evaporate. And in Offen-

* Karl Kraus translated and edited Offenbach's *La Vie Parisienne.*—ED.

bach's operetta the bourgeois trinity of true, beautiful, and good is brought together, freshly rehearsed and with musical accompaniment, in its star turn on the trapeze of stupidity. Nonsense is true, stupidity beautiful, weakness good. This is Offenbach's secret: how in the deep nonsense of public discipline—whether it be of the upper ten thousand, a dance floor, or a military state—the deep sense of private licentiousness opens a dreamy eye. And what as language might have been judicial strictness, renunciation, discrimination, becomes cunning and evasion, obstruction and postponement, as music. Music as the preserver of the moral order? Music as the police of a world of pleasure? Yes, that is the splendor that falls on the old Paris ballrooms, on the Grande Chaumière, the Clôserie des Lilas in his performance of *La Vie Parisienne*. "And the inimitable duplicity of this music, which simultaneously puts a plus and a minus sign before everything it says, betraying idyll to parody, mockery to lyricism; the abundance of musical devices ready to perform all duties, uniting pain and pleasure—this gift is here developed to its purest pitch." Anarchy as the only international constitution that is moral and worthy of man becomes the true music of these operettas. The voice of Kraus speaks, rather than sings, this inner music. It whistles bitingly about the peaks of dizzying stupidity, reverberates shatteringly from the abyss of the absurd, and in Frescata's lines it hums, like the wind in the chimney, a requiem to the generation of our grandfathers. Offenbach's work is touched by the pangs of death. It contracts, rids itself of everything superfluous, passes through the dangerous span of this existence and re-emerges saved, more real than before. For where this fickle voice is heard, the lightning flashes of the advertisements and the thunder of the Métro cleave the Paris of the omnibuses and the gas flames. And the work gives him all this in return. For at moments it is transformed into a curtain, and with the wild gestures of a fairground showman with which he accompanies the whole performance, Kraus tears aside this curtain and suddenly reveals the interior of his cabinet of horrors. There they stand: Schober, Bekessy, Kerr, and the other skits, no longer enemies but curiosities, heirlooms from the world of Offenbach or Nestroy, no, older, rarer still, lares of the troglodytes, household gods of stupidity from prehistoric times. Kraus, in his recitals, does not speak the words of Offenbach or Nestroy: they speak from him. And now and then a breathtaking, half-blank, half-glittering whoremonger's glance falls on the crowd before him, inviting them to the unholy marriage with the masks in which they do not recognize themselves, and for the last time invokes his evil privilege of ambiguity.

It is only now that the satirist's true face, or rather true mask, is revealed. It is the mask of Timon, the misanthrope. "Shakespeare had foreknowledge of everything"—yes. But above all of Kraus. Shakespeare portrays inhuman figures— and Timon as the most inhuman of them—and says: Nature would produce such a creature if she wished to create something befitting the world as your kind have fashioned it, something worthy of it. Such a creature is Timon; such is Kraus. Neither has, or wants, anything in common with men. "An animal feud is on, and so we renounce humanity"; from a remote village in the Swiss mountains Kraus throws down this challenge to mankind, and Timon wants only the sea to weep at his grave. Like Timon's verse, Kraus's poetry stands opposite the colon of the *dramatis persona,* of the role. A fool, a Caliban, a Timon—no more thoughtful, no more dignified or better—but, nevertheless, his own Shakespeare. All the figures thronging about him should be seen as originating in Shakespeare. Always he is the model, whether Kraus speaks with Weininger about man or with Altenberg about women, with Wedekind about the stage or with Loos about food, with Else Lasker-Schüler about the Jews or with Theodor Haecker about the Christians. The power of the demon ends in this realm. His demi- or subhuman traits are conquered by a truly inhuman being, a monster. Kraus hinted at this in the words "In me a capacity for psychology is united with the greater

capacity to ignore the psychological." It is the inhuman quality of the actor that he pre-empts in these words: the cannibal
quality. For in each of his roles the actor assimilates bodily
a human being, and in Shakespeare's baroque tirades—when
the cannibal is unmasked as the better man, the hero as an
actor, when Timon plays the rich man, Hamlet the madman
—it is as if his lips dripped blood. So Kraus, following
Shakespeare's example, wrote himself parts that let him taste
blood. The endurance of his convictions is persistence in a
role, in its stereotypes, its cues. His experiences are in their
entirety nothing but this: cues. This is why he insists on them,
demanding them of existence like an actor who never forgives
a partner for denying him his cue.

The Offenbach readings, the recital of couplets from Nestroy, are bereft of all musical means. The word never gives
way to the instrument; but by extending its boundaries
further and further it finally enfeebles itself, dissolving into
a merely animal voice: a humming that is to the word what his
smile is to the joke is the holy of holies of this performer's art.
In this smile, this humming in which, as in a crater lake amid
the most mostrous crags and cinders, the world is peacefully
and contentedly mirrored, irrupts the deep complicity with his
listeners and models that Kraus has never allowed to enter his
words. His service to the world permits no compromise. But
as soon as he turns his back on it, he is ready for a good many.
Then is felt the tormenting, inexhaustible charm of these recitals: that of seeing the distinction between like and unlike
minds annulled, and the homogeneous mass of false friends
created, that sets the tone of these performances. Kraus confronts a world of enemies, seeks to coerce them to love and yet
coerces them to nothing but hypocrisy. His defenselessness
before the latter has a precise connection to the subversive
dilettantism that is particularly predominant in the Offenbach
performances. Here Kraus confines music to limits narrower
than were ever dreamed of in the manifestoes of the George
school. This cannot, of course, obscure the antithesis between

the linguistic gestures of both men. Rather, an exact correlation exists between the factors that give Kraus access to the two poles of linguistic expression—the enfeebled pole of humming and the armed pole of pathos—and those which forbid his sanctification of the word to take on the forms of the Georgean cult of language. To the cosmic rising and falling that for George "deifies the body and embodies the divine," language is only the Jacob's ladder with its ten thousand word-rungs. Kraus's language, by contrast, has done away with all hieratic moments. It is the medium neither of clairvoyance nor of domination. It is the theater of a sanctification of the name— with this Jewish certainty it sets itself against the theurgy of the "word-body." Very late, with a decisiveness that must have matured in years of silence, Kraus entered the lists against the great partner whose work had arisen at the same time as his own, beneath the threshold of the century. George's first published book and the first volume of *Die Fackel* are dated 1899. And only retrospectively, "After Thirty Years," in 1929, did Kraus issue the challenge. There, as the zealot, he confronts George, the object of worship,

> who in the temple dwells from which
> he never had to drive the traders and the lenders,
> nor yet the pharisees and scribes
> who, therefore, camped about the place, describe it.
> *Profanum vulgus* praises this renouncer
> who never told it what it ought to hate.
> And he who found the goal before the way
> did not come from the source.

"You came from the source—the source is the goal" is received by the "Dying Man" as God's comfort and promise. To this Kraus alludes here, as does Viertel when, in the same way as Kraus, he calls the world a "wrong, deviating, circuitous way back to paradise." "And so," he continues in this most important passage of his essay on Kraus, "I attempt to interpret the development of this remarkable talent: intellectuality as a deviation . . . leading back to immediacy; publicity—a false trail back to language; satire—a detour to poetry." This "source"—the phenomenon's seal of authenticity—is the subject of a discovery that has a curious element of rediscovery. The theater of this philosophical recognition scene in Kraus's work is poetry, and its language rhyme: "A word that never lies at source" and that, just as blessedness has its source at the end of time, has its at the end of the line. Rhyme—two *putti* bearing the demon to its grave. It died at its source because it came into the world as a hybrid of mind and sexuality. Its sword and shield—concept and guilt—have fallen from its hands to become emblems beneath the feet of the angel that killed it. This is a poetic, martial angel with a foil in his hand, as only Baudelaire knew him: "practicing alone fantastic swordsmanship,"

> *Flairant dans tous les coins les hasards de la rime,*
> *Trébuchant sur les mots comme sur les pavés,*
> *Heurtant parfois des vers depuis longtemps rêvés.*
> (Scenting rhyme's hazards in every corner,
> Stumbling on words as on uneven pavements,
> Jostling now and then long-dreamed-of lines.)

Also a licentious angel, to be sure, "here chasing a metaphor that has just turned the corner, there coupling words like a procurer, perverting phrases, infatuated with similarities, blissfully abusing chiastic embraces, always on the lookout for adventure, impatient and hesitant to consummate in joy and torment." So finally the hedonistic moment of the work finds its purest expression in this melancholy and fantastic relationship to existence in which Kraus, in the Viennese tradition of Raimund and Girardi, arrives at a conception of happiness that is as resigned as it is sensual. This must be borne in mind if one is to understand the urgency with which he opposed the dancing pose affected by Nietzsche—not to mention the wrath with which the monster was bound to greet the Superman.

The child recognizes by rhyme that it has reached the summit of language, from which it can hear at their source the rushing of all springs. Up there creaturely existence is at home;

after so much dumbness in the animal and so much lying in the whore, it has found its tongue in the child. "A good brain must be capable of imagining each fiber of childhood with all its phenomena so intensely that temperature is raised"—in statements such as this Kraus aims further than it appears. He himself, at any rate, satisfied this requirement to the extent that he never envisaged the child as the object of education but, in an image from his own youth, as the antagonist of education who is educated by this antagonism, not by the educator. "Not the cane was to be abolished, but the teacher who uses it badly." Kraus wants to be nothing except the teacher who uses it better. The limit of his philanthropy, his pity, is marked by the cane, which he first felt in the same class at school to which he owes his best poems.

"I am only one of the late followers"—Kraus is a late follower of the school anthologies. "The German Boy's Table Grace," "Siegfried's Sword," "The Grave in the Busento," "Kaiser Karl Inspects a School"—these were his models, poetically re-created by the attentive pupil who learned them. So the "Steeds of Gravelotte" became the poem "To Eternal Peace," and even the most incandescent of his hate poems were ignited by Hölty's "Forest Fire," the glow of which pervaded the anthologies of our school days. And if on the last day not only the graves but the school anthologies open, to the tune of "How the trumpets blow, Hussars away," the true Pegasus of the little folk will burst from them and, a shriveled mummy, a puppet of cloth or yellowish ivory, hanging dead and dried up over the shoulders of his horse, this unparalleled fashioner of verses will go careening off; but the two-edged saber in his hand, polished as his rhymes and incisive as on the First Day, will belabor the green woods, and blooms of style bestrew the ground.

Language has never been more perfectly distinguished from mind, never more intimately bound to Eros, than by Kraus in the observation "The more closely you look at a word the more distantly it looks back." This is a Platonic love of language.

The only closeness from which the word cannot escape, however, is rhyme. So the primal erotic relationship between closeness and distance is given voice in his language: as rhyme and
name. As rhyme, language rises up from the creaturely world;
as name, it draws all creation up to it. In "The Forsaken" the
most ardent interpenetration of language and Eros, as Kraus
experienced them, expresses itself with an innocent grandeur
that recalls the perfect Greek epigrams and vase pictures. "The
Forsaken" are forsaken by each other. But—this is their great
solace—also with each other. On the threshold between dying
and rebirth they pause. With head turned back, joy "in un-
heard-of fashion" takes her eternal leave; turned from her the
soul "in unwonted fashion" silently sets foot in an alien world.
Thus forsaken with each other are joy and soul, but also language and Eros, also rhyme and name. To "The Forsaken" the
fifth volume of *Words in Verse* is dedicated. Only the dedica-
tion now reaches them, which is nothing other than avowal of
Platonic love, which does not satisfy its desire in what it loves,
but possesses and holds it in name. This self-obsessed man
knows no other self-renunciation than giving thanks. His love
is not possession, but gratitude. Thanking and dedicating—
for to thank is to put feelings under a name. How the beloved
grows distant and lustrous, how her minuteness and her glow
withdraw into name, that is the only experience of love known
to *Words in Verse*. And, therefore, "To live without women,
how easy—to have lived without women, how hard."

From within the linguistic compass of the man, and only
from within it, can we discern Kraus's basic polemical procedure: quotation. To quote a word is to call it by its name.
So Kraus's achievement exhausts itself at its highest level by
making even the newspaper quotable. He transports it to his
own sphere, and the empty phrase is suddenly forced to recognize that even in the deepest dregs of the journals it is not
safe from the voice that swoops on the wings of the word to
drag it from its darkness. How wonderful, if this voice approaches not to punish but to save, as it does on the Shake-

spearean wings of the lines in which, before Arras, someone sends word home of how in the early morning, on the last blasted tree before the fortifications, a lark began to sing. A single line, and not even one of his, is enough to enable Kraus to descend, as savior, into this inferno, a single italicization: "It was a nightingale and not a lark which sat there on the pome*granate* tree and sang."* In the quotation that both saves and chastises, language proves the matrix of justice. It summons the word by its name, wrenches it destructively from its context, but precisely thereby calls it back to its origin. It appears, now with rhyme and reason, sonorously, congruously in the structure of a new text. As rhyme it gathers the similar into its aura; as name it stands alone and expressionless. In quotation the two realms—of origin and destruction—justify themselves before language. And conversely, only where they interpenetrate—in quotation—is language consummated. In it is mirrored the angelic tongue in which all words, startled from the idyllic context of meaning, have become mottoes in the book of Creation.

From its two poles—classical and materialist humanism—the whole world of this man's culture is embraced by quotation. Schiller, admittedly unnamed, stands beside Shakespeare: "There is also a moral nobility. Mean natures pay / With that which they do, noble with that which they are"—this classical distich characterizes, in the convergence of manorial *noblesse* and cosmopolitan rectitude, the utopian vanishing point where Weimar humanism was at home, and which was finally fixed by Stifter. It is decisive for Kraus that he locates origin at exactly this vanishing point. It is his program to reverse the development of bourgeois-capitalist affairs to a condition that was never theirs. But he is nonetheless the last bourgeois to claim his justification from Being, and Expressionism was portentous for him because in it this attitude had for the first time to prove its worth in face of a revolutionary situation. It was precisely the attempt to do justice to this situation not

* *Granat* means "pomegranate"; *Granate*, "grenade" or "shell."—TRANS.

by actions but by Being that led Expressionism to its clenched ensteepments. So it became the last historical refuge of personality. The guilt that bowed it and the purity it proclaimed —both are part of the phantom of the unpolitical or "natural" man who emerges at the end of that regression and was unmasked by Marx. "Man as member of bourgeois society," writes Marx, "the unpolitical man, necessarily appears as the natural man.... Political revolution dissolves bourgeois life into its component parts without revolutionizing or criticizing these components themselves. It stands to bourgeois society, to the world of needs, work, private interests, private right, in the same relation as to the foundation of its existence ...and therefore to its natural basis.... The real man is acknowledged only in the form of the egoistical individual, the true man only in the form of the abstract *citoyen*.... Only when the really individual man takes back into himself the abstract citizen and, as an individual man, has become in his empirical life, in his individual work, in his individual circumstances a species-being...and therefore no longer separates social power from himself in the form of political power, only then is human emancipation complete." The materialist humanism which Marx here opposes to its classical counterpart manifests itself for Kraus in the child, and the developing human being raises his face against the idols of ideal man— the romantic child of nature as much as the dutiful citizen. For the sake of such development Kraus revised the school anthology, investigated German education, and found it tossing helplessly on the waves of journalistic caprice. Hence the "Lyric of the Germans": "He who can is their man and not he who must, / they strayed from being to seeming. / Their lyrical case was not Claudius / but Heine." The fact, however, that the developing man actually takes form not within the natural sphere but in that of mankind, in the struggle for liberation, and that he is recognized by the posture that the fight with exploitation and poverty stamp upon him, that there is no idealistic but only a materialistic deliverance from myth, and

that at the origin of creation stands not purity but purification
—all this did not leave its trace on Kraus's materialist humanism until very late. Only in despair did he discover in quotation the power not to preserve but to purify, to tear from
context, to destroy; the only power in which hope still resides that something might survive this age—because it was
wrenched from it.

Here we find confirmation that all the martial energies of
this man are innate civic virtues; only in the *mêlée* did they
take on their combative aspect. But already no one recognizes
them any more; no one can grasp the necessity that compelled
this great bourgeois character to become a comedian, this
guardian of Goethean linguistic values a polemicist, or why this
irreproachably honorable man went berserk. This, however,
was bound to happen, since he thought fit to begin changing
the world with his own class, in his own home, in Vienna. And
when, recognizing the futility of his enterprise, he abruptly
broke it off, he placed the matter back in the hands of nature
—this time destructive, not creative nature:

> Let time stand still! Sun, be consummate!
> Make great the end! Announce eternity!
> Rise up with menace, let your light boom thunder,
> that our strident death be silenced.
>
> You golden bell, melt in your own heat,
> Make yourself a gun against the cosmic foe!
> Shoot firebrands in his face! Had I but Joshua's power,
> I tell you, Gibeon would be again!

On this unfettered nature Kraus's later political credo is
founded, though in antithesis to Stifter's patriarchal code; it
is a confession that is in every respect astonishing, but incomprehensible only in the fact that it has not been preserved in
Die Fackel's largest type, and that this most powerful of postwar bourgeois prose must be sought in a vanished edition of
the issue of November 1920:

"What I mean is—and now for once I shall speak plainly to
this dehumanized brood of owners of property and blood, and

all their followers, because they do not understand German and from my 'contradictions' are incapable of deducing my true intention ... —what I mean is: Communism as a reality is only the obverse of their own life-violating ideology, admittedly by the grace of a purer ideal origin, a deranged remedy with a purer ideal purpose—the devil take its practice, but God preserve it as a constant threat over the heads of those who have property and would like to compel all others to preserve it, driving them, with the consolation that worldly goods are not the highest, to the fronts of hunger and patriotic honor. God preserve it, so that this rabble who are beside themselves with brazenness do not grow more brazen still, and so that the society of those exclusively entitled to enjoyment, who believe it is loving subordinate humanity enough if they give it syphilis, may at least go to bed with a nightmare! So that at least they may lose their appetite for preaching morality to their victims, take less delight in ridiculing them!"

A human, natural, noble language—particularly in the light of a noteworthy declaration by Loos: "If human work consists only of destruction, it is truly human, natural, noble work." For far too long the accent was placed on creativity. People are only creative to the extent that they avoid tasks and supervision. Work as a supervised task—its model: political and technical work—is attended by dirt and detritus, intrudes destructively into matter, is abrasive to what is already achieved, critical toward its conditions, and is in all this opposite to that of the dilettante luxuriating in creation. His work is innocent and pure, consuming and purifying masterliness. And therefore the monster stands among us as the messenger of a more real humanism. He is the conqueror of the empty phrase. He feels solidarity not with the slender pine but with the plane that devours it, not with the precious ore but with the blast furnace that purifies it. The average European has not succeeded in uniting his life with technology, because he has clung to the fetish of creative existence. One must have followed Loos in his struggle with the dragon "ornament," heard the stellar Esperanto of Scheerbart's creations, or seen Klee's *New Angel*, who preferred to free men by taking from them, rather than make them happy by giving to them, to understand a humanity that proves itself by destruction.

Justice, therefore, is destructive in opposing the constructive ambiguities of law, and destructively Kraus did justice to his own work: "All my errors stay behind to lead." This is a sober language that bases its dominance on permanence, and the writings of Kraus have already begun to last, so that he might furnish them with an epigraph from Lichtenberg, who dedicated one of his most profound works to "Your Majesty Forgetfulness." So his modesty now appears—bolder than his former self-assertion, which dissolved in demonic self-reflection. Neither purity nor sacrifice mastered the demon; but where origin and destruction come together, his rule is over. Like a creature sprung from the child and the cannibal his conqueror stands before him: not a new man; a monster, a new angel. Perhaps one of those who, according to the Talmud, are at each moment created anew in countless throngs, and who, once they have raised their voices before God, cease and pass into nothingness. Lamenting, chastising, or rejoicing? No matter—on this evanescent voice the ephemeral work of Kraus is modeled. Angelus—that is the messenger in the old engravings.

FOUR

Critique of Violence

The task of a critique of violence can be summarized as that of expounding its relation to law and justice. For a cause, however effective, becomes violent, in the precise sense of the word, only when it bears on moral issues. The sphere of these issues is defined by the concepts of law and justice. With regard to the first of these, it is clear that the most elementary relationship within any legal system is that of ends to means, and, further, that violence can first be sought only in the realm of means, not of ends. These observations provide a critique of violence with more—and certainly different—premises than perhaps appears. For if violence is a means, a criterion for criticizing it might seem immediately available. It imposes itself in the question whether violence, in a given case, is a means to a just or an unjust end. A critique of it would then be implied in a system of just ends. This, however, is not so. For what such a system, assuming it to be secure against all doubt, would contain is not a criterion for violence itself as a principle, but, rather, the criterion for cases of its use. The question would remain open whether violence, as a principle, could be a moral means even to just ends. To resolve this question a more exact criterion is needed, which would discriminate within the sphere of means themselves, without regard for the ends they serve.

The exclusion of this more precise critical approach is perhaps the predominant feature of a main current of legal philosophy: natural law. It perceives in the use of violent means to just ends no greater problem than a man sees in his "right" to move his body in the direction of a desired goal. According to this view (for which the terrorism in the French Revolution provided an ideological foundation), violence is a product of nature, as it were a raw material, the use of which is in no way problematical, unless force is misused for unjust ends. If, according to the theory of state of natural law, people give up all their violence for the sake of the state, this is done on the assumption (which Spinoza, for example, states explicitly in his *Tractatus Theologico-Politicus*) that the individual, before the conclusion of this rational contract, has *de jure* the right to use at will the violence that is *de facto* at his disposal. Perhaps these views have been recently rekindled by Darwin's biology, which, in a thoroughly dogmatic manner, regards violence as the only original means, besides natural selection, appropriate to all the vital ends of nature. Popular Darwinistic philosophy has often shown how short a step it is from this dogma of natural history to the still cruder one of legal philosophy, which holds that the violence that is, almost alone, appropriate to natural ends is thereby also legal.

This thesis of natural law that regards violence as a natural datum is diametrically opposed to that of positive law, which sees violence as a product of history. If natural law can judge all existing law only in criticizing its ends, so positive law can judge all evolving law only in criticizing its means. If justice is the criterion of ends, legality is that of means. Notwithstanding this antithesis, however, both schools meet in their common basic dogma: just ends can be attained by justified means, justified means used for just ends. Natural law attempts, by the justness of the ends, to "justify" the means, positive law to "guarantee" the justness of the ends through the justification of the means. This antinomy would prove insoluble if the common dogmatic assumption were false, if justified means on the one hand and just ends on the other were in irreconcilable conflict. No insight into this problem could be gained, however, until the circular argument had been broken, and mutually independent criteria both of just ends and of justified means were established.

The realm of ends, and therefore also the question of a

criterion of justness, is excluded for the time being from this study. Instead, the central place is given to the question of the justification of certain means that constitute violence. Principles of natural law cannot decide this question, but can only lead to bottomless casuistry. For if positive law is blind to the absoluteness of ends, natural law is equally so to the contingency of means. On the other hand, the positive theory of law is acceptable as a hypothetical basis at the outset of this study, because it undertakes a fundamental distinction between kinds of violence independently of cases of their application. This distinction is between historically acknowledged, so-called sanctioned violence, and unsanctioned violence. If the following considerations proceed from this it cannot, of course, mean that given forms of violence are classified in terms of whether they are sanctioned or not. For in a critique of violence, a criterion for the latter in positive law cannot concern its uses but only its evaluation. The question that concerns us is, what light is thrown on the nature of violence by the fact that such a criterion or distinction can be applied to it at all, or, in other words, what is the meaning of this distinction? That this distinction supplied by positive law is meaningful, based on the nature of violence, and irreplaceable by any other, will soon enough be shown, but at the same time light will be shed on the sphere in which alone such a distinction can be made. To sum up: if the criterion established by positive law to assess the legality of violence can be analyzed with regard to its meaning, then the sphere of its application must be criticized with regard to its value. For this critique a standpoint outside positive legal philosophy but also outside natural law must be found. The extent to which it can only be furnished by a historico-philosophical view of law will emerge.

The meaning of the distinction between legitimate and illegitimate violence is not immediately obvious. The misunderstanding in natural law by which a distinction is drawn between violence used for just and unjust ends must be emphatically rejected. Rather, it has already been indicated that positive law demands of all violence a proof of its historical origin, which under certain conditions is declared legal, sanctioned. Since the acknowledgment of legal violence is most tangibly evident in a deliberate submission to its ends, a hypothetical distinction between kinds of violence must be based on the presence or absence of a general historical acknowledgment of its ends. Ends that lack such acknowledgment may be called natural ends, the other legal ends. The differing function of violence, depending on whether it serves natural or legal ends, can be most clearly traced against a background of specific legal conditions. For the sake of simplicity, the following discussion will relate to contemporary European conditions. Characteristic of these, as far as the individual as legal subject is concerned, is the tendency not to admit the natural ends of such individuals in all those cases in which such ends could, in a given situation, be usefully pursued by violence. This means: this legal system tries to erect, in all areas where individual ends could be usefully pursued by violence, legal ends that can only be realized by legal power. Indeed, it strives to limit by legal ends even those areas in which natural ends are admitted in principle within wide boundaries, like that of education, as soon as these natural ends are pursued with an excessive measure of violence, as in the laws relating to the limits of educational authority to punish. It can be formulated as a general maxim of present-day European legislation that all the natural ends of individuals must collide with legal ends if pursued with a greater or lesser degree of violence. (The contradiction between this and the right of self-defense will be resolved in what follows.) From this maxim it follows that law sees violence in the hands of individuals as a danger undermining the legal system. As a danger nullifying legal ends and the legal executive? Certainly not; for then violence as such would not be condemned, but only that directed to illegal ends. It will be argued that a system of legal ends cannot be maintained if natural ends are anywhere still pursued violently. In the first place, however, this is a mere dogma. To counter it one might perhaps consider the suprising possibility that the law's interest in a monopoly of violence vis-à-vis individuals is not explained by the intention of preserving legal ends but, rather, by that of preserving the law itself; that violence, when not in the hands of the law, threatens it not by the ends that it may pursue but by its mere existence outside the law. The same may be more drastically suggested if one reflects how often the figure of the "great" criminal, however repellent his ends may have been, has aroused the secret admiration of the public. This cannot result from his deed, but only from the violence to which it bears witness. In this case, therefore, the violence of which present-day law is seeking in all areas of activity to deprive the individual appears really threatening, and arouses even in defeat the sympathy of the mass against law. By what function violence can with reason seem so threatening to law, and be so feared by it, must be especially evident where its application, even in the present legal system, is still permissible.

This is above all the case in the class struggle, in the form of the workers' guaranteed right to strike. Organized labor is, apart from the state, probably today the only legal subject entitled to exercise violence. Against this view there is certainly the objection that an omission of actions, a nonaction, which a strike really is, cannot be described as violence. Such a consideration doubtless made it easier for a state power to conceive the right to strike, once this was no longer avoidable. But its truth is not unconditional, and therefore not unrestricted. It is true that the omission of an action, or service, where it amounts simply to a "severing of relations," can be an entirely nonviolent, pure means. And as in the view of the state, or the law, the right to strike conceded to labor is certainly not a right to exercise violence but, rather, to escape from a violence indirectly exercised by the employer, strikes conforming to this may undoubtedly occur from time to time and involve only a "withdrawal" or "estrangement" from the employer. The moment of violence, however, is necessarily introduced, in the

f extortion, into such an omission, if it takes place in the
t of a conscious readiness to resume the suspended
action under certain circumstances that either have nothing
whatever to do with this action or only superficially modify it.
Understood in this way, the right to strike constitutes in the
view of labor, which is opposed to that of the state, the right to
use force in attaining certain ends. The antithesis between the
two conceptions emerges in all its bitterness in face of a revolutionary general strike. In this, labor will always appeal to its
right to strike, and the state will call this appeal an abuse,
since the right to strike was not "so intended," and take emergency measures. For the state retains the right to declare that a
simultaneous use of strike in all industries is illegal, since the
specific reasons for strike admitted by legislation cannot be
prevalent in every workshop. In this difference of interpretation is expressed the objective contradiction in the legal situation, whereby the state acknowledges a violence whose ends, as
natural ends, it sometimes regards with indifference, but in a
crisis (the revolutionary general strike) confronts inimically.
For, however paradoxical this may appear at first sight, even
conduct involving the exercise of a right can nevertheless, under certain circumstances, be described as violent. More specifically, such conduct, when active, may be called violent if it
exercises a right in order to overthrow the legal system that has
conferred it; when passive, it is nevertheless to be so described
if it constitutes extortion in the sense explained above. It
therefore reveals an objective contradiction in the legal situation, but not a logical contradiction in the law, if under certain
circumstances the law meets the strikers, as perpetrators of
violence, with violence. For in a strike the state fears above all
else that function of violence which it is the object of this study
to identify as the only secure foundation of its critique. For if
violence were, as first appears, merely the means to secure
directly whatever happens to be sought, it could fulfill its end
as predatory violence. It would be entirely unsuitable as a basis
for, or a modification to, relatively stable conditions. The

strike shows, however, that it can be so, that it is able to found and modify legal conditions, however offended the sense of justice may find itself thereby. It will be objected that such a function of violence is fortuitous and isolated. This can be rebutted by a consideration of military violence.

The possibility of military law rests on exactly the same objective contradiction in the legal situation as does that of strike law, that is to say, on the fact that legal subjects sanction violence whose ends remain for the sanctioners natural ends, and can therefore in a crisis come into conflict with their own legal or natural ends. Admittedly, military violence is in the first place used quite directly, as predatory violence, toward its ends. Yet it is very striking that even—or, rather, precisely —in primitive conditions that know hardly the beginnings of constitutional relations, and even in cases where the victor has established himself in invulnerable possession, a peace cere-mony is entirely necessary. Indeed, the word "peace," in the sense in which it is the correlative to the word "war" (for there is also a quite different meaning, similarly unmetaphor-ical and political, the one used by Kant in talking of "Eternal Peace"), denotes this a priori, necessary sanctioning, regardless of all other legal conditions, of every victory. This sanction consists precisely in recognizing the new conditions as a new "law," quite regardless of whether they need *de facto* any guarantee of their continuation. If, therefore, conclusions can be drawn from military violence, as being primordial and para-digmatic of all violence used for natural ends, there is inherent in all such violence a lawmaking character. We shall return later to the implications of this insight. It explains the above-mentioned tendency of modern law to divest the individual, at least as a legal subject, of all violence, even that directed only to natural ends. In the great criminal this violence con-fronts the law with the threat of declaring a new law, a threat that even today, despite its impotence, in important instances horrifies the public as it did in primeval times. The state, however, fears this violence simply for its lawmaking character, being obliged to acknowledge it as lawmaking whenever external powers force it to concede them the right to conduct warfare, and classes the right to strike.

If in the last war the critique of military violence was the starting point for a passionate critique of violence in general—which taught at least one thing, that violence is no longer exercised and tolerated naïvely—nevertheless, violence was not only subject to criticism for its lawmaking character, but was also judged, perhaps more annihilatingly, for another of its functions. For a duality in the function of violence is characteristic of militarism, which could only come into being through general conscription. Militarism is the compulsory, universal use of violence as a means to the ends of the state. This compulsory use of violence has recently been scrutinized as closely as, or still more closely than, the use of violence itself. In it violence shows itself in a function quite different from its simple application for natural ends. It consists in the use of violence as a means of legal ends. For the subordination of citizens to laws—in the present case, to the law of general conscription—is a legal end. If that first function of violence is called the lawmaking function, this second will be called the law-preserving function. Since conscription is a case of law-preserving violence that is not in principle distinguished from others, a really effective critique of it is far less easy than the declamations of pacifists and activists suggest. Rather, such a critique coincides with the critique of all legal violence—that is, with the critique of legal or executive force—and cannot be performed by any lesser program. Nor, of course—unless one is prepared to proclaim a quite childish anarchism—is it achieved by refusing to acknowledge any constraint toward persons and declaring "What pleases is permitted." Such a maxim merely excludes reflection on the moral and historical spheres, and thereby on any meaning in action, and beyond this on any meaning in reality itself, which cannot be constituted if "action" is removed from its sphere. More important is the fact that even the appeal, so frequently attempted, to the categorical imperative, with its doubtless incontestable minimum program—act in such a way that at all times you use humanity both in your person and in the person of all others as an end, and never merely as a means—is in itself inadequate for such a critique.* For positive law, if conscious of its roots, will certainly claim to acknowledge and promote the interest of mankind in the person of each individual. It sees this interest in the representation and preservation of an order imposed by fate. While this view, which claims to preserve law in its very basis, cannot escape criticism, nevertheless all attacks that are made merely in the name of a formless "freedom" without being able to specify this higher order of freedom, remain impotent against it. And most impotent of all when, instead of attacking the legal system root and branch, they impugn particular laws or legal practices that the law, of course, takes under the protection of its power, which resides in the fact that there is only one fate and that what exists, and in particular what threatens, belongs inviolably to its order. For law-preserving violence is a threatening violence. And its threat is not intended as the deterrent that uninformed liberal theorists interpret it to be. A deterrent in the exact sense would require a certainty that contradicts the nature of a threat and is not attained by any law, since there is always hope of eluding its arm. This makes it all the more threatening, like fate, on which depends whether the criminal is apprehended. The deepest purpose of the uncertainty of the legal threat will emerge from the later consideration of the sphere of fate in which it originates. There is a useful pointer to it in the sphere of punishments. Among them, since the validity of positive law has been called into question, capital punishment has provoked more criticism than all others. However superficial the arguments may in most cases have been, their motives were and are rooted in principle. The opponents of these critics

* One might, rather, doubt whether this famous demand does not contain too little, that is, whether it is permissible to use, or allow to be used, oneself or another in any respect as a means. Very good grounds for such doubt could be adduced.

felt, perhaps without knowing why and probably involuntarily, that an attack on capital punishment assails, not legal measure, not laws, but law itself in its origin. For if violence, violence crowned by fate, is the origin of law, then it may be readily supposed that where the highest violence, that over life and death, occurs in the legal system, the origins of law jut manifestly and fearsomely into existence. In agreement with this is the fact that the death penalty in primitive legal systems is imposed even for such crimes as offenses against property, to which it seems quite out of "proportion." Its purpose is not to punish the infringement of law but to establish new law. For in the exercise of violence over life and death more than in any other legal act, law reaffirms itself. But in this very violence something rotten in law is revealed, above all to a finer sensibility, because the latter knows itself to be infinitely remote from conditions in which fate might imperiously have shown itself in such a sentence. Reason must, however, attempt to approach such conditions all the more resolutely, if it is to bring to a conclusion its critique of both lawmaking and lawpreserving violence.

In a far more unnatural combination than in the death penalty, in a kind of spectral mixture, these two forms of violence are present in another institution of the modern state, the police. True, this is violence for legal ends (in the right of disposition), but with the simultaneous authority to decide these ends itself within wide limits (in the right of decree). The ignominy of such an authority, which is felt by few simply because its ordinances suffice only seldom for the crudest acts, but are therefore allowed to rampage all the more blindly in the most vulnerable areas and against thinkers, from whom the state is not protected by law—this ignominy lies in the fact that in this authority the separation of lawmaking and lawpreserving violence is suspended. If the first is required to prove its worth in victory, the second is subject to the restriction that it may not set itself new ends. Police violence is emancipated from both conditions. It is lawmaking, for its characteristic function is not the promulgation of laws but the assertion of legal claims for any decree, and law-preserving, because it is at the disposal of these ends. The assertion that the ends of police violence are always identical or even connected to those of general law is entirely untrue. Rather, the "law" of the police really marks the point at which the state, whether from impotence or because of the immanent connections within any legal system, can no longer guarantee through the legal system the empirical ends that it desires at any price to attain. Therefore the police intervene "for security reasons" in countless cases where no clear legal situation exists, when they are not merely, without the slightest relation to legal ends, accompanying the citizen as a brutal encumbrance through a life regulated by ordinances, or simply supervising him. Unlike law, which acknowledges in the "decision" determined by place and time a metaphysical category that gives it a claim to critical evaluation, a consideration of the police institution encounters nothing essential at all. Its power is formless, like its nowhere tangible, all-pervasive, ghostly presence in the life of civilized states. And though the police may, in particulars, everywhere appear the same, it cannot finally be denied that their spirit is less devastating where they represent, in absolute monarchy, the power of a ruler in which legislative and executive supremacy are united, than in democracies where their existence, elevated by no such relation, bears witness to the greatest conceivable degeneration of violence.

All violence as a means is either lawmaking or law-preserving. If it lays claim to neither of these predicates, it forfeits all validity. It follows, however, that all violence as a means, even in the most favorable case, is implicated in the problematic nature of law itself. And if the importance of these problems cannot be assessed with certainty at this stage of the investigation, law nevertheless appears, from what has been said, in so ambiguous a moral light that the question poses itself whether there are no other than violent means for regulating conflicting human interests. We are above all obligated to note

that a totally nonviolent resolution of conflicts can never lead
to a legal contract. For the latter, however peacefully it may
have been entered into by the parties, leads finally to possible
violence. It confers on both parties the right to take recourse
to violence in some form against the other, should he break
the agreement. Not only that; like the outcome, the origin of
every contract also points toward violence. It need not be
directly present in it as lawmaking violence, but is represented
in it insofar as the power that guarantees a legal contract is in
turn of violent origin even if violence is not introduced into
the contract itself. When the consciousness of the latent presence of violence in a legal institution disappears, the institution falls into decay. In our time, parliaments provide an
example of this. They offer the familiar, woeful spectacle because they have not remained conscious of the revolutionary
forces to which they owe their existence. Accordingly, in Germany in particular, the last manifestation of such forces bore
no fruit for parliaments. They lack the sense that a lawmaking
violence is represented by themselves; no wonder that they
cannot achieve decrees worthy of this violence, but cultivate
in compromise a supposedly nonviolent manner of dealing with
political affairs. This remains, however, a "product situated
within the mentality of violence, no matter how it may disdain
all open violence, because the effort toward compromise is
motivated not internally but from outside, by the opposing
effort, because no compromise, however freely accepted, is conceivable without a compulsive character. 'It would be better
otherwise' is the underlying feeling in every compromise."*
Significantly, the decay of parliaments has perhaps alienated
as many minds from the ideal of a nonviolent resolution of
political conflicts as were attracted to it by the war. The pacifists are confronted by the Bolsheviks and Syndicalists. These
have effected an annihilating and on the whole apt critique
of present-day parliaments. Nevertheless, however desirable
and gratifying a flourishing parliament might be by compari-

* Unger, *Politik und Metaphysik*, Berlin, 1921, p. 8.

son, a discussion of means of political agreement that are in principle nonviolent cannot be concerned with parliamentarianism. For what parliament achieves in vital affairs can only be those legal decrees that in their origin and outcome are attended by violence.

Is any nonviolent resolution of conflict possible? Without doubt. The relationships of private persons are full of examples of this. Nonviolent agreement is possible wherever a civilized outlook allows the use of unalloyed means of agreement. Legal and illegal means of every kind that are all the same violent may be confronted with nonviolent ones as unalloyed means. Courtesy, sympathy, peaceableness, trust, and whatever else might here be mentioned, are their subjective preconditions. Their objective manifestation, however, is determined by the law (the enormous scope of which cannot be discussed here) that unalloyed means are never those of direct, but always those of indirect solutions. They therefore never apply directly to the resolution of conflict between man and man, but only to matters concerning objects. The sphere of nonviolent means opens up in the realm of human conflicts relating to goods. For this reason technique in the broadest sense of the word is their most particular area. Its profoundest example is perhaps the conference, considered as a technique of civil agreement. For in it not only is nonviolent agreement possible, but also the exclusion of violence in principle is quite explicitly demonstrable by one significant factor: there is no sanction for lying. Probably no legislation on earth originally stipulated such a sanction. This makes clear that there is a sphere of human agreement that is nonviolent to the extent that it is wholly inaccessible to violence: the proper sphere of "understanding," language. Only late and in a peculiar process of decay has it been penetrated by legal violence in the penalty placed on fraud. For whereas the legal system at its origin, trusting to its victorious power, is content to defeat lawbreaking wherever it happens to show itself, and deception, having itself no trace of power about it, was, on the principle *ius civile* *vigilantibus scriptum est,* exempt from punishment in Roman and ancient Germanic law, the law of a later period, lacking confidence in its own violence, no longer felt itself a match for that of all others. Rather, fear of the latter and mistrust of itself indicate its declining vitality. It begins to set itself ends, with the intention of sparing law-preserving violence more taxing manifestations. It turns to fraud, therefore, not out of moral considerations, but for fear of the violence that it might unleash in the defrauded party. Since such fear conflicts with the violent nature of law derived from its origins, such ends are inappropriate to the justified means of law. They reflect not only the decay of its own sphere, but also a diminution of pure means. For, in prohibiting fraud, law restricts the use of wholly nonviolent means because they could produce reactive violence. This tendency of law has also played a part in the concession of the right to strike, which contradicts the interests of the state. It grants this right because it forestalls violent actions the state is afraid to oppose. Did not workers previously resort at once to sabotage and set fire to factories? To induce men to reconcile their interests peacefully without involving the legal system, there is, in the end, apart from all virtues, one effective motive that often enough puts into the most reluctant hands pure instead of violent means; it is the fear of mutual disadvantages that threaten to arise from violent confrontation, whatever the outcome might be. Such motives are clearly visible in countless cases of conflict of interests between private persons. It is different when classes and nations are in conflict, since the higher orders that threaten to overwhelm equally victor and vanquished are hidden from the feelings of most, and from the intelligence of almost all. Space does not here permit me to trace such higher orders and the common interests corresponding to them, which constitute the most enduring motive for a policy of pure means.* We can therefore only point to pure means in politics as analogous

* But see Unger, pp. 18 ff.

to those which govern peaceful intercourse between private persons.

As regards class struggles, in them strike must under certain conditions be seen as a pure means. Two essentially different kinds of strike, the possibilities of which have already been considered, must now be more fully characterized. Sorel has the credit—from political, rather than purely theoretical, considerations—of having first distinguished them. He contrasts them as the political and the proletarian general strike. They are also antithetical in their relation to violence. Of the partisans of the former he says: "The strengthening of state power is the basis of their conceptions; in their present organizations the politicians (viz. the moderate socialists) are already preparing the ground for a strong centralized and disciplined power that will be impervious to criticism from the opposition, capable of imposing silence, and of issuing its mendacious decrees."* "The political general strike demonstrates how the state will lose none of its strength, how power is transferred from the privileged to the privileged, how the mass of producers will change their masters." In contrast to this political general strike (which incidentally seems to have been summed up by the abortive German revolution), the proletarian general strike sets itself the sole task of destroying state power. It "nullifies all the ideological consequences of every possible social policy; its partisans see even the most popular reforms as bourgeois." "This general strike clearly announces its indifference toward material gain through conquest by declaring its intention to abolish the state; the state was really ... the basis of the existence of the ruling group, who in all their enterprises benefit from the burdens borne by the public." While the first form of interruption of work is violent since it causes only an external modification of labor conditions, the second, as a pure means, is nonviolent. For it takes place not in readiness to resume work following external concessions and this

* Sorel, *Réflexions sur la violence*, 5th ed., Paris, 1919, p. 250.

or that modification to working conditions, but in the determination to resume only a wholly transformed work, no longer enforced by the state, an upheaval that this kind of strike not so much causes as consummates. For this reason, the first of these undertakings is lawmaking but the second anarchistic. Taking up occasional statements by Marx, Sorel rejects every kind of program, of utopia—in a word, of lawmaking—for the revolutionary movement: "With the general strike all these fine things disappear; the revolution appears as a clear, simple revolt, and no place is reserved either for the sociologists or for the elegant amateurs of social reforms or for the intellectuals who have made it their profession to think for the proletariat." Against this deep, moral, and genuinely revolutionary conception, no objection can stand that seeks, on grounds of its possibly catastrophic consequences, to brand such a general strike as violent. Even if it can rightly be said that the modern economy, seen as a whole, resembles much less a machine that stands idle when abandoned by its stoker than a beast that goes berserk as soon as its tamer turns his back, nevertheless the violence of an action can be assessed no more from its effects than from its ends, but only from the law of its means. State power, of course, which has eyes only for effects, opposes precisely this kind of strike for its alleged violence, as distinct from partial strikes which are for the most part actually extortionate. The extent to which such a rigorous conception of the general strike as such is capable of diminishing the incidence of actual violence in revolutions, Sorel has explained with highly ingenious arguments. By contrast, an outstanding example of violent omission, more immoral and cruder than the political general strike, akin to a blockade, is the strike by doctors, such as several German cities have seen. In this is revealed at its most repellent an unscrupulous use of violence that is positively depraved in a professional class that for years, without the slightest attempts at resistance, "secured death its prey," and then at the first opportunity abandoned life of its own free will. More clearly than in recent class struggles, the means of nonviolent agreement have developed in thousands of years of the history of states. Only occasionally does the task of diplomats in their transactions consist of modifications to legal systems. Fundamentally they have, entirely on the analogy of agreement between private persons, to resolve conflicts case by case, in the names of their states, peacefully and without contracts. A delicate task that is more robustly performed by referees, but a method of solution that in principle is above that of the referee because it is beyond all legal systems, and therefore beyond violence. Accordingly, like the intercourse of private persons, that of diplomats has engendered its own forms and virtues, which were not always mere formalities, even though they have become so.

Among all the forms of violence permitted by both natural law and positive law there is not one that is free of the gravely problematic nature, already indicated, of all legal violence. Since, however, every conceivable solution to human problems, not to speak of deliverance from the confines of all the world-historical conditions of existence obtaining hitherto, remains impossible if violence is totally excluded in principle, the question necessarily arises as to other kinds of violence than all those envisaged by legal theory. It is at the same time the question of the truth of the basic dogma common to both theories: just ends can be attained by justified means, justified means used for just ends. How would it be, therefore, if all the violence imposed by fate, using justified means, were of itself in irreconcilable conflict with just ends, and if at the same time a different kind of violence came into view that certainly could be either the justified or the unjustified means to those ends, but was not related to them as means at all but in some different way? This would throw light on the curious and at first discouraging discovery of the ultimate insolubility of all legal problems (which in its hopelessness is perhaps comparable only to the possibility of conclusive pronouncements on "right" and "wrong" in evolving languages). For it is never reason that decides on the justification of means and the justness of ends, but fate-imposed violence on the former and God on the latter. And insight that is uncommon only because of the stubborn prevailing habit of conceiving those just ends as ends of a possible law, that is, not only as generally valid (which follows analytically from the nature of justice), but also as capable of generalization, which, as could be shown, contradicts the nature of justice. For ends that for one situation are just, universally acceptable, and valid, are so for no other situation, no matter how similar it may be in other respects. The nonmediate function of violence at issue here is illustrated by everyday experience. As regards man, he is impelled by anger, for example, to the most visible outbursts of a violence that is not related as a means to a preconceived end. It is not a means but a manifestation. Moreover, this violence has thoroughly objective manifestations in which it can be subjected to criticism. These are to be found, most significantly, above all in myth.

Mythical violence in its archetypal form is a mere manifestation of the gods. Not a means to their ends, scarcely a manifestation of their will, but first of all a manifestation of their existence. The legend of Niobe contains an outstanding example of this. True, it might appear that the action of Apollo and Artemis is only a punishment. But their violence establishes a law far more than it punishes for the infringement of one already existing. Niobe's arrogance calls down fate upon itself not because her arrogance offends against the law but because it challenges fate—to a fight in which fate must triumph, and can bring to light a law only in its triumph. How little such divine violence was to the ancients the law-preserving violence of punishment is shown by the heroic legends in which the hero—for example, Prometheus—challenges fate with dignified courage, fights it with varying fortunes, and is not left by the legend without hope of one day bringing a new law to men. It is really this hero and the legal violence of the myth native to him that the public tries to picture even now in admiring the miscreant. Violence therefore bursts upon Niobe from the uncertain, ambiguous sphere of fate. It is not actually destructive. Although it brings a cruel death to Niobe's children, it stops short of the life of their mother, whom it leaves behind, more guilty than before through the death of the children, both as an eternally mute bearer of guilt and as a boundary stone on the frontier between men and gods. If this immediate violence in mythical manifestations proves closely related, indeed identical to lawmaking violence, it reflects a problematic light on lawmaking violence, insofar as the latter was characterized above, in the account of military violence, as merely a mediate violence. At the same time this connection promises further to illuminate fate, which in all cases underlies legal violence, and to conclude in broad outline the critique of the latter. For the function of violence in lawmaking is twofold, in the sense that lawmaking pursues as its end, with violence as the means, *what* is to be established as law, but at the moment of instatement does not dismiss violence; rather, at this very moment of lawmaking, it specifically establishes as law not an end unalloyed by violence, but one necessarily and intimately bound to it, under the title of power. Lawmaking is power making, and, to that extent, an immediate manifestation of violence. Justice is the principle of all divine end making, power the principle of all mythical lawmaking.

An application of the latter that has immense consequences is to be found in constitutional law. For in this sphere the establishing of frontiers, the task of "peace" after all the wars of the mythical age, is the primal phenomenon of all lawmaking violence. Here we see most clearly that power, more than the most extravagant gain in property, is what is guaranteed by all lawmaking violence. Where frontiers are decided the adversary is not simply annihilated; indeed, he is accorded rights even when the victor's superiority in power is complete. And these are, in a demonically ambiguous way, "equal" rights: for both parties to the treaty it is the same line that may not be crossed. Here appears, in a terribly primitive form, the same mythical ambiguity of laws that may not be "infringed" to which Anatole France refers satirically when he says, "Poor and rich are equally forbidden to spend the night under the bridges." It also appears that Sorel touches not merely on a cultural-historical but also on a metaphysical truth in surmising that in the beginning all right was the prerogative of the kings or the nobles—in short, of the mighty; and that, *mutatis mutandis,* it will remain so as long as it exists. For from the point of view of violence, which alone can guarantee law, there is no equality, but at the most equally great violence. The act of fixing frontiers, however, is also significant for an understanding of law in another respect. Laws and unmarked frontiers remain, at least in primeval times, unwritten laws. A man can unwittingly infringe upon them and thus incur retribution. For each intervention of law that is provoked by an offense against the unwritten and unknown law is called, in contradistinction to punishment, retribution. But however unluckily it may befall its unsuspecting victim, its occurrence is, in the understanding of the law, not chance, but fate showing itself once again in its deliberate ambiguity. Hermann Cohen, in a brief reflection on the ancients' conception of fate, has spoken of the "inescapable realization" that it is "fate's orders themselves that seem to cause and bring about this infringement, this offense."* To this spirit of law even the modern principle that ignorance of a law is not protection against punishment testifies, just as the struggle over written law in the early period of the ancient Greek communities is to be understood as a rebellion against the spirit of mythical statutes.

Far from inaugurating a purer sphere, the mythical manifestation of immediate violence shows itself fundamentally identical with all legal violence, and turns suspicion concerning the latter into certainty of the perniciousness of its historical function, the destruction of which thus becomes

---

* Hermann Cohen, *Ethik des reinen Willens,* 2nd ed., Berlin, 1907, p. 362.

obligatory. This very task of destruction poses again, in the last resort, the question of a pure immediate violence that might be able to call a halt to mythical violence. Just as in all spheres God opposes myth, mythical violence is confronted by the divine. And the latter constitutes its antithesis in all respects. If mythical violence is lawmaking, divine violence is law-destroying; if the former sets boundaries, the latter boundlessly destroys them; if mythical violence brings at once guilt and retribution, divine power only expiates; if the former threatens, the latter strikes; if the former is bloody, the latter is lethal without spilling blood. The legend of Niobe may be confronted, as an example of this violence, with God's judgment on the company of Korah. It strikes privileged Levites, strikes them without warning, without threat, and does not stop short of annihilation. But in annihilating it also expiates, and a deep connection between the lack of bloodshed and the expiatory character of this violence is unmistakable. For blood is the symbol of mere life. The dissolution of legal violence stems, as cannot be shown in detail here, from the guilt of more natural life, which consigns the living, innocent and unhappy, to a retribution that "expiates" the guilt of mere life—and doubtless also purifies the guilty, not of guilt, however, but of law. For with mere life the rule of law over the living ceases. Mythical violence is bloody power over mere life for its own sake, divine violence pure power over all life for the sake of the living. The first demands sacrifice, the second accepts it.

This divine power is attested not only by religious tradition but is also found in present-day life in at least one sanctioned manifestation. The educative power, which in its perfected form stands outside the law, is one of its manifestations. These are defined, therefore, not by miracles directly performed by God, but by the expiating moment in them that strikes without bloodshed and, finally, by the absence of all law-making. To this extent it is justifiable to call this violence, too, annihilating; but it is so only relatively, with regard to goods, right, life, and suchlike, never absolutely, with regard to the soul of the living. The premise of such an extension of pure or divine power is sure to provoke, particularly today, the most violent reactions, and to be countered by the argument that taken to its logical conclusion it confers on men even lethal power against one another. This, however, cannot be conceded. For the question "May I kill?" meets its irreducible answer in the commandment "Thou shalt not kill." This commandment precedes the deed, just as God was "preventing" the deed. But just as it may not be fear of punishment that enforces obedience, the injunction becomes inapplicable, incommensurable once the deed is accomplished. No judgment of the deed can be derived from the commandment. And so neither the divine judgment, nor the grounds for this judgment, can be known in advance. Those who base a condemnation of all violent killing of one person by another on the commandment are therefore mistaken. It exists not as a criterion of judgment, but as a guideline for the actions of persons or communities who have to wrestle with it in solitude and, in exceptional cases, to take on themselves the responsibility of ignoring it. Thus it was understood by Judaism, which expressly rejected the condemnation of killing in self-defense. But those thinkers who take the opposed view refer to a more distant theorem, on which they possibly propose to base even the commandment itself. This is the doctrine of the sanctity of life, which they either apply to all animal or even vegetable life, or limit to human life. Their argumentation, exemplified in an extreme case by the revolutionary killing of the oppressor, runs as follows: "If I do not kill I shall never establish the world dominion of justice ... that is the argument of the intelligent terrorist. ... We, however, profess that higher even than the happiness and justice of existence stands existence itself."* As certainly as this last proposition is false, indeed ignoble, it shows the necessity of seeking the reason for the commandment no longer

* Kurt Hiller in a yearbook of *Das Ziel.*

in what the deed does to the victim, but in what it does to God and the doer. The proposition that existence stands higher than a just existence is false and ignominious, if existence is to mean nothing other than mere life—and it has this meaning in the argument referred to. It contains a mighty truth, however, if existence, or, better, life (words whose ambiguity is readily dispelled, analogously to that of freedom, when they are referred to two distinct spheres), means the irreducible, total condition that is "man"; if the proposition is intended to mean that the nonexistence of man is something more terrible than the (admittedly subordinate) not-yet-attained condition of the just man. To this ambiguity the proposition quoted above owes its plausibility. Man cannot, at any price, be said to coincide with the mere life in him, no more than with any other of his conditions and qualities, not even with the uniqueness of his bodily person. However sacred man is (or that life in him that is identically present in earthly life, death, and afterlife), there is no sacredness in his condition, in his bodily life vulnerable to injury by his fellow men. What, then, distinguishes it essentially from the life of animals and plants? And even if these were sacred, they could not be so by virtue only of being alive, of being in life. It might be well worth while to track down the origin of the dogma of the sacredness of life. Perhaps, indeed probably, it is relatively recent, the last mistaken attempt of the weakened Western tradition to seek the saint it has lost in cosmological impenetrability. (The antiquity of all religious commandments against murder is no counterargument, because these are based on other ideas than the modern theorem.) Finally, this idea of man's sacredness gives grounds for reflection that what is here pronounced sacred was according to ancient mythical thought the marked bearer of guilt: life itself.

The critique of violence is the philosophy of its history—the "philosophy" of this history, because only the idea of its development makes possible a critical, discriminating, and decisive approach to its temporal data. A gaze directed only at what is close at hand can at most perceive a dialectical rising and falling in the lawmaking and law-preserving formations of violence. The law governing their oscillation rests on the circumstance that all law-preserving violence, in its duration, indirectly weakens the lawmaking violence represented by it, through the suppression of hostile counterviolence. (Various symptoms of this have been referred to in the course of this study.) This lasts until either new forces or those earlier suppressed triumph over the hitherto lawmaking violence and thus found a new law, destined in its turn to decay. On the breaking of this cycle maintained by mythical forms of law, on the suspension of law with all the forces on which it depends as they depend on it, finally therefore on the abolition of state power, a new historical epoch is founded. If the rule of myth is broken occasionally in the present age, the coming age is not so unimaginably remote that an attack on law is altogether futile. But if the existence of violence outside the law, as pure immediate violence, is assured, this furnishes the proof that revolutionary violence, the highest manifestation of unalloyed violence by man, is possible, and by what means. Less possible and also less urgent for humankind, however, is to decide when unalloyed violence has been realized in particular cases. For only mythical violence, not divine, will be recognizable as such with certainty, unless it be in incomparable effects, because the expiatory power of violence is not visible to men. Once again all the eternal forms are open to pure divine violence, which myth bastardized with law. It may manifest itself in a true war exactly as in the divine judgment of the multitude on a criminal. But all mythical, lawmaking violence, which we may call executive, is pernicious. Pernicious, too, is the law-preserving, administrative violence that serves it. Divine violence, which is the sign and seal but never the means of sacred execution, may be called sovereign violence.

The Destructive Character

It could happen to someone looking back over his life that he realized that almost all the deeper obligations he had endured in its course originated in people on whose "destructive character" everyone was agreed. He would stumble on this fact one day, perhaps by chance, and the heavier the blow it deals him, the better are his chances of picturing the destructive character.

The destructive character knows only one watchword: make room; only one activity: clearing away. His need for fresh air and open space is stronger than any hatred.

The destructive character is young and cheerful. For destroying rejuvenates in clearing away the traces of our own age; it cheers because everything cleared away means to the destroyer a complete reduction, indeed eradication, of his own condition. But what contributes most of all to this Apollonian image of the destroyer is the realization of how immensely the world is simplified when tested for its worthiness of destruction. This is the great bond embracing and unifying all that exists. It is a sight that affords the destructive character a spectacle of deepest harmony.

The destructive character is always blithely at work. It is nature that dictates his tempo, indirectly at least, for he must forestall her. Otherwise she will take over the destruction herself.

No vision inspires the destructive character. He has few needs, and the least of them is to know what will replace what has been destroyed. First of all, for a moment at least, empty space, the place where the thing stood or the victim lived.

Someone is sure to be found who needs this space without its being filled.

The destructive character does his work, the only work he avoids is being creative. Just as the creator seeks solitude, the destroyer must be constantly surrounded by people, witnesses to his efficacy.

The destructive character is a signal. Just as a trigonometric sign is exposed on all sides to the wind, so is he to rumor. To protect him from it is pointless.

The destructive character has no interest in being understood. Attempts in this direction he regards as superficial. Being misunderstood cannot harm him. On the contrary he provokes it, just as oracles, those destructive institutions of the state, provoked it. The most petit bourgeois of all phenomena, gossip, comes about only because people do not wish to be misunderstood. The destructive character tolerates misunderstanding; he does not promote gossip.

The destructive character is the enemy of the etui-man. The etui-man looks for comfort, and the case is its quintessence. The inside of the case is the velvet-lined track that he has imprinted on the world. The destructive character obliterates even the traces of destruction.

The destructive character stands in the front line of the traditionalists. Some pass things down to posterity, by making them untouchable and thus conserving them, others pass on situations, by making them practicable and thus liquidating them. The latter are called the destructive.

The destructive character has the consciousness of historical man, whose deepest emotion is an insuperable mistrust of the course of things and a readiness at all times to recognize that everything can go wrong. Therefore the destructive character is reliability itself.

The destructive character sees nothing permanent. But for this very reason he sees ways everywhere. Where others encounter walls or mountains, there, too, he sees a way. But because he sees a way everywhere, he has to clear things from it everywhere. Not always by brute force; sometimes by the most refined. Because he sees ways everywhere, he always positions himself at crossroads. No moment can know what the next will bring. What exists he reduces to rubble, not for the sake of the rubble, but for that of the way leading through it.

The destructive character lives from the feeling, not that life is worth living, but that suicide is not worth the trouble.

Fate and Character

Fate and character are commonly regarded as causally connected, character being the cause of fate. The idea underlying this is the following: if, on the one hand, the character of a person, the way in which he reacts, were known in all its details, and if, on the other, all the events in the areas entered by that character were known, both what would happen to him and what he would accomplish could be exactly predicted. That is, his fate would be known. Contemporary ideas do not permit immediate logical access to the idea of fate, and therefore modern men accept the idea of reading character from, for example, the physical features of a person, finding knowledge of character as such somehow generally present within themselves, whereas the notion of analogously reading a person's fate from the lines in his hand seems unacceptable. This appears as impossible as "to predict the future"; for under this category the foretelling of fate is unceremoniously subsumed, while character appears as something existing in the present and the past and therefore as perceptible. It is, however, precisely the contention of those who profess to predict men's fate from no matter what signs, that for those able to perceive it (who find an immediate knowledge of fate as such in themselves) it is in some way present, or more cautiously stated, accessible. The supposition that some "accessibility" of future fate contradicts neither that concept itself nor the human powers of perception predicting it is not, as can be shown, nonsensical. Like character, fate, too, can be apprehended only through signs, not in itself, for—even if this or that character trait, this or that link of fate, is directly in view, it is nevertheless a relationship that is meant by these concepts, never accessible except through signs because it is situated above the immediately visible level. The system of characterological signs is generally confined to the body, if we disregard the characterological significance of those signs investigated by the horoscope, whereas in the traditional view all the phenomena of external life, in addition to bodily ones, can become signs of fate. However, the connection between the sign and the signified constitutes in both spheres an equally hermetic and difficult problem, though different in other respects, because despite all the superficial observation and false hypostasizing of the signs, they do not in either system signify character or fate on the basis of causal connections. A nexus of meaning can never be founded causally, even though in the present case the existence of the signs may have been produced causally by fate and character. The inquiry that follows is not concerned with what such a system of signs for character and fate is like, but merely with what it signifies.

It emerges that the traditional conception of the nature and the relationship of character and fate not only remains problematic insofar as it is incapable of making the possibility of a prediction of fate rationally comprehensible, but that it is false, because the distinction on which it rests is theoretically untenable. For it is impossible to form an uncontradictory concept of the exterior of an active human being the core of whom is taken to be character. No definition of the external world can disregard the limits set by the concept of the active man. Between the active man and the external world all is interaction, their spheres of action interpenetrate; no matter how different their conceptions may be, their concepts are inseparable. Not only is it impossible to determine in a single case what finally is to be considered a function of character and what a function of fate in a human life (this would make no difference here if the two only merged in experience); the external world that the active man encounters can also in principle be reduced, to any desired degree, to his inner world, and his inner world similarly to his outer world, indeed regarded in principle as one and the same thing. Considered in this way character and fate, far from being theoretically distinct, coincide. Such is the case when Nietzsche says, "If a man has character, he has an experience that constantly recurs." That means: if a man has character his fate is essentially constant. Admittedly, it also means: he has no fate—a conclusion drawn by the Stoics.

If a concept of fate is to be attained, therefore, it must be clearly distinguished from that of character, which in turn cannot be achieved until the latter has been more exactly defined. On the basis of this definition the two concepts will become wholly divergent; where there is character there will, with certainty, not be fate, and in the area of fate character will not be found. In addition care must be taken to assign both concepts to spheres in which they do not, as happens in common speech, usurp the rank of higher spheres and concepts. For character is usually placed in an ethical, fate in a religious context. We must banish them from both regions by revealing the error by which they were placed there. This error is caused, as regards the concept of fate, through association with that of guilt. Thus, to mention a typical case, fate-imposed misfortune is seen as the response of God or the gods to a religious offense. Doubts concerning this are aroused, however, by the absence of any corresponding relation of the concept of fate to the concept that necessarily accompanies that of guilt in the ethical sphere, namely that of innocence. In the Greek classical development of the idea of fate, the happiness granted to a man is by no means understood as confirmation of an innocent conduct of life, but as a temptation to the most grievous offense, *hubris*. There is, therefore, no relation of fate to innocence. And—this question strikes even deeper—has fate any reference to good fortune, to happiness? Is happiness, as misfortune doubtless is, an intrinsic category of fate? Happiness is, rather, what releases the fortunate man from the embroilment of the Fates and from the net of his own fate. Hölderlin does not for nothing call the bliss-

ful gods "fateless." Happiness and bliss are therefore no more
part of the sphere of fate than is innocence. But an order the
sole intrinsic concepts of which are misfortune and guilt, and
within which there is no conceivable path of liberation (for
insofar as something is fate, it is misfortune and guilt)—such
an order cannot be religious, no matter how the misunderstood
concept of guilt appears to suggest the contrary. Another
sphere must therefore be sought in which misfortune and
guilt alone carry weight, a balance on which bliss and innocence are found too light and float upward. This balance
is the scale of law. The laws of fate—misfortune and guilt—
are elevated by law to measures of the person; it would be
false to assume that only guilt is present in a legal context; it
is demonstrable that all legal guilt is nothing other than
misfortune. Mistakenly, through confusing itself with the
realm of justice, the order of law, which is only a residue of
the demonic stage of human existence when legal statutes
determined not only men's relationships but also their relation
to the gods, has preserved itself long past the time of the victory over the demons. It was not in law but in tragedy that
the head of genius lifted itself for the first time from the mist
of guilt, for in tragedy demonic fate is breached. But not by
having the endless pagan chain of guilt and atonement superseded by the purity of man who has expiated and is with the
pure god. Rather, in tragedy pagan man becomes aware that
he is better than his god, but the realization robs him of
speech, remains unspoken. Without declaring itself, it seeks
secretly to gather its forces. Guilt and atonement it does not
measure justly in the balance, but mixes indiscriminately.
There is no question of the "moral world order" being restored; instead, the moral hero, still dumb, not yet of age—
as such he is called a hero—wishes to raise himself by shaking
that tormented world. The paradox of the birth of genius in
moral speechlessness, moral infantility, is the sublimity of
tragedy. It is probably the basis of all sublimity, in which
genius, rather than God, appears. Fate shows itself, therefore,

in the view of life, as condemned, as having, at bottom, first been condemned and then become guilty. Goethe summarizes both phases in the words "The poor man you let become guilty." Law condemns, not to punishment but to guilt. Fate is the guilt context of the living. It corresponds to the natural condition of the living, that illusion not yet wholly dispelled from which man is so far removed that, under its rule, he was never wholly immersed in it, but only invisible in his best part. It is not therefore really man who has a fate; rather, the subject of fate is indeterminable. The judge can perceive fate wherever he pleases; with every judgment he must blindly dictate fate. It is never man but only the life in him that it strikes—the part involved in natural guilt and misfortune by virtue of illusion. In the manner of fate, this life can be coupled to cards as to planets, and the clairvoyante makes use of the simple technique of placing it in the context of guilt by means of the first calculable, definite things that come to hand (things unchastely pregnant with certainty). Thereby she discovers in signs something about a natural life in man that she seeks to substitute for the head of genius mentioned earlier; as, on his side, the man who visits her gives way to the guilty life within himself. The guilt context is temporal in a totally inauthentic way, very different in its kind and measure from the time of redemption, or of music, or of truth. On determining the particular nature of time in fate depends the complete elucidation of these matters. The fortuneteller who uses cards and the palmist teach us at least that this time can at every moment be made simultaneous with another (not present). It is not an autonomous time, but is parasitically dependent on the time of a higher, less natural life. It has no present, for fateful moments exist only in bad novels, and past and future it knows only in curious variations.

There is therefore a concept of fate—and it is the genuine concept, the only one that embraces equally fate in tragedy and the intentions of the fortuneteller—that is completely independent of that of character, having its foundation in an entirely different sphere. The concept of character must be developed to a similar level. It is no accident that both orders are connected with interpretative practices and that in chiromancy character and fate coincide authentically. Both concern the natural man—or, better, the nature of man, the very being that makes its appearance in signs that either occur spontaneously or are experimentally produced. The foundation of the concept of character will therefore need likewise to be related to a natural sphere and to have no more to do with ethics or morality than fate has with religion. On the other hand, the concept of character will have to be divested of those features that constitute its erroneous connection to that of fate. This connection is effected by the idea of a network that can be tightened by knowledge at will into a dense fabric, for this is how character appears to superficial observation. Along with the broad underlying traits, the trained eye of the connoisseur of men is supposed to perceive finer and closer connections, until what looked like a net is tightened into cloth. In the threads of this weft a weak understanding believes it possesses the moral nature of the character concerned and can distinguish its good and bad qualities. But, as moral philosophy is obliged to demonstrate, only actions and never qualities can be of moral importance. Appearances are admittedly to the contrary. Not just "thievish," "extravagant," "courageous" seem to imply moral valuations (even leaving aside the apparent moral coloration of the concepts), but above all words like "self-sacrificing," "malicious," "vengeful," "envious" seem to indicate character traits that cannot be abstracted from moral valuation. Nevertheless, such abstraction is in all cases not only possible but necessary in order to grasp the meaning of the concept. This abstraction must be such that valuation itself is fully preserved; only its moral accent is withdrawn, to give way to such conditional evaluations, in either a positive or a negative sense, as are expressed by the morally indifferent descriptions of qualities of the intellect (such as "clever" or "stupid").

The true sphere to which these pseudo-moral character descriptions are to be consigned is shown by comedy. At its center, as the main protagonist in a comedy of character, stands often enough a person whom, if we were confronted by his actions in life instead of by his person on the stage, we would call a scoundrel. On the comic stage, however, his actions take on only the interest shed with the light of character, and the latter is, in classical examples, the subject not of moral condemnation but of high amusement. It is never in themselves, never morally, that the actions of the comic hero affect his public; his deeds are interesting only insofar as they reflect the light of character. Moreover, one notes that the great comic playwright—for example, Molière—does not seek to define his creations by the multiplicity of their character traits. On the contrary, psychological analysis is denied any access to his work. It has nothing to do with the concerns of psychology if miserliness or hypochondria, in *L'avare* or *Le malade imaginaire*, are hypostasized as the foundation of all action. About hypochondria and miserliness these dramas teach nothing; far from making them comprehensible, they depict them with an intensifying crassness; if the object of psychology is the inner life of man understood empirically, Molière's characters are of no use to it even as means of demonstration. Character is unfolded in them like a sun, in the brilliance of its single trait, which allows no other to remain visible in its proximity. The sublimity of character comedy rests on this anonymity of man and his morality, alongside the utmost development of individuality through its exclusive character trait. While fate unfolds the immense complexity of the guilty person, the complications and bonds of his guilt, character gives this mystical enslavement of the person to the guilt context the answer of genius. Complication becomes simplicity, fate freedom. For the character of the comic figure is not the scarecrow of the determinist; it is the beacon in whose beams the freedom of his actions becomes visible. To the dogma of the natural guilt of human life, of original guilt, the irredeemable nature of which constitutes the doc-trine, and its occasional redemption the cult, of paganism, genius opposes a vision of the natural innocence of man. This vision remains for its part likewise in the realm of nature, yet moral insights are still at a proximity to its essence that is attained by the opposed idea only in the form of tragedy, which is not its only form. The vision of character, on the other hand, is liberating in all its forms: it is linked to free-dom, as cannot be shown here, by way of its affinity to logic. The character trait is not therefore the knot in the net. It is the sun of individuality in the colorless (anonymous) sky of man, which casts the shadow of the comic action. (This places Cohen's profound dictum that every tragic action, however sublimely it strides upon its cothurnus, casts a comic shadow, in its most appropriate context.)

Physiognomic signs, like other mantic symbols, serve for the ancients primarily the exploration of fate, in accordance with the dominance of the pagan belief in guilt. The study of physiognomy, like comedy, was a manifestation of the new age of genius. Modern physiognomics reveals its connection with the old art of divination in the unfruitful, morally evaluative accent of its concepts, as also in the striving for analytical com-plexity. In precisely this respect the ancient and medieval physiognomists saw things more clearly, in recognizing that character can only be grasped through a small number of morally indifferent basic concepts, like those, for example, that the doctrine of temperaments tried to identify.

Theologico-Political Fragment

Only the Messiah himself consummates all history, in the sense that he alone redeems, completes, creates its relation to the Messianic. For this reason nothing historical can relate itself on its own account to anything Messianic. Therefore the Kingdom of God is not the *telos* of the historical dynamic; it cannot be set as a goal. From the standpoint of history it is not the goal, but the end. Therefore the order of the profane cannot be built up on the idea of the Divine Kingdom, and therefore theocracy has no political, but only a religious meaning. To have repudiated with utmost vehemence the political significance of theocracy is the cardinal merit of Bloch's *Spirit of Utopia.*

The order of the profane should be erected on the idea of happiness. The relation of this order to the Messianic is one of the essential teachings of the philosophy of history. It is the precondition of a mystical conception of history, containing a problem that can be represented figuratively. If one arrow points to the goal toward which the profane dynamic acts, and another marks the direction of Messianic intensity, then certainly the quest of free humanity for happiness runs counter to the Messianic direction; but just as a force can, through acting, increase another that is acting in the opposite direction, so the order of the profane assists, through being profane, the coming of the Messianic Kingdom. The profane, therefore, although not itself a category of this Kingdom, is a decisive category of its quietest approach. For in happiness all that is earthly seeks its downfall, and only in good fortune is its downfall destined to find it. Whereas, admittedly, the immediate Messianic intensity of the heart, of the inner man in isolation, passes through misfortune, as suffering. To the spiritual *restitutio in integrum,* which introduces immortality, corresponds a worldly restitution that leads to the eternity of downfall, and the rhythm of this eternally transient worldly existence, transient in its totality, in its spatial but also in its temporal totality, the rhythm of Messianic nature, is happiness. For nature is Messianic by reason of its eternal and total passing away.

To strive after such passing, even for those stages of man that are nature, is the task of world politics, whose method must be called nihilism.

On Language as Such and on the Language of Man

Every expression of human mental life can be understood as a kind of language, and this understanding, in the manner of a true method, everywhere raises new questions. It is possible to talk about a language of music and of sculpture, about a language of justice that has nothing directly to do with those in which German or English legal judgments are couched, about a language of technology that is not the specialized language of technicians. Language in such contexts means the tendency inherent in the subjects concerned—technology, art, justice, or religion—toward the communication of mental meanings. To sum up: all communication of mental meanings is language, communication in words being only a particular case of human language and of the justice, poetry, or whatever underlying it or founded on it. The existence of language, however, is not only coextensive with all the areas of human mental expression in which language is always in one sense or another inherent, but with absolutely everything. There is no event or thing in either animate or inanimate nature that does not in some way partake of language, for it is in the nature of all to communicate their mental meanings. This use of the word "language" is in no way metaphorical. For to think that we cannot imagine anything that does not communicate its mental nature in its expression is entirely meaningful; the greater or lesser degree of consciousness that is apparently (or really) involved in such communication cannot alter the fact that we cannot imagine a total absence of language in anything. An existence entirely without relationship to language is an idea; but this idea can bear no fruit even within that realm of Ideas whose circumference defines the idea of God.

All that is asserted here is that all expression, insofar as it is a communication of mental meaning, is to be classed as language. And expression, by its whole innermost nature, is certainly to be understood only as *language;* on the other hand, to understand a linguistic entity it is always necessary to ask of which mental entity it is the direct expression. That is to say: the German language, for example, is by no means the expression of everything that we could—theoretically— express *through* it, but is the direct expression of that which communicates *itself* in it. This "itself" is a mental entity. It is therefore obvious at once that the mental entity that communicates itself in language is not language itself but something to be distinguished from it. The view that the mental essence of a thing consists precisely in its language— this view, taken as a hypothesis, is the great abyss into which all linguistic theory threatens to fall,* and to survive suspended precisely over this abyss is its task. The distinction between a mental entity and the linguistic entity in which it communicates is the first stage of any study of linguistic theory, and this distinction seems so unquestionable that it is, rather, the frequently asserted identity between mental and linguistic being that constitutes a deep and incomprehensible paradox, the expression of which is found in the ambiguity of the word logos. Nevertheless, this paradox has a place, as a solution, at the center of linguistic theory, but remains a paradox, and insoluble, if placed at the beginning.

What does language communicate? It communicates the mental being corresponding to it. It is fundamental that this mental being communicates itself *in* language and not *through*

---

* Or is it, rather, the temptation to place at the outset a hypothesis that constitutes an abyss for all philosophizing?

language. Languages therefore have no speaker, if this means someone who communicates *through* these languages. Mental being communicates itself in, not through, a language, which means: it is not outwardly identical with linguistic being. Mental is identical with linguistic being only insofar as it is capable of communication. What is communicable in a mental entity is its linguistic entity. Language therefore communicates the particular linguistic being of things, but their mental being only insofar as this is directly included in their linguistic being, insofar as it is capable of being communicated.

Language communicates the linguistic being of things. The clearest manifestation of this being, however, is language itself. The answer to the question "*What* does language communicate?" is therefore "All language communicates itself." The language of this lamp, for example, does not communicate the lamp (for the mental being of the lamp, insofar as it is *communicable,* is by no means the lamp itself), but: the language-lamp, the lamp in communication, the lamp in expression. For in language the situation is this: *the linguistic being of all things is their language*. The understanding of linguistic theory depends on giving this proposition a clarity that annihilates even the appearance of tautology. This proposition is untautological, for it means: that which in a mental entity is communicable *is* its language. On this "is" (equivalent to "is immediately") everything depends. Not that which *appears* most clearly in its language is communicable in a mental entity, as was just said by way of transition, but this *capacity* for communication is language itself. Or: the language of a mental entity is directly that which is communicable in it. What is communicable *of* a mental entity, *in* this it communicates itself. Which signifies: all language communicates itself. Or more precisely: all language communicates itself *in* itself; it is in the purest sense the "medium" of the communication. Mediation, which is the immediacy of all mental communication, is the fundamental problem of linguistic theory, and if one chooses to call this immediacy magic, then the primary problem of language is its magic. At the same time, the notion of the magic of language points to something else: its infiniteness. This is conditional on its immediacy. For just because nothing is communicated *through* language, what is communicated *in* language cannot be externally limited or measured, and therefore all language contains its own incommensurable, uniquely constituted infinity. Its linguistic being, not its verbal meanings, defines its frontier.

The linguistic being of things is their language; this proposition, applied to man, means: the linguistic being of man is his language. Which signifies: man communicates his own mental being *in* his language. However, the language of man speaks in words. Man therefore communicates his own mental being (insofar as it is communicable) by *naming* all other things. But do we know any other languages that name things? It should not be accepted that we know of no languages other than that of man, for this is untrue. We only know of no *naming* language other than that of man; to identify naming language with language as such is to rob linguistic theory of its deepest insights. *It is therefore the linguistic being of man to name things.*

Why name them? To whom does man communicate himself? But is this question, as applied to man, other than as applied to other communications (languages)? To whom does the lamp communicate itself? The mountain? The fox? But here the answer is: to man. This is not anthropomorphism. The truth of this answer is shown in knowledge and perhaps also in art. Furthermore, if the lamp and the mountain and the fox did not communicate themselves to man, how should he be able to name them? And he names them; *he* communicates himself by naming *them*. To whom does he communicate himself?

Before this question can be answered we must again inquire: how does man communicate himself? A profound distinction is to be made, a choice presented, in face of which an intrinsically false understanding of language is certain to give itself away. Does man communicate his mental being *by* the names that he gives things? Or *in* them? In the paradoxical nature of these questions lies their answer. Anyone who believes that man communicates his mental being *by* names cannot also assume that it is his mental being that he communicates, for this does not happen through the names of things, that is, through the words by which he denotes a thing. And, equally, the advocate of such a view can only assume that man is communicating factual subject matter to other men, for that does happen through the word by which he denotes a thing. This view is the bourgeois conception of language, the invalidity and emptiness of which will become increasingly clear in what follows. It holds that the means of communication is the word, its object factual, its addressee a human being. The other conception of language, in contrast, knows no means, no object, and no addressee of communication. It means: *in naming the mental being of man communicates itself to God.*

Naming, in the realm of language, has as its sole purpose and its incomparably high meaning that it is the innermost nature of language itself. Naming is that by which nothing beyond it is communicated, and *in* which language itself communicates itself absolutely. In naming the mental entity that communicates itself is *language*. Where mental being in its communication is language itself in its absolute wholeness, only there is the name, and only the name is there. Name as the heritage of human language therefore vouches for the fact *that language as such* is the mental being of man; and only for this reason is the mental being of man, alone among all mental entities, communicable without residue. On this is founded the difference between human language and the language of things. But because the mental being of man is language itself, he cannot communicate himself by it but only in it. The quintessence of this intensive totality of language as the mental being of man is naming. Man is the namer, by this we recognize that through him pure language speaks. All nature, insofar as it communicates itself, communicates itself in language, and so finally in man. Hence he is the lord of nature and can give names to things. Only through the linguistic being of things can he gain knowledge of them from within himself—in name. God's creation is completed when things receive their names from man, from whom in name language alone speaks. Man can call name the language of language (if the genitive refers to the relationship not of a means but of a medium) and in this sense certainly, because he speaks in name, man is the speaker of language, and for this very reason its only speaker. In terming man the speaker (which, however, according to the Bible, for example, clearly means the name giver: "As man should name all kinds of living creatures, so should they be *called*"), many languages imply this metaphysical truth.

Name, however, is not only the last utterance of language but also the true call of it. Thus in name appears the essential law of language, according to which to express oneself and to address everything else amounts to the same. Language—and in it a mental entity—only expresses itself purely where it speaks in name, that is, in its universal naming. So in name culminate both the intensive totality of language, as the absolutely communicable mental entity, and the extensive totality of language, as the universally communicating (naming) entity. By virtue of its communicating nature, its universality, language is incomplete where the mental entity that speaks from it is not in its whole structure linguistic, that is, communicable. *Man alone has a language that is complete both in its universality and in its intensiveness.*

In the light of this, a question may now be asked without the risk of confusion, a question that, though of the highest metaphysical importance, can be clearly posed first of all as one of terminology. It is whether mental being—not only of man (for that is necessary) but also of things, and thus mental being as such—can from the point of view of linguistic theory be described as of linguistic nature. If mental being is identical with linguistic, then a thing, by virtue of its mental being, is a medium of communication, and what is communicated in it is—in accordance with its mediating relationship—precisely this medium (language) itself. Language is thus the mental being of things. Mental being is therefore postulated at the outset as communicable, or, rather, is situated *within* the communicable, and the thesis that the linguistic being of things is identical with the mental, insofar as the latter is communicable, becomes in its "insofar" a tautology. *There is no such thing as a meaning of language; as communication, language communicates a mental entity, i.e., something communicable per se.* The differences between languages are those of media that are distinguished as it were by their density, that is, gradually; and this with regard to the density both of the communicating (naming) and of the communicable (name) aspects of communication. These two spheres, which are clearly distinguished yet united only in the name language of man, are naturally constantly interrelated.

For the metaphysics of language the equation of mental with linguistic being, which knows only gradual differences, produces a graduation of all mental being in degrees. This graduation, which takes place within mental being itself, can no longer be embraced by any higher category and so leads to the graduation of all being, both mental and linguistic, by degrees of existence or being, such as was already familiar to scholasticism with regard to mental being. However, the equation of mental and linguistic being is of great metaphysical moment to linguistic theory because it leads to the concept that has again and again, as if of its own accord, elevated itself to the center of linguistic philosophy and constituted its most intimate connection with the philosophy of religion. This is the concept of revelation. Within all linguistic formation a conflict is waged between what is expressed and expressible and what is inexpressible and unexpressed. On considering this conflict one sees, in the perspective of the inexpressible, at the same time the last mental entity. Now it is clear that in the equation of mental and linguistic being the notion of an inverse proportionality between the two is disputed. For this latter thesis runs: the deeper, i.e., the more existent and real the mind, the more it is inexpressible and unexpressed, whereas it is consistent with the equation proposed above to make the relation between mind and language thoroughly unambiguous, so that the expression that is linguistically most existent (i.e., most fixed) is linguistically the most rounded and definitive; in a word, the most expressed is at the same time the purely mental. Exactly this, however, is meant by the concept of revelation, if it takes the inviolability of the word as the only and sufficient condition and characteristic of the divinity of the mental being that is expressed in it. The highest mental region of religion is (in the concept of revelation) at the same time the only one that does not know the inexpressible. For it is addressed in name and expresses itself as revelation. In this, however, notice is given that only the highest mental being, as it appears in religion, rests solely on man and on the language in him, whereas all art, not excluding poetry, does not rest on the ultimate essence of language-mind, but on language-mind confined to things, even if in consummate beauty. *"Language, the mother* of reason and *revelation,* its alpha and omega," says Hamann.

Language itself is not perfectly expressed in things themselves. This proposition has a double meaning in its metaphorical and literal senses: the languages of things are imperfect, and they are dumb. Things are denied the pure formal principle of language—sound. They can only communicate to one another through a more or less material community. This community is immediate and infinite, like every linguistic communication; it is magical (for there is also a magic of matter). The incomparable feature of human language is that its magical community with things is immaterial and purely mental, and the symbol of this is sound. The Bible expresses this symbolic fact when it says that God breathes his breath into man: this is at once life and mind and language.

If in what follows the nature of language is considered on

the basis of the first chapter of Genesis, the object is neither
biblical interpretation, nor subjection of the Bible to objective
consideration as revealed truth, but the discovery of what
emerges of itself from the biblical text with regard to the nature of language; and the Bible is only *initially* indispensable
for this purpose because the present argument broadly follows
it in presupposing language as an ultimate reality, perceptible
only in its manifestation, inexplicable and mystical. The Bible,
in regarding itself as a revelation, must necessarily evolve the
fundamental linguistic facts. The second version of the story
of the Creation, which tells of the breathing of God's breath
into man, also reports that man was made from earth. This is,
in the whole story of the Creation, the only reference to the
material in which the Creator expresses his will, which is
doubtless otherwise thought of as creation without mediation.
In this second story of the Creation the making of man did
not take place through the word: God spoke—and there was—
but this man, who is not created from the word, is now in-
vested with the *gift* of language and is elevated above nature.

This curious revolution in the act of creation, where it
concerns man, is no less clearly recorded, however, in the first
story of the Creation, and in an entirely different context
it vouches, with the same certainty, for a special relationship
between man and language resulting from the act of creation.
The manifold rhythm of the act of creation in the first chapter
establishes a kind of basic form from which the act that creates
man diverges significantly. Admittedly this passage nowhere
expressly refers to a relationship either of man or of nature
to the material from which they were created; and the question whether the words "He made" envisages a creation out of
material must here be left open, but the rhythm by which the
creation of nature (in Genesis 1) is accomplished is: Let there
be—He made (created)—He named. In individual acts of creation (1:3; 1:11) only the words "Let there be" occur. In this
"Let there be" and in the words "He named" at the beginning
and end of the act, the deep and clear relation of the creative

act to language appears each time. With the creative omnipotence of language it begins, and at the end language as it
were assimilates the created, names it. Language is therefore
both creative and the finished creation, it is word and name.
In God name is creative because it is word, and God's word
is cognizant because it is name. "And he saw that it was good";
that is: He had cognized it through name. The absolute relation of name to knowledge exists only in God, only there is
name, because it is inwardly identical with the creative word,
the pure medium of knowledge. That means: God made things
knowable in their names. Man, however, names them according to knowledge.

In the creation of man the threefold rhythm of the creation
of nature has given way to an entirely different order. In it,
therefore, language has a different meaning: the trinity of the
act is here preserved, but in this very parallelism the diver-
gence is all the more striking: in the threefold "He created"
of 1:27. God did not create man from the word, and he did
not name him. He did not wish to subject him to language,
but in man God set language, which had served *Him* as
medium of creation, free. God rested when he had left his
creative power to itself in man. This creativity, relieved of its
divine actuality, became knowledge. Man is the knower in the
same language in which God is creator. God created him in
his image, he created the knower in the image of the creator.
Therefore the proposition that the mental being of man is
language needs explanation. His mental being is the language
in which creation took place. In the word creation took place,
and God's linguistic being is the word. All human language
is only reflection of the word in name. Name is no closer to
the word than knowledge to creation. The infinity of all human language always remains limited and analytical in nature
in comparison to the absolutely unlimited and creative infinity
of the divine word.

The deepest images of this divine word and the point where
human language participates most intimately in the divine

infinity of the pure word, the point at which it cannot become finite word and knowledge, are the human name. The theory of proper names is the theory of the frontier between finite and infinite language. Of all beings man is the only one who himself names his own kind, as he is the only one whom God did not name. It is perhaps bold, but scarcely impossible, to mention the second part of 2:20 in this context: that man named all beings, "*but* for man there was not found a helper fit for him." Accordingly, Adam names his wife as soon as he receives her (woman in the second chapter, Eve in the third). By giving names, parents dedicate their children to God; the names they give do not correspond—in a metaphysical, not etymological sense—to any knowledge, for they name newborn children. In a strict sense, no name ought (in its etymological meaning) to correspond to any person, for the proper name is the word of God in human sounds. By it each man is guaranteed his creation by God, and in this sense he is himself creative, as is expressed by mythological wisdom in the idea (which doubtless not infrequently comes true) that a man's name is his fate. The proper name is the communion of man with the *creative* word of God. (Not the only one, however; man knows a further linguistic communion with God's word.) Through the word man is bound to the language of things. The human word is the name of things. Hence it is no longer conceivable, as the bourgeois view of language maintains, that the word has an accidental relation to its object, that it is a sign for things (or knowledge of them) agreed by some convention. Language never gives *mere* signs. However, the rejection of bourgeois by mystical linguistic theory equally rests on a misunderstanding. For according to mystical theory the word is simply the essence of the thing. That is incorrect, because the thing in itself has no word, being created from God's word and known in its name by a human word. This knowledge of the thing, however, is not spontaneous creation, it does not emerge from language in the absolutely unlimited and infinite manner of creation; rather, the name that man gives to language depends on how language is communicated to him. In name the word of God has not remained creative; it has become in one part receptive, even if receptive to language. Thus fertilized, it aims to give birth to the language of things themselves, from which in turn, soundlessly, in the mute magic of nature, the word of God shines forth.

For conception and spontaneity together, which are found in this unique union only in the linguistic realm, language has its own word, and this word applies also to that conception which is enacted by the nameless in names. It is the translation of the language of things into that of man. It is necessary to found the concept of translation at the deepest level of linguistic theory, for it is much too far-reaching and powerful to be treated in any way as an afterthought, as has happened occasionally. Translation attains its full meaning in the realization that every evolved language (with the exception of the word of God) can be considered as a translation of all the others. By the relation, mentioned earlier, of languages as between media of varying densities, the translatability of languages into one another is established. Translation is removal from one language into another through a continuum of transformations. Translation passes through continua of transformation, not abstract areas of identity and similarity.

The translation of the language of things into that of man is not only a translation of the mute into the sonic; it is also the translation of the nameless into name. It is therefore the translation of an imperfect language into a more perfect one, and cannot but add something to it, namely knowledge. The objectivity of this translation is, however, guaranteed by God. For God created things; the creative word in them is the germ of the cognizing name, just as God, too, finally named each thing after it was created. But obviously this naming is only an expression of the identity of the creative word and the cognizing name in God, not the prior solution of the task that God expressly assigns to man himself: that of naming things. In receiving the unspoken nameless language of things and

converting it by name into sounds, man performs this task. It
would be insoluble were not the name-language of man and
the nameless one of things related in God and released from
the same creative word, which in things became the communication of matter in magic communion, and in man the language of knowledge and name in blissful mind. Hamann says:
"Everything that man heard in the beginning, saw with his
eyes, and felt with his hands was the living word; for God
was the word. With this word in his mouth and in his heart,
the origin of language was as natural, as close, and as easy as
a child's game...." Friedrich Müller, in his poem "Adam's
Awakening and First Blissful Nights," has God summon man
to name giving in these words: "Man of the earth step near,
in gazing grow more perfect, more perfect through the word."
By this combination of contemplation and naming is implied
the communicating muteness of things (animals) toward the
word language of man, which receives them in name. In the
same chapter of the poem, the poet expresses the realization
that only the word from which things are created permits man
to name them, by communicating itself in the manifold languages of animals, even if mutely, in the image: God gives
each beast in turn a sign, whereupon they step before man to
be named. In an almost sublime way the linguistic community
of mute creation with God is thus conveyed in the image of
the sign.

As the unspoken word in the existence of things falls infinitely short of the naming word in the knowledge of man,
and as the latter in turn must fall short of the creative word
of God, there is reason for the multiplicity of human languages. The language of things can pass into the language of
knowledge and name only through translation—as many translations, so many languages—once man has fallen from the
paradisiac state that knew only one language. (According to the
Bible, this consequence of the expulsion from paradise admittedly came about only later.) The paradisiac language of man
must have been one of perfect knowledge; whereas later all

knowledge is again infinitely differentiated in the multiplicity of language, was indeed forced to differentiate itself on a lower level as creation in name. For that the language of paradise was fully cognizant, even the existence of the tree of knowledge cannot conceal. Its apples were supposed to impart knowledge of good and evil. But on the seventh day, God had already cognized with the words of creation. And God saw that it was good. The knowledge to which the snake seduces, that of good and evil, is nameless. It is vain in the deepest sense, and this very knowledge is itself the only evil known to the paradisiac state. Knowledge of good and evil abandons name, it is a knowledge from outside, the uncreated imitation of the creative word. Name steps outside itself in this knowledge: the Fall marks the birth of the *human word,* in which name no longer lives intact, and which has stepped out of name language, the language of knowledge, from what we may call its own immanent magic, in order to become expressly, as it were externally, magic. The word must communicate *something* (other than itself). That is really the Fall of language-mind. The word as something externally communicating, as it were a parody by the expressly mediate word of the expressly immediate, the creative word of God, and the decay of the blissful, Adamite language-mind that stand between them. For in reality there exists a fundamental identity between the word that, after the promise of the snake, knows good and evil, and the externally communicating word. The knowledge of things resides in name, whereas that of good and evil is, in the profound sense in which Kierkegaard uses the word, "prattle," and knows only one purification and elevation, to which the prattling man, the sinner, was therefore submitted: judgment. Admittedly, the judging word has direct knowledge of good and evil. Its magic is different from that of name, but equally magical. This judging word expels the first human beings from paradise; they themselves have aroused it in accordance with the immutable law by which this judging word punishes —and expects—its own awakening as the only, the deepest guilt. In the Fall, since the eternal purity of names was violated, the sterner purity of the judging word arose. For the essential composition of language the Fall has a threefold significance (without mentioning its other meanings). In stepping outside the purer language of name, man makes language a means (that is, a knowledge inappropriate to him), and therefore also, in one part at any rate, a *mere* sign; and this later results in the plurality of languages. The second meaning is that from the Fall, in exchange for the immediacy of name damaged by it, a new immediacy arises, the magic of judgment, which no longer rests blissfully in itself. The third meaning that can perhaps be tentatively ventured is that the origin of abstraction, too, as a faculty of language-mind, is to be sought in the Fall. For good and evil, being unnamable, nameless, stand outside the language of names, which man leaves behind precisely in the abyss opened by this question. Name, however, with regard to existing language, offers only the ground in which its concrete elements are rooted. But the abstract elements of language—we may perhaps surmise—are rooted in the word of judgment. The immediacy (which, however, is the linguistic root) of the communicability of abstraction resides in judgment. This immediacy in the communication of abstraction came into being as judgment, when, in the Fall, man abandoned immediacy in the communication of the concrete, name, and fell into the abyss of the mediateness of all communication, of the word as means, of the empty word, into the abyss of prattle. For—it must be said again—the question as to good and evil in the world after creation was empty prattle. The tree of knowledge did not stand in the garden of God in order to dispense information on good and evil, but as an emblem of judgment over the questioner. This immense irony marks the mythical origin of law.

After the Fall, which, in making language mediate, laid the foundation for its multiplicity, it could be only a step to linguistic confusion. Since men had injured the purity of name, the turning away from that contemplation of things in which their language passes into man needed only to be completed in order to deprive men of the common foundation of an already shaken language-mind. *Signs* must become confused where things are entangled. The enslavement of language in prattle is joined by the enslavement of things in folly almost as its inevitable consequence. In this turning away from things, which was enslavement, the plan for the tower of Babel came into being, and linguistic confusion with it.

The life of man in pure language-mind was blissful. Nature, however, is mute. True, it can be clearly felt in the second chapter of Genesis how this muteness, named by man, itself became bliss, only of lower degree. Friedrich Müller has Adam say to the animals that leave him after he has named them, "And saw by the nobility with which they leaped away from me that the man had given them a name." After the Fall, however, when God's word curses the ground, the appearance of nature is deeply changed. Now begins its other muteness, which we mean by the deep sadness of nature. It is a metaphysical truth that all nature would begin to lament if it were endowed with language. (Though to "endow with language" is more than to "make able to speak.") This proposition has a double meaning. It means, first: she would lament language itself. Speechlessness: that is the great sorrow of nature (and for the sake of her redemption the life and language of *man*—not only, as is supposed, of the poet—are in nature). This proposition means, secondly: she would lament. Lament, however, is the most undifferentiated, impotent expression of language; it contains scarcely more than the sensuous breath; and even where there is only a rustling of plants, in it there is always a lament. Because she is mute, nature mourns. Yet the inversion of this proposition leads even further into the essence of nature; the sadness of nature makes her mute. In all mourning there is the deepest inclination to speechlessness, which is infinitely more than inability or disinclination to communicate. That which mourns feels itself thoroughly known by the unknowable. To be named—even when the namer is Godlike and blissful—perhaps always remains an intimation of mourning. But how much more melancholy to be named not from the one blessed, paradisiac language of names, but from the hundred languages of man, in which name has already withered, yet which, according to God's pronouncement, have knowledge of things. Things have no proper names except in God. For in his creative word, God called them into being, calling them by their proper names. In the language of men, however, they are over-named. There is, in the relation of human languages to that of things, something that can be approximately described as "over-naming": over-naming as the deepest linguistic reason for all melancholy and (from the point of view of the thing) of all deliberate muteness. Over-naming as the linguistic being of melancholy points to another curious relation of language: the overprecision that obtains in the tragic relationship between the languages of human speakers.

There is a language of sculpture, of painting, of poetry. Just as the language of poetry is partly, if not solely, founded on the name language of man, it is very conceivable that the language of sculpture or painting is founded on certain kinds of thing languages, that in them we find a translation of the language of things into an infinitely higher language, which may still be of the same sphere. We are concerned here with nameless, nonacoustic languages, languages issuing from matter; here we should recall the material community of things in their communication.

Moreover, the communication of things is certainly communal in a way that grasps the world as such as an undivided whole.

For an understanding of artistic forms it is of value to attempt to grasp them all as languages and to seek their connection with natural languages. An example that is appropriate because it is derived from the acoustic sphere is the kinship between song and the language of birds. On the other hand, it is certain that the language of art can be understood only in the deepest relationship to the doctrine of signs. Without the latter any linguistic philosophy remains entirely fragmentary, because the relationship between language and sign (of which that between human language and writing offers only a very particular example) is original and fundamental.

This provides an opportunity to describe another antithesis that permeates the whole sphere of language and has important relations to the antithesis already mentioned between language in a narrower sense and signs, with which, of course, language by no means necessarily coincides. For language is in every case not only communication of the communicable but also, at the same time, a symbol of the noncommunicable. This symbolic side of language is connected to its relation to signs, but extends more widely, for example, in certain respects, to name and judgment. These have not only a communicating function, but most probably also a closely connected symbolic function, to which, at least explicitly, no reference has here been made.

These considerations therefore leave us a purified concept of language, even though it may still be an imperfect one. The language of an entity is the medium in which its mental being is communicated. The uninterrupted flow of this communication runs through the whole of nature from the lowest forms of existence to man and from man to God. Man communicates himself to God through name, which he gives to nature and (in proper names) to his own kind, and to nature he gives names according to the communication that he receives from her, for the whole of nature, too, is imbued with a nameless, unspoken language, the residue of the creative word of God, which is preserved in man as the cognizing name and above man as the judgment suspended over him. The language of nature is comparable to a secret password that each sentry passes to the next in his own language, but the meaning of the password is the sentry's language itself. All higher language is a translation of those lower, until in ultimate clarity the word of God unfolds, which is the unity of this movement made up of language.

On the Mimetic Faculty

Nature creates similarities. One need only think of mimicry. The highest capacity for producing similarities, however, is man's. His gift of seeing resemblances is nothing other than a rudiment of the powerful compulsion in former times to become and behave like something else. Perhaps there is none of his higher functions in which his mimetic faculty does not play a decisive role.

This faculty has a history, however, in both the phylogenetic and the ontogenetic sense. As regards the latter, play is for many its school. Children's play is everywhere permeated by mimetic modes of behavior, and its realm is by no means limited to what one person can imitate in another. The child plays at being not only a shopkeeper or teacher but also a windmill and a train. Of what use to him is this schooling of his mimetic faculty?

The answer presupposes an understanding of the phylogenetic significance of the mimetic faculty. Here it is not enough to think of what we understand today by the concept of similarity. As is known, the sphere of life that formerly seemed to be governed by the law of similarity was comprehensive; it ruled both microcosm and macrocosm. But these natural correspondences are given their true importance only if seen as stimulating and awakening the mimetic faculty in man. It must be borne in mind that neither mimetic powers nor mimetic objects remain the same in the course of thousands of years. Rather, we must suppose that the gift of producing similarities—for example, in dances, whose oldest function this was—and therefore also the gift of recognizing them, have changed with historical development.

The direction of this change seems definable as the increasing decay of the mimetic faculty. For clearly the observable world of modern man contains only minimal residues of the magical correspondences and analogies that were familiar to ancient peoples. The question is whether we are concerned with the decay of this faculty or with its transformation. Of the direction in which the latter might lie some indications may be derived, even if indirectly, from astrology.

We must assume in principle that in the remote past the processes considered imitable included those in the sky. In dance, on other cultic occasions, such imitation could be produced, such similarity manipulated. But if the mimetic genius was really a life-determining force for the ancients, it is not difficult to imagine that the newborn child was thought to be in full possession of this gift, and in particular to be perfectly molded on the structure of cosmic being.

Allusion to the astrological sphere may supply a first reference point for an understanding of the concept of nonsensuous similarity. True, our existence no longer includes what once made it possible to speak of this kind of similarity: above all, the ability to produce it. Nevertheless we, too, possess a canon according to which the meaning of nonsensuous similarity can be at least partly clarified. And this canon is language.

From time immemorial the mimetic faculty has been conceded some influence on language. Yet this was done without foundation: without consideration of a further meaning, still less a history, of the mimetic faculty. But above all such notions remained closely tied to the commonplace, sensuous area of similarity. All the same, imitative behavior in language formation was acknowledged under the name of onomatopoeia. Now if language, as is evident, is not an agreed system of signs, we shall be constantly obliged to have recourse to the kind of thoughts that appear in their most primitive form as the onomatopoeic mode of explanation. The question is whether this can be developed and adapted to improved understanding.

"Every word—and the whole of language," it has been asserted, "is onomatopoeic." It is difficult to conceive in any detail the program that might be implied by this proposition. However, the concept of nonsensuous similarity is of some relevance. For if words meaning the same thing in different languages are arranged about that thing as their center, we have to inquire how they all—while often possessing not the slightest similarity to one another—are similar to what they signify at their center. Yet this kind of similarity may be explained not only by the relationships between words meaning the same thing in different languages, just as, in general, our reflections cannot be restricted to the spoken word. They are equally concerned with the written word. And here it is noteworthy that the latter—in some cases perhaps more vividly than the spoken word—illuminates, by the relation of its written form to what it signifies, the nature of nonsensuous similarity. In brief, it is nonsensuous similarity that establishes the ties not only between the spoken and the signified but also between the written and the signified, and equally between the spoken and the written.

Graphology has taught us to recognize in handwriting images that the unconscious of the writer conceals in it. It may be supposed that the mimetic process that expresses itself in this way in the activity of the writer was, in the very distant times in which script originated, of utmost importance for writing. Script has thus become, like language, an archive of nonsensuous similarities, of nonsensuous correspondences.

This aspect of language as script, however, does not develop in isolation from its other, semiotic aspect. Rather, the mimetic element in language can, like a flame, manifest itself only through a kind of bearer. This bearer is the semiotic element. Thus the coherence of words or sentences is the bearer through which, like a flash, similarity appears. For its production by man—like its perception by him—is in many cases, and particularly the most important, limited to flashes. It flits past. It is not improbable that the rapidity of writing and reading heightens the fusion of the semiotic and the mimetic in the sphere of language.

"To read what was never written." Such reading is the most ancient: reading before all languages, from the entrails, the stars, or dances. Later the mediating link of a new kind of reading, of runes and hieroglyphs, came into use. It seems fair to suppose that these were the stages by which the mimetic gift, which was once the foundation of occult practices, gained admittance to writing and language. In this way language may be seen as the highest level of mimetic behavior and the most complete archive of nonsensuous similarity: a medium into which the earlier powers of mimetic production and comprehension have passed without residue, to the point where they have liquidated those of magic.

Editor's Note

The present translation in some instances follows separate publications and individual gatherings of Benjamin's essays, which all appeared under the Suhrkamp (Frankfurt) imprint. These texts and publications include:

"A Berlin Chronicle" (*Berliner Chronik*, 1970); "One-Way Street" (selections from *Einbahnstrasse*, 1955); "Paris, Capital of the Nineteenth Century" (in *Illuminationen*, 1961); "Surrealism" (in *Über Literatur*, 1969); "Brecht's *Threepenny Novel*," "Conversations with Brecht," and "The Author as Producer" (in *Versuche über Brecht*, 1975); "Karl Kraus" (in *Über Literatur*, 1969); "Critique of Violence (in *Angelus Novus*, 1966); "Theologico-Political Fragment" (in *Illuminationen*, 1961); "On Language as Such and on the Language of Man" and "On the Mimetic Faculty" (in *Angelus Novus*, 1966). All other texts were translated from Walter Benjamin, *Gesammelte Schriften*, ed. Rolf Tiedemann and Hermann Schweppenhäuser (Frankfurt: Suhrkamp, 1972–77).

The first publications of the essays published in this collection are as follows:

"A Berlin Chronicle": *Berliner Chronik*, ed. Gershom Scholem, Frankfurt, Suhrkamp, 1970.

"One-Way Street": selections from *Einbahnstrasse*, Berlin, Rowohlt, 1928.

"Moscow": in *Die Kreatur*, II, 1927, pp. 71–101.

"Marseilles": in *Neue Schweizer Rundschau*, XXII, 1929, pp. 291–95.

"Hashish in Marseilles": in *Frankfurter Zeitung*, LXXVII, December 4, 1932.

"Paris, Capital of the Nineteenth Century": in *Schriften*, ed. Theodor W. and Gretel Adorno, with Friedrich Podszus, Frankfurt, Suhrkamp, 1955.

"Naples": in *Frankfurter Zeitung*, LXX, August 19, 1925.

"Surrealism," *Literarische Welt,* V, 1929, in four installments.

"Brecht's *Threepenny Novel*": in *Bertolt Brechts Dreigroschenbuch,* ed., Siegfried Unseld, Frankfurt, Suhrkamp, 1960, pp. 187–93.

"Conversations with Brecht" and "The Author as Producer": in *Versuche über Brecht,* Frankfurt, Suhrkamp, 1975.

"Karl Kraus," *Frankfurter Zeitung,* LXXVI, 1931, in four installments.

"Critique of Violence": in *Archiv für Sozialwissenschaft und Sozialpolitik,* XLVII, 1920/21, pp. 809–32.

"The Destructive Character": in *Frankfurter Zeitung,* LXXVI, November 20, 1931.

"Fate and Character": in *Die Argonauten,* I, 1921, pp. 187–96.

"Theologico-Political Fragment," "On Language as Such and on the Language of Man," and "On the Mimetic Faculty": in *Schriften* (1955).

Useful Further Readings

Adorno, Theodor W., "A Portrait of Walter Benjamin," in *Prisms*, trans. Samuel and Shierry Weber, London, Neville Spearman, 1967, pp. 229–41.

Arendt, Hannah, "Introduction: Walter Benjamin 1892–1940," in Walter Benjamin, *Illuminations*, New York, Harcourt Brace Jovanovich, 1968, pp. 1–55.

Buck-Morss, Susan, *The Origins of Negative Dialectics: Theodor W. Adorno, Walter Benjamin, and the Frankfurt Institute*, New York, The Free Press, 1977.

Durzak, Manfred, "*Walter Benjamin und die Literaturwissenschaft,*" *Monatshefte für den deutschen Unterricht*, LVIII, 1966, 217–32. Concentrates on Benjamin's scholarly studies, especially his volume on the baroque "Play of Lament."

Heissenbüttel, Helmut, "*Vom Zeugnis des Fortlebens in Briefen,*" *Merkur*, XXI, 1967, pp. 232–44. On reconsidering Brecht's friendship with Benjamin.

Jameson, Fredric, *Marxism and Form: Twentieth Century Dialectical Theories of Literature*, Princeton University Press, 1971, pp. 60–83.

Jay, Martin, *The Dialectical Imagination: A History of the Frankfurt School and the Institute of Social Research 1923–1950*, London, Heinemann, 1973, chaps. 6, 8, and elsewhere.

Rosen, Charles, "The Ruins of Walter Benjamin," *New York Review of Books*, XXIV, 17, 1977, pp. 31–40; XXIV, 18, pp. 30–38.

Scholem, Gershom, "Walter Benjamin," *The Leo Baeck Institute Yearbook*, X, New York: East and West Library, 1965, pp. 117–36.

Scholem, Gershom, *Walter Benjamin—die Geschichte einer Freundschaft*, Frankfurt, Suhrkamp, 1975.

Tiedemann, Rolf, *Studien zur Philosophie Walter Benjamins*, Frankfurt, Suhrkamp, 1973. A unified interpretation from an Adornian point of view.

Weber, Shierry M., "Walter Benjamin: Commodity Fetishism, the Modern, and the Experience of History," in *The Unknown Dimension: European Marxism Since Lenin*, ed. Dick Howard and Karl E. Klare, New York, Basic Books, 1972, pp. 249–75.

Wellek, René, "The Early Literary Criticism of Walter Benjamin," *Rice University Studies*, LVII, 1971, pp. 123–34.

Wellek, René, "Walter Benjamin's Literary Criticism in His Marxist Phase," in *The Personality of the Critic*, ed. Joseph P. Strelka, *Yearbook of Comparative Criticism*, VI, State Park, Pennsylvania University Press, 1973, pp. 168–78.

Zur Aktualität Walter Benjamins: Interpretationen von Jürgen Habermas, Gershom Scholem, und anderen, Frankfurt, Suhrkamp, 1972.

Index

Abraham a Santa Clara, 1644–1709, German court preacher, 254

Adorno, Theodor Wiesengrund, 1903–69, German philosopher and sociologist, vii–ix, xiii–xiv, xix, xxxix

Allen, Woody (Allen Konigsberg), 1935– , American writer, actor, and film director, xxxv

Altenberg, Peter, 1859–1919, German writer, 247, 263

Antonioni, Michelangelo, 1912– , Italian film director, xvi

Apollinaire, Guillaume, 1880–1918, French prose writer, art critic, and modernist poet, 179, 182, 184–85, 189

Apollo, 294

Arago, Dominique François, 1786–1853, French physicist and astronomer, 150

Aragon, Louis, 1897– , French poet, novelist, and journalist, 177–79, 182, 185, 186, 191, 236, 237

Hannah Arendt, 1906–75, vii, ix, xv, xxxii

Artemis, 294

Auerbach, Erich, 1892–1957, German philologist and critic, 181

Bakunin, Mikhail Aleksandrovich, 1814–76, Russian anarchist, 189

Balzac, Honoré de, 1799–1850, 146, 161

Bartram, director of Russian toy museum, 104

Baudelaire, Charles, 1821–67, xii, xiv, xxxix, 64, 67, 137, 154, 156–58, 214, 258, 266

Becher, Johannes R., 1891–1958, German writer and editor, 203–04

Bekessy, Imre, 1866–1951, Austro-Hungarian journalist, 263

Benjamin, Dora, Walter Benjamin's sister, x

Benjamin, Dora, née Kellner, d. 1964, Walter Benjamin's wife, xi–xii

Benjamin, Georg, physician, Walter Benjamin's brother, x

Benjamin, Hilde, née Lange, 1902– , Georg Benjamin's wife, later minister of justice of the German Democratic Republic, x

Béraud, Henri, 1885–1958, French novelist and journalist, 186

Bernhard, Lucian, interior decorator and poster artist, 23

Berrichon, Paterne, 1855–1922, French writer, 188

Bloch, Ernst, 1885–1959, German philosopher and writer, vii, 312

Bloy, Léon, 1846–1917, French writer, 261

Böhle, Franz, author of *Theatrical Catechism*, 159

Bötticher, architectural theorist, 147

Brahe, Tycho, 1546–1601, Danish astronomer, 92

Brecht, Bertolt, 1898–1956, German playwright and poet, viii, xiv, xvi, xxviii, xxxiii–xxxiv, xl, 193–